HANDBOOK OF COMPUTER IN LIBRARY SERVICES

About the Book

Library Services is constantly evolving, incorporating new topics like Database Management, Information Architecture and Knowledge Management, for example. There is no generally agreed distinction between library science, library and information science and librarianship. To a certain extent they can be considered equivalent terms, perhaps adopted to increase the "science" aspect, or improve the popular image of librarians. The term library and information science (LIS) is sometimes used; most librarians consider it as only a terminological variation, intended to emphasize the scientific and technical foundations of the subject and its relationship with information science. LIS should not be confused with information theory, the mathematical study of the concept of information, or information science, a field related to computer science and cognitive science.

About the Author

Dr.Lamba is presently working as Chief Librarian in H.K.B.K. College of Engineering, Bangalore and Previouly he was as Librarian in Al-Ameen Dental College,Vijayapura,Bijapur. He has done his MLIS.c, from Karnataka University, Dharwad, M.Phil from Vinayaka Missions University,Thirumanimuthar,Tamil Nadu and PhD from Mysore University, he is an active member of various professional bodies like Indian Society for Technical Education, New Delhi, Indian Library Association and Society for the advancement of Library and Information Sciences, Chennai. He has designed and Maintained Eng-Lib-Forum for Engineering College Librarains. He hosted a number of traning workshops for school Librarians and Teacher Librarians. He is a member of American Library Association and British Council Library.

HANDBOOK OF COMPUTER IN LIBRARY SERVICES

DR. LAMBA

AMIGA PRESS INC.

DELHI (INDIA)

AMIGA PRESS INC.
H.O.: 28-A, Indra Park, Chander Nagar
Delhi-110051 (India)
Tel.: 011-22504028, +91-98736-57000
E-mail: amigapress@gmail.com
amigapub@gmail.com
Website : www.amigapress.co.in

This edition is published by Amiga Press Inc.

ISBN: 978-93-84533-44-1

First Published 2019

Printed and bound in India by Replika Press Pvt. Ltd.

Preface

Library and information science (LIS) is the study of issues related to libraries. This includes academic studies (most often surveys) about how library resources are used and how people interact with library systems. These studies tend to be specific to certain libraries at certain times. The organization of knowledge for efficient retrieval of relevant information is also a major research goal of LIS. Basic topics in library science include the acquisition, classification and preservation of library materials. In a more present-day view, a fervent outgrowth of LIS is information architecture. LIS should not be confused with information theory, the mathematical study of the concept of information.

Library science is distinct from librarianship, which is the practical services rendered by librarians in their day-to-day attempt to meet the needs of library patrons. Librarianship tends not to create new knowledge, nor to strive to advance any field or discipline. Librarians only rarely engage in library science and then usually outside their jobs as librarians. But the study of library science is part of the requisite training of librarians. "Information" and "documentation" means non-book materials that university libraries deal with, such as magazines, scientific journals, technical reports and access to online databases.

Library science is constantly evolving, incorporating new topics like Database Management, Information Architecture and Knowledge Management, for example. There is no generally agreed distinction between library science, library and information science and librarianship. To a certain extent they can be considered equivalent terms, perhaps adopted to increase the "science" aspect, or improve the popular image of librarians. The term library and information science (LIS) is sometimes used; most librarians consider it as only a terminological variation, intended to emphasize the scientific and technical foundations of the subject and its relationship with information science. LIS should not be confused with information theory, the mathematical study of the concept of information, or information science, a field related to computer science and cognitive science.

The library and information services are responsible for supporting promoting and enhancing teaching, learning and research programme of universities and colleges by providing varieties of information materials in different format, in house and in remote location and providing training to use in house materials as well as access to information available at different location.

Preservation is a branch of Library and Information Science concerned with maintaining or restoring access to artifacts, documents and records through the study, diagnosis, treatment and prevention of decay and damage. It should be distinguished from conservation which refers to the treatment and repair of individual items to slow decay or restore them to a usable state. Conservation is occasionally used interchangeably with preservation, particularly outside the professional literature.

The information technology explosion and its applications in every aspect of life have changed the entire scenario of the present world. The IT revolution and information explosion has led to the emergence of electronic information era. The present day electronic and information technology are mutually reinforcing phenomena; and one of the key aspects of living in the information conscious society is the growing level of interactions we have with this complex and increasingly electronic environment.

A digital library is a library in which a significant proportion of the resources are available in machine-readable format, accessible by means of computers. The digital content may be locally held or accessed remotely via computer networks. Library Science is a modern discipline. Earlier regarded as storehouses for preservation of manuscripts and books for reading and reference purposes, publicly or privately, the functions of library today have assumed multifold dimensions today.

This is a reference book. All the matter is just compiled and edited in nature, taken from the various sources which are in public domain.

This book fulfills the long felt necessity of a text dealing with concepts of this subject.

—Editor

Contents

Introduction

Library Science

Library science, not to be confused with librarianship (non-science), is an interdisciplinary science incorporating the humanities, law and applied science to study topics related to libraries, the collection, organization and dissemination of information resources and the political economy of information. Historically, library science has also included Archival science. "The distinction between a library and an archive is relatively modern".

This includes how information resources are organized to serve the needs of select user groups, how people interact with classification systems and technology, how information is acquired, evaluated and applied by people in and outside of libraries as well as cross-culturally, how people are trained and educated for careers in libraries, the ethics that guide library service and organization, the legal status of libraries and information resources and the applied science of computer technology used in documentation and records management. Academic courses in library science typically include Collection management, Information Systems and Technology, Cataloging and classification, Reference, Statistics and Management.

Library science is constantly evolving, incorporating new topics like Database Management, Information Architecture and Knowledge Management, for example. There is no generally agreed distinction between library science, library and information science and librarianship. To a certain extent they can be considered equivalent terms, perhaps adopted to increase the "science" aspect, or improve the popular image of librarians. The term library and information science (LIS) is sometimes used; most librarians consider it as only a terminological variation, intended to emphasize the scientific and technical foundations of the subject and its relationship with information science. LIS should not be confused with information theory, the mathematical study of the concept of information, or information science, a field related to computer science and cognitive science.

One operational view, implied by some of the textbooks, is that librarianship means the professional aspects of work as a librarian, such as certification, in-service training and issues of gender equality.

History

Library and information science, it may be argued, began with the first effort to organize a collection of information and provide access to that information.

Early History: At Ugarit in Syria excavations have revealed a palace library, temple library and two private libraries which date back to around 1200 BCE, containing diplomatic texts as well as poetry and other literary forms. In the 7th century, King Ashurbanipal of Assyria assembled what is considered "the first systematically collected library" at Nineveh; previous collections functioned more as passive archives. The legendary Library of Alexandria is perhaps the best known example of an early library, flourishing in the 3rd century BC and possibly inspired by Demetrius Phalereus.

Ancient Information Retrieval: One of the curators of the imperial library in the Han Dynasty is believed to have been the first to establish a library classification system and the first book notation system. At this time the library catalogue was written on scrolls of fine silk and stored in silk bags.

Jefferson's Method: Thomas Jefferson, whose library at Monticello consisted of thousands of books, devised a classification system inspired by the Baconian method which grouped books more or less by subject rather than alphabetically, as it was previously done. Jefferson's collection became the nucleus of our national collection when it was transferred to the United States Congress after a fire destroyed Congress' library during the War of 1812. The Jefferson collection was the start of what we now know as the Library of Congress.

20th Century: The term "library science" first appeared in the early 1930's, in the title of S. R. Ranganathan's The Five Laws of Library Science, published in 1931 and in the title of Lee Pierce Butler's 1933 book, An introduction to library science (University of Chicago Press). Butler's new approach advocated research using quantitative methods and ideas in the social sciences with the aim of using librarianship to address society's information needs. This research agenda went against the more procedure-based approach of "library economy," which was mostly confined to practical problems in the administration of libraries. While Ranganathan's approach was philosophical it was tied more to the day- to-day business of running a library.

In more recent years, with the growth of digital technology, the field has been greatly influenced by information science concepts. Although a basic understanding is critical to both library research and practical work, the area of information science has remained largely distinct both in training and in research interests.

Training in Librarianship

Most professional library jobs require a professional post-baccalaureate degree in library science, or one of its equivalent terms, library and information science as a basic credential. In the United States and Canada the certification usually comes from a Master's degree granted by an ALA -accredited institution, so even non-scholarly librarians have an originally academic background. In the United Kingdom, however, there have been moves to broaden the entry requirements to professional library posts, such that qualifications in, or experience of, a number of other disciplines have become more acceptable.

Subdisciplines: Subdisciplines of library science include the study of:

- Human Information Behaviours (information-seeking, search strategies and use)
- Knowledge Organization (which includes bibliographies, cataloging, classification, indexing & abstracting, metadata, semantic & syntactic analysis (controlled vocabularies, etc.))
- Digital libraries
- Collection development
- Public reference and other services
- Scholarly communication (includes bibliometrics, informetrics, scientometrics, webmetrics)

Types of library science professionals:

- Librarian
- Curator
- Archivist
- Computer, Data and Information Systems professionals
- Metadata Architects
- Cataloger
- Indexers
- Information broker
- Information architect
- Metadata Managers

Librarians in Different Types of Libraries

Public: The study of librarianship for public libraries covers issues such as cataloging, collection development for a diverse community, information literacy, community standards, public services-focused librarianship, serving a diverse community of adults, children and teens, Intellectual freedom, Censorship and legal and budgeting issues.

School: The study of school librarianship covers library services for children in schools up until (but not including) university. In some regions, the local government may have stricter standards for the education and certification of school librarians (who are often considered a special case of teacher), than for other librarians and the educational programme will include those local standards. School librarianship may also include issues of intellectual freedom; pedagogy; and how to build a cooperative curriculum with the teaching staff.

Academic: The study of academic librarianship covers library services for colleges and universities. Issues of special importance to the field may include copyright; technology, digital libraries and digital repositories; academic freedom; open access to scholarly works; as well as specialized knowledge of subject areas important to the institution and the relevant reference works. Some academic librarians are considered faculty and hold similar academic ranks as professors, while others are not. In either case, the minimal qualification is a Master's degree in Library Studies or Library Science and, in some cases, a Master's degree in another field.

Archives: The study of archives covers the training of archivists, librarians specially trained to maintain and build archives of records intended for historical preservation. Special issues include physical preservation of materials and mass deacidification; specialist catalogues; solo work; access; and appraisal. Many archivists are also trained historians specializing in the period covered by the archive.

Special: Special librarians include almost any other form of librarianship, including those who serve in medical libraries (and hospitals or medical schools), corporations, news agency libraries, or other special collections. The issues at these libraries will be specific to the industries they inhabit, but may include solo work; corporate financing; specialized collection development; and extensive self-promotion to potential patrons.

Preservation: Preservation librarians most often work in academic libraries. Their focus is on the management of preservation activities that seek to maintain access to content within books, manuscripts, archival materials and other library resources. Examples of activities managed by preservation librarians include binding, conservation, digital and analog reformatting, digital preservation and environmental monitoring.

Theory and Practice: Many practicing librarians do not contribute to LIS scholarship but focus on daily operations of their own library systems. Other practicing librarians, particularly in academic libraries, do perform original scholarly LIS research and contribute to the academic end of the field.

On this basis, it has sometimes been proposed that LIS is distinct from librarianship, in a way analogous to the difference between medicine and doctoring. In this view, librarianship, the application of library science, would comprise the practical services rendered by librarians in their day-to-day attempts to meet the needs of library patrons. Other uses of these terms do not make the distinction and treat them as synonyms. Powell's widely used introductory textbook does not make a formal distinction, but its bibliography uses the word librarianship as the heading for articles about the library profession.

Current Issues in LIS:

- Education for librarianship
- Information policy
- Information communication technologies (ICT's)
- Information Society
- Equity of Access
- Sustainability and ICT's
- Children's Internet Protection Act
- Censorship
- Information explosion
- Information literacy
- Government Information
- Decreased funding for established libraries
- Copyright
- Intellectual property rights
- Intellectual freedom
- Digital divide
- Open access
- Patriot Act
- Public lending right
- Slow fires
- Serials crisis
- Current digital/scanning technologies
- Remote access

LIBRARY AND INFORMATION STUDIES

Prospective students should consider several factors when choosing a graduate programme for a master's degree in library and information studies. These include both personal and professional considerations such as career plans, interest in various specializations, geographic mobility, distance learning opportunities and financial resources. These guidelines suggest some information gathering techniques to assist prospective students in choosing a programme.

The master's degree in library and information studies is frequently referred to as the MLS; however, ALA-accredited programmes offer degrees with names such as Master of Arts, Master of Librarianship, Master of Library and Information Studies, or Master of Science. The ALA Office for Human Resource Development and Recruitment offers information on careers in library and information studies and on selecting an ALA-accredited programme.

Accreditation: Graduating from an ALA-accredited programme enhances your career mobility and provides greater flexibility in the types of libraries, information centres and jobs for which you can apply. The majority of employers require an ALA-accredited master's for professional positions. Some states require an ALA-accredited degree to work as a professional librarian in public or school libraries.

ALA accredits master's programmes in library and information studies in the United States, Canada and Puerto Rico. ALA policy recognizes the ALA-accredited master's degree as the appropriate professional degree for librarians and information professionals. For school library media specialists, a master's degree with a specialty in school library media from an educational unit accredited by the National Council for the Accreditation of Teacher Education (NCATE) is also appropriate. ALA's policy states that "The master's degree in librarianship from a programme accredited by the American Library Association or a master's degree with a specialty in school library media from an educational unit accredited by the National Council for the Accreditation of Teacher Education is the appropriate first professional degree." (ALA Policy 54.2.2)

ALA accreditation indicates that the programme has undergone a self-evaluation process, been reviewed by peers and meets the Standards for Accreditation of Master's Programmes in Library and Information Studies that were established by the Committee on Accreditation and adopted by the ALA Council in 1992. The Committee on Accreditation evaluates each programme for conformity to the Standards, which address mission, goals and objectives, curriculum, faculty, students, administration and financial support and physical resources and facilities.

Gathering Basic Information: Although all programmes accredited by ALA's COA meet the Standards, there is a considerable diversity among programmes. We encourage prospective students to contact programmes directly for specific information. To help in your decision we suggest that you review the programme's web site; talk to the faculty, students and alumni; and ask librarians in your area to answer questions about your specific interests and concerns.

To get the latest information about the programmes in which you are interested, visit the programme's web site or request a print catalogue. These resources provide information on the programme's mission, goals and objectives, curriculum, current and future course schedules, application deadlines and admission requirements and procedures.

Visiting the schools you are considering can help you select the programme that best meets your goals. While you are on-site, investigate university facilities such as computer and library resources. The general campus environment, availability of affordable on-campus housing or housing near the university, child care facilities and extra-curricular activities may be important to some prospective students. If you notify a programme of your intention to visit, meetings can be arranged with administrators, faculty members and/or students.

The ALA's Office for Human Resource Development and Recruitment web site also provides links to many resources to help you obtain information when selecting a programme. At this site you will find information on scholarships, placement, salaries and general career information.

Admission Requirements: Individual institutions and programmes establish their own admission requirements, which vary from programme to programme. Generally, programmes require a bachelor's degree from a regionally accredited institution and a minimum grade point average of 3.0 on a 4.0 scale (or equivalent, e.g., B average). Many programmes require Graduate Record Examination (GRE) scores; a few accept the Miller Analogies Test or have no test requirements. Students from outside the United States may be required to take The Test of English as a Foreign Language (TOEFL). Most programmes request that students provide several letters of recommendation and a statement of educational and professional objectives. Some programmes may also require a personal interview. Entering students may be required to demonstrate computer skills or successful completion of remedial computer courses early in the programme.

Curriculum: Considerable variation exists in curricula offered by the programmes, such as the number and types of required courses. The number of academic credit hours required for a master's degree also varies from 36 semester hours to 72 quarter hours. Some programmes emphasize full-time studies, while others have a larger percentage of part-time students; however, most have a time limit for completing a degree.

Many programmes can be completed in one calendar year with full- time attendance; some require two academic years to complete the programme. Programmes requiring a thesis or practicum may require more time to complete.

Choosing a Specialization: Some students enter a master's programme knowing what they want to do when they graduate, some have not made a decision and some see their interests shift once they are exposed to the wide variety of types and settings in which librarians and information professionals work. Plan a programme of study based on an assessment of your past experiences, education, personal strengths and interests, geographic mobility, intended career path and future plans. Although you should be aware of job market opportunities, you should not necessarily let them dictate your choice to specialize. Faculty advisors can help in the process of developing a programme of study that fits your needs.

All ALA-accredited programmes have required courses to provide general preparation to practice in the profession. Some programmes also offer specialized tracks or courses that permit or encourage concentration in a specific area of library and information studies (for example, school librarianship, art librarianship, health science librarianship, database design, or archives). The opportunity to specialize depends on the availability of relevant courses, on focused class project/paper opportunities and the availability of practica or student employment options.

Flexibility and Distance Learning: Flexibility in fulfilling course requirements may be important to students who work or live away from a campus or in an area that does not have an ALA-accredited programme. Most programmes allow students to take independent studies, courses in other schools, graduate departments, or universities and apply the credits towards the master's in library and information studies.

Many ALA-accredited programmes provide distance learning opportunities for students through a variety of delivery methods. In some cases students can complete the entire programme can be at a distance; in other cases some on-campus courses or regional residency may be required. Because these offerings change very frequently, prospective students should contact the programme directly for the latest information on distance learning options.

Financial Aid: Financial aid can consist of scholarships, teaching and research assistantships, grants, work-study programmes, loans and tuition assistance. The programme administers some financial aid opportunities while others are administered through the general university financial aid office. There may be reciprocal tuition agreements between states that can reduce tuition or provide tuition waivers. In addition, some employers provide tuition assistance as a fringe benefit to employees.

Prospective students should contact the institution and programme to obtain information on financial aid and scholarships. In addition to work-study, other part-time positions may be available at local area libraries or information settings. Work in an information setting not only helps finance your education-it also provides valuable experience.

Financial Assistance for Library and Information Studies, an annual compilation available from the ALA Committee on Education, provides listings of financial aid from a variety of sources. In Canada, prospective students should also contact the Canadian Library Association. Scholarship application deadlines vary and may be as early as a year in advance of the term of enrollment.

Placement Services

Most programmes offer some type of job placement service for both current students and alumni. Some have a designated placement officer, while others use faculty for job search advising. Most programmes receive job listings from around the country, although some programmes may be better able to help graduates find jobs in the local area. You may wish to inquire to the programme about placement statistics to learn about the types of jobs obtained by recent graduates. The ALA Office for Human Resource Development and Recruitment web site also provides information on placement, salaries and general career information.

The job market for library and information professionals is cyclical and varies by type of institution, job function and geographical area. The availability of positions may be dependent on available funding resources and replacement needs. Many graduates also find positions in settings other than traditional libraries; these may include special libraries, software or hardware development companies, information management firms, indexing and abstracting agencies and information technology firms.

How Can I Learn about Law Librarianship as a Career?

What do law librarians do? Law librarians are professionally trained people who work in various legal settings, including law schools, private law firms and government libraries.

The American Association of Law Libraries (AALL) has published a booklet, entitled "Finding Your Way in the Information Age" that explains the many roles of law librarians as well as the kinds of skills needed to be successful in this profession. You can request a free copy from AALL.

If you are interested in learning about the profession, you should also look at the two major publications of the American Association of Law Libraries, AALL Spectrum and the Law Library Journal. AALL is a professional organization representing 5,000 law librarians. The association exists to promote and enhance the value of law libraries to the public, the legal community and the world; to foster the profession of law librarianship; and to provide leadership in the field of legal information. A review of AALLNET will help you understand this profession and the kinds of work we do. We recommend that you talk to librarians in the field about the profession. Contact your local law school library, law firm, or local public law library. Most law librarians will be happy to talk to you about our profession and answer your questions. Many large cities and several regions of the country have local organizations of law librarians, called AALL chapters. Communicate with them to identify law librarians to talk with; attend their meetings; educate yourself!

What are the Academic Qualifications for a Law Librarian? There are several different routes to take to obtain the education needed to work as a law librarian. 85% of those working as law librarians have a graduate degree in library science. Most jobs require a master's degree from an American Library Association (ALA) accredited institution. The names of the degrees vary MLS, MLIS, MSIS, ML, MA in LS but all reflect an appropriate entry level educational requirement for careers in the law librarianship profession.

Nearly 30% of all law librarians also have a JD or LLB degree. Most positions require that this degree be earned from a law school accredited by the American Bar Association (ABA).

Less than 20% of the law librarian jobs being filled require both degrees. (National searches are routinely conducted by academic law libraries so most academic jobs will be posted on the webpage. Conversely the sectors where law degrees are rarely required most often do not search nationally, so most of those jobs are not advertised through the national sources like AALLNET.)

Some jobs will require the graduate degree in library science but state a preference for the law degree as well. Experience working in a law library is often as important as having a law degree.

Several schools offer a joint JD/MLS degree where a student can earn a law degree and a library degree simultaneously. Check with the individual school to understand the number of credit hours required. Most of these programmes will require at least 4 years of study. In sum, to qualify for virtually any professional job in law libraries you must have a graduate degree in library science. You may want to consider also earning your law degree. Armed with JD and MLS degrees, you will be qualified for more positions in law librarianship.

Typically, directors of academic law libraries have faculty status so they must have a law degree. In addition, many (but not all) reference librarian positions in law schools require a law degree. Ordinarily, there is no law degree requirement for law librarian positions in law firms, corporations or public, county and government law libraries.

If you already have a law degree but no graduate library degree, should you invest in another 1-2 years of professional education? From the surveys done in the law librarianship profession and from close examination of the job postings for the last few years, a law degree alone would rarely qualify you for jobs in any kind of law library. There are some exceptions, especially if you are interested in eventually obtaining the library degree. The best advice is to encourage you to get the graduate library science degree. On its face you will be qualified for many more positions in law libraries. In addition, you will be much better prepared to assume the challenges and changes of librarianship in today and tomorrow's environment.

How do I Evaluate Library and Information Science Programmes for a Career in Law Librarianship? You have many factors to consider when evaluating a graduate programme in library and information science, including the location of the school, tuition and cost of living and your ultimate career goals. There are many fine ALA approved institutions that offer a master's degree in library and information science (often designated as an MLS or MLIS). Today, there are fifty-one accredited programmes to choose from. You may also be interested in the top twenty library schools as ranked by US News.

However, in selecting the library science programme that you think will meet your needs for a career in law librarianship, you will also need some subject specialization in the law. The AALL Guidelines for Graduate Programmes suggest that you will need both general competencies and subject competencies.

General competencies include reference and research services, library management, collection management and organization and classification. These competencies can be obtained through any of the various library and information science schools.

Subject competencies include an understanding of the legal system; a knowledge of the legal profession and its terminology, including legal abbreviations and citation systems; a knowledge of the literature of the law, including the legal documents that are published and issued by the various branches of government; and an understanding of the legal requirements and ethical considerations of the legal profession and librarianship. You will find a list of thirty-one competencies for law librarian professionals titled "Credentialing Survey Confirms Law Librarian Competencies and Training Needs" in the April, 1998 issue of AALL Spectrum. These competencies were identified on the AALL Credentialing Survey and provide a solid core of what law librarians do.

These law-related subject competencies can be obtained in several ways. Locate a graduate programme in library science that offers courses in law librarianship. Some schools offer one course, others offer two courses and others offer more in-depth study by offering at least three courses. While a graduate programme that offers only one course in law librarianship does not give you an in depth exposure to law librarianship, you may be able to supplement the course with independent studies, internships for academic credit that give you experience working in a law library, or work in a law library while you are in school. Presently, some library schools do not offer any courses in law librarianship, however, this situation could change and you should check directly with the school.

The Special Libraries Association issued a Library and Information Studies Programmes Survey which compares the competencies developed for special librarians and the corresponding courses that are offered in graduate library programmes.

View a complete list of the graduate programmes in library and information science with some offering coursework in law librarianship. You may also be interested in the top twenty library schools as ranked by US News, which now also ranks programmes in law librarianship.

What Type of Curriculum Should I Expect? Many masters programmes in Library and Information Science can be completed in one calendar year with full-time attendance, but the number of academic credit hours required for a master's degree varies from school to school. Some programmes can take as long as two years and may require a thesis and/or fieldwork. Most schools permit part-time attendance and many now have some distance education opportunities. According to the Association for Library and Information Science Education's Statistical Report for 1998, forty-two (75%) of the library schools offered one or more distance courses in 1996-97. No two library science distance education programmes are exactly alike, for they offer various methods of delivery: e-mail, satellite transmission, correspondence courses and the Internet.

Check the breadth and depth of their law librarianship course offerings. A group of law librarians known as the Conference of Law Library Educators teach courses in library schools. Syllabi for many courses offered in law librarianship can be found on their webpage.

Law librarians must have skills in legal research, legal bibliography, organization of legal materials, law library administration and knowledge of legal information systems. Most graduate programmes focus on technology's role in storing and accessing information, or offer coursework in understanding and utilizing the latest technology. A good foundation in technology is essential for law librarianship. Law librarians should be familiar with online databases, such as WESTLAW, LEXIS and Dialog. Law Librarians must be able to help patrons obtain desired information and facilitate access to library material through cataloging and classification.

You may want to look at the course offerings in other academic departments of the University you are considering. Internship and fieldwork opportunities are also an important consideration. You may also want to look at the school's computer and technical resources, such as the size and hours of the computer lab and the number and types of courses offered in online technology and information system management. Check out the school's placement or career services department? How will they help you get a job after you earn your degree?

As with any other profession, competition is fierce for well-paying jobs and you should acquire as many marketable skills as possible.

DEVELOPMENT OF LIBRARY AND INFORMATION SCIENCE

Library and information science (LIS) is the study of issues related to libraries. This includes academic studies (most often surveys) about how library resources are used and how people interact with library systems. These studies tend to be specific to certain libraries at certain times. The organization of knowledge for efficient retrieval of relevant information is also a major research goal of LIS. Basic topics in library science include the acquisition, classification and preservation of library materials. In a more present-day view, a fervent outgrowth of LIS is information architecture. LIS should not be confused with information theory, the mathematical study of the concept of information.

Library science is distinct from librarianship, which is the practical services rendered by librarians in their day-to-day attempt to meet the needs of library patrons. Librarianship tends not to create new knowledge, nor to strive to advance any field or discipline. Librarians only rarely engage in library science and then usually outside their jobs as librarians. But the study of library science is part of the requisite training of librarians. "Information" and "documentation" means non-book materials that university libraries deal with, such as magazines, scientific journals, technical reports and access to online databases.

The term library and information science should not be broken into these separate pieces. Library and Information Science is a hybrid academic field that grew from library schools' fight for survival in the electronic age. The politics of academia, issues of status and prestige, issues of perceived obsolescence and other forces created these programmes. Programmes in library and information science are interdisciplinary, overlapping with the fields of systems' analysis, computer science, statistics and various parts of the social sciences.

The field of library and information science is not defined by its output of information specialists, but by the "information specialists" who remain in academia teaching and doing research, by its literature, its journals and all the other ways in which an academic discipline is defined, the study of which, by the way, falls within the scope of Library and Information Science.

Important LIS institutions and resources:

- The National Information Standards Organization
- Indiana University SLIS.
- Syracuse University School of Information Studies.
- University of Michigan School of Information.
- University of Pittsburgh School of Information Sciences.
- University of California Berkeley School of Information Management & Systems.
- University of Washington Information School.
- University of North Carolina at Chapel Hill School of Information and Library Science.
- University of North Texas School of Library and Information Sciences.
- Dominican University (River Forest, IL).
- University of Illinois Graduate School of Library and Information Science.
- University of Rhode Island Graduate School of Library and Information Studies.
- Simmons College Graduate School of Library & Information Science.
- OCLC (Online Computer Library Center).
- American Library Association.
- Canadian Library Association.
- Australian Library and Information Association.
- American Society for Information Science and Technology.
- International Federation of Library Associations and Institutions (IFLA).

Some current LIS issues:

- childhood internet protection act
- information explosion
- information retrieval
- Library Instruction
- knowledge management
- reference sources
- information storage
- information literacy
- slow fires
- mass deacidification
- information architecture
- public lending right
- Patriot Act

Library Management: Basic tasks in library management include:

- planning the acquistion of materials
- classification of materials
- preservation of materials (especially rare and fragile materials such as manuscripts)
- borrowing materials
- developing and administering library computer systems

More long-term issues include the planning of the construction of new libraries or extensions to existing ones.

The School of Information Studies prepares students for careers in library and information professions. The School provides students with the opportunity to develop attitudes associated with progressive information services and to develop an understanding of the value, role and application of modern technology as it relates to library operations and the transfer of information. The School's graduate programme is fully accredited by the American Library Association.

In harmony with the mission of the University of Wisconsin-Milwaukee, a major urban research institute, the School of Information Studies strives to make significant contributions towards extending and enhancing the quality of information services and the promotion of information and technological literacy to a diverse society. The School of Information Studies is committed to excellence in instruction, research and service. Goals of the school are:

1. To prepare professionals who are able to provide leadership and adapt to change in a technological and knowledge-based environment for careers in libraries, school media centres, information systems and related areas, according to accepted professional standards.

2. To enrich the library and information science profession through recruitment of students with strong academic skills from diverse cultural, geographic and subject backgrounds.
3. To enable undergraduate students to achieve qualifications to pursue degree and certificate programmes.
4. To enable students to develop specializations in the information professions at the graduate level through the provision of single and dual degree programmes.
5. To promote a research orientation through participation in the Doctor of Philosophy degree programme.
6. To contribute to the international knowledge base of library and information science through research and publication.
7. To facilitate the development, provision and evaluation of library and information services through consultation services to individual organizations and leadership in professional associations locally, statewide, nationally and internationally.
8. To offer opportunities for professionals and the wider community to update their skills and knowledge through advanced and continuing education courses, workshops and programmes offered nationally and internationally.

The purpose of the MLIS programme is to prepare librarians and information professionals who are able to manage change in an urbanized, technologically oriented and knowledge-based society. The MLIS programme provides a systematic course of study which enables individuals with a strong service orientation to apply principles of library and information science, use current methods and tools and recognize the value of research. Students may elect to specialize according to the type of library or information service which best meets their needs: i.e., school, public, academic, or special; or to follow a more generalized approach.

Graduates of the Master of Library and Information Science degree programme are expected to demonstrate the following competencies:

1. To apply scientific principles in developing and managing information resources designed to meet user needs and interests.
2. To analyze, describe and organize resources for effective and efficient retrieval and dissemination of information.
3. To utilize knowledge of information sources, services and systems to meet the informational needs of users.
4. To apply management principles in planning, developing, marketing and evaluating library and information services.
5. To work in specialized areas of library and information service, utilizing knowledge obtained from concentrations within the School and in other disciplines.

6. To build upon current knowledge of information and communication theories and technologies in planning, design, development and delivery of information services.

The master's degree programme is designed to support each of these objectives with appropriate coursework and educational experiences. The School of Information Studies in collaboration with the School of Education offers post-bachelor's programmes leading to State of Wisconsin licensing as Initial Instructional Library Media Specialist, Instructional Library Media Specialist and Instructional Library Media Supervisor.

Students admitted to the Master of Library and Information Science degree programme can incorporate in their degree programme the courses for these licenses to the extent that these courses satisfy the degree requirements, either as required core courses or as electives. Licenses will be granted only to those persons who are eligible to hold a Wisconsin license to teach in the elementary or secondary schools or who have completed an approved elementary or secondary classroom teacher preparation programme. For additional information about these licenses and their relationship to the master's degree, consult the School Library Media Coordinator.

The advanced courses offered by the School of Information Studies may be elected on a non-degree basis by postmaster's students who wish to continue their professional education or special competence in some phase of urban library and information services. The School's graduate courses are also open to graduate students in other fields of study, provided that they have completed the appropriate basic courses (or their equivalent).

Coordinated Degree Programmes: In cooperation with the Department of Music in the Peck School of the Arts and the Departments of Anthropology, English, Geography and History, the Urban Studies programme and the Foreign Language and Literature programme in the College of Letters and Science, the School of Information Studies offers the following coordinated degree programmes:

MM/MLIS. Master of Music/Master of Library and Information Studies programme to prepare students for positions as music librarians. Students in the MM degree programme will pursue a concentration in Music History and Literature, 54 credits.

MA/MLIS. A Master of Arts in Geography/Master of Library and Information Science programme to prepare students for positions as map librarians, 48 credits.

MA/MLIS. A Master of Arts in History/Master of Library and archivists, 48 credits.

MS/MLIS. A Master of Science in Urban Studies/Master of Library and Information Science programme to prepare students for positions as urban information specialists, 54 credits.

MAFLL/MLIS. A Master of Arts in Foreign Language and Literature/ Master of Library and Information Science programme to prepare students for positions as librarians in a variety of libraries and curators of special subject collections, 51 credits.

MA/MLIS. A Master of Arts in English/Master of Library and Information Science programme to prepare students for positions as humanities librarians and curators of special subject collections in the humanities, 51 credits.

MS/MLIS. A Master of Science in Anthropology/Master of Library and Information Science to prepare students for positions as curators of museum libraries and as information specialists and researchers for local history collections and state historical societies, 51 credits.

Prerequisite to the award of either degree in these coordinated programmes is the simultaneous award of its counterpart degree. For additional information on these programmes, see the Music, Geography, History, Urban Studies, Foreign Language and Literature, English and Anthropology sections of this Bulletin. Under the auspices of the doctoral programme in Urban Education, the School of Information Studies provides doctoral training with a specialization in Educational and Media Technology. Prospective doctoral students wishing to specialize in Educational and Media Technology must first be admitted to the Urban Education Doctoral Programme. Admission and general programme requirements can be obtained from the Director of Doctoral Studies in Urban Education. This specialization is described in detail in the Urban Education section of this Bulletin.

BIBLIOMETRICS OF ELECTRONIC JOURNALS IN INFORMATION SCIENCE

The Internet has rapidly become a global publishing platform, and electronic journals covering a wide range of subject areas are now available. Information science is no exception, and we now find a significant portion of its literature appearing in e-journals. This article presents some bibliometric data on the currently available e-journals in the field and the articles appearing in them.

The first thing one must do in conducting a study of this type is to determine the corpus of journals and define what is meant by an "electronic journal".

With the advent of the Internet and World Wide Web, anyone with a home page can be regarded as a publisher, and even simple newsletters published erratically and infrequently might be regarded as "e-journals." (Note 1) At the other end of the publishing spectrum are high quality, rigorously edited, peer-reviewed scholarly publications that are made available on the Web. Some of these electronic publications replicate existing print publications; others exist only in electronic form.

For the purposes of this study, e-journals were defined to be publications available in electronic form only and having an International Standard Serial Number (ISSN). The presence of an ISSN helps to lend an air of legitimacy to a publication and weed out more ephemeral publications such as newsletters and informal magazines, which tend not to apply for an ISSN. (Imposing a requirement that journals be peer reviewed serves the same purpose, but it is often difficult to ascertain whether a journal is peer reviewed or not.)

Two surveys of e-journals in information science have already been published. Joglekar and Sen (1999) identified 15 information science e-journals and presented some bibliometric data on them. According to their definition, an e-journal contains original work which is subject to a peer review process, and is published only on the Web at no cost.

Jacso (2001) studied the coverage of e-journals (he prefers the term "digital journal") in databases covering library and information science. His definition of an e-journal is similar to that of Joglekar and Sen. Jacso chose 10 information science e-journals and reported on their coverage in six online databases.

Koehler et al. (2000) compared some of the bibliometric characteristics of three information science e-journals and a leading print journal, Journal of the American Society for Information Science (JASIS). They found that JASIS articles tended to have more citations, and its articles were typically longer than e-journal articles. They also observed that JASIS and Information Research (IR) seem to be perceived by authors as archival journals, while the other two e-journals they studied tended to publish reports of work in process. In addition, they reported that JASIS authors were mostly from North America, and IR authors, originally mainly of UK origin, have become more geographically dispersed. Koehler et al. suggested that this means that IR was becoming a more mature journal.

Data Collection

Candidate e-journals for this study were obtained from the sources mentioned above, a directory of peer-reviewed scholarly e-journals published by the Association of Research Libraries (2000), and the excellent and comprehensive directory of information science e-journals maintained at the Thomas Parry Library at the University of Wales, Aberytswyth (2001). Other Web-available directories were consulted (including the one available on the Web site of this publication), and the Goggle search engine was also used to identify likely e-journal sites.

As the e-journals were identified, they were processed for inclusion in the Information Science Abstracts (ISA) database. The entire run of each journal was examined, and articles relevant to the subject of information science, and published since 1995, were selected.

Special efforts were made to ensure that ISA comprehensively covers all the relevant e-journals. A new Document Type (DT=E-Journal Article) was added to the database to facilitate retrieval of articles from these journals. Coverage of e-journals began in ISA Volume 35, Issue 8 (November 2000), which was a special issue devoted entirely to e-journal articles. That issue contained 557 articles from the first several e-journals that had been processed; since then, e-journals have been added to the ISA database on a regular basis. Many e-journals offer an e-mail service to alert readers when new issues become available; these services are extremely helpful and have been used when offered to facilitate the timely updating of the database.

ISA is maintained and produced using the Microsoft Access platform. For this work, the records tagged as e-journal articles were extracted from the master ISA database and copied into a separate Access database (the "e-journal database") (Note 2). Counts and analyses were then obtained by means of Access queries.

Data Analysis

Journals: As of August 2001, 1,120 articles on information science subjects have been published in the 28 e-journals listed in the Appendix to this article. Note that this is not the total number of articles published by these journals; they often carry articles on subjects that are on topics other than information science. The Appendix shows the publisher, publication frequency, ISSN, URL, and starting date of each e-journal.

In common with many other disciplines, information science has witnessed a flurry of activity in the e-journal area. The first information science e-journals appeared in the early 1990s; since 1995, three to four new journals, on average, have appeared each year. However, the number of articles appearing in information science e-journals is still only a small fraction of the total. The ISA database currently contains approximately 135,000 abstracts, so the 1,120 e-journal articles represent 0.8% of the total.

During the period in which e-journals have been published (since 1995), the ISA database contains approximately 24,000 abstracts, so the e-journals represent approximately 5% of the database for this period. If we limit these data to journal articles only (ISA contains approximately 73,000 abstracts with a Document Type of "Journal Article or "E-Journal Article"), the above percentages become 1.5% and 5.2%, respectively. As awareness of e-journals spreads and as authors begin to regard them as legitimate publication media, we can expect the number of e-journal articles to grow. (Recent research indicates that this is beginning to occur. Lawrence (2001) found that highly cited recent computer science articles are more likely to be online than in print.)

E-journals differ from print journals in several significant aspects. They are disseminated completely in electronic form, and access to them is frequently free to the user. It is therefore simple to start a publication and just as simple to kill it. When publication ceases, there are no subscription liabilities to concern the publisher because no funds have been collected from the users. None of the titles shown in the Appendix are published by commercial for-profit companies. There are therefore no subscriptions, and access to them all is freely available to anyone using the Internet.

In the relatively short time (chronologically, but not in "Internet time") since it became possible to publish electronically on the Web, three information science e-journals have already ceased publication, and two others are currently inactive. (Data on these five journals are, however, included in the statistics below.) All of these e-journals except ICSTI Forum have been in electronic form since their inception. ICSTI Forum is an interesting example of a journal that began as a print journal and then transformed to an electronic-only journal by ceasing to produce the print version.

THE UNIQUE CONCERN OF LIBRARY AND INFORMATION SCIENCE

"Concern for people becoming informed is not unique to LIS, and thus is insufficient to differentiate LIS from other fields. LIS are a part of a Larger enterprise." The unique concern of LIS is recognized as: Statement of the core concern of LIS: Humans becoming informed (constructing meaning) via intermediation between inquirers and instrumented records. No other field has this as its concern. "

"Note that the promiscuous term information does not appear in the above statement circumscribing the field's central concerns: The detrimental effects of the ambiguity this term provokes. Furner has shown that discourse in the field is improved where specific terms are utilized in place of the i- word for specific senses of that term." Michael Buckland wrote: "Educational programs in library, information and documentation are concerned with what people know, are not limited to technology, and require wide-ranging expertise. They differ fundamentally and importantly from computer science programs and from the information systems programs found in business schools.".

LIS Theories

Julian Warner suggests that—"Two paradigms, the cognitive and the physical, have been distinguished in information retrieval research, but they share the assumption of the value of delivering relevant records. For the purpose of discussion here, they can be considered a single heterogeneous paradigm, linked but not united by this common assumption. The value placed on query transformation is dissonant with common practice, where users may prefer to explore an area and may value fully informed exploration. Some dissenting research discussions have been more congruent with practice, advocating explorative capability - the ability to explore and make discriminations between representations of objects - as the fundamental design principle for information retrieval systems".

The domain analytic approach (e.g., Hjørland 2010) suggests that the relevant criteria for making discriminations in information retrieval are scientific and scholarly criteria. In some fields (e.g. evidence based medicine) the relevant distinctions are very explicit. In other cases they are implicit or unclear. At the basic level, the relevance of bibliographical records are determined by epistemological criteria of what constitutes knowledge.

The Big Picture: Structure of Information Science

Any field is structured along some distinct, larger areas or subdisciplines of enquiry or practice. Think of a number of areas of medicine, computer science, librarianship, and so forth. Information science is not an exception. It has a distinct, two-partite structure. A number of authors observed that the work in information science falls in two large areas or subdisciplines, each, of course, with further subareas or specialties.

White and McCain conducted a monumental bibliometric study of the domain of information science by providing extensive analysis of co-citation patterns for 120 authors over a period of 23 years. Borrowing from White and McCain, visualize a map of information science as an ellipse with authors inside, distributed or clustered according to their connections. There are two large clusters at each end of the ellipse, with only a few authors spanning both. In other words, there are two major areas or subdisciplines.

I liked their metaphor:

As Things Turn Out, Information Science Looks Rather like Australia: Heavily coastal in its development, with a sparsely settled interior.

In one of the coastal sections, fall authors that worked on analytical study of literatures; their structures; studies of texts as content-bearing objects; communication in various populations, particularly scientific communication; social context of information; information uses; information seeking and behaviour; various theories of information and related topics. As yet, there is no good label for that cluster. Some call it "information analysis." For simplicity, lets call this the domain cluster, as did White and McCain, although "basic" may be a good label. In the other coastal section are authors who concentrated on IR theory and retrieval algorithms; practical IR processes and systems; human-computer interaction; user studies; library systems; OPACs; and related topics.

Let's call this cluster the *retrieval cluster*, although "applied" may also be a good label. Basically, most of the areas in the domain cluster are about study of fundamental manifes-tations and behaviour of phenomena and objects that information science is all about. They are centered on the phenomenon of information and its manifestations in literature. The retrieval cluster deals, by and large, with a variety of implementations, on both practical and theoretical levels. It is about implementation, behaviour, and effects of the interface between literatures and people, including, of course, all kinds of retrieval aspects. Unfortunately, these two main clusters are largely unconnected.

Only a very small number of authors spanned the two clusters. In other words, there are very few integrating works. The last text that undertook an integrative approach encom-passing both clusters. A rare example of such an effort in research is the last work by Tague-Sutcliffe, where she related the notion of informative-ness with evaluation of IR systems.

In part, this is due to availability of funds for given topics—not surprisingly, research goes after moneyed topics. By and large, over the last decade or so, major granting agencies funded only applied research in information science. For instance, I have been unable to identify a single grant addressing any of the topics in the domain or basic cluster from NSF Division of Information and Intelligent Systems since its preceding Division of Information Science and Technology was reorganized and included in the Directorate for Computer and Information Science and Engineering (CISE) in 1985. In de Solla Price's concepts and words, the domain cluster is "little science", while the retrieval cluster is "big science," and the connection between the two has presently no science.

PROBLEMS ADDRESSED

General

Webster routinely defines information science as "the science dealing with the efficient collection, storage, and retrieval of information." It is a general definition of problems addressed by information science. The definition follows pretty much an early and popular one given by Borko as a part of a wide discussion and controversy about the nature of the field in the 1960s. More specifically, information science is a field of professional practice and scientific enquiry addressing the problem of effective communication of knowledge records—"literature"—among humans in the context of social, organizational, and individual need for and use of information. The key orientation here is the problem of need for and use of information, as involving knowledge records.

To provide for that need, information science deals with specifically, oriented information techniques, procedures, and systems. To elaborate, the specific concentration of information science is on human knowledge records as content-bearing objects, in all forms, shapes, and media. The primary emphasis is on content of these objects, in terms of their potential for conveying information. "Literature" may be used as a generic term for these knowledge records, but "literature" has many other connotations, thus requiring a careful restriction in its use in information science. Because of these connotations, "literature" will not become popular in information science.

Realizing this, I am using the term here only as a shorthand, as did White and McCain, when they elegantly stated:

> *"The proper study of information science is the interface between people and literature ... modeling the world of publications with a practical goal of being able to deliver their content to enquirers on demand ... While many scientists seek to understand communication between persons, information scientists seek to understand communication between persons and certain valued surrogates for persons that literature comprises.*

In all of this there is a technological imperative, reflected in efforts to take advantage of modern information technology. While information science is not about technology, the problem of providing effective computer applications pervades the field. Following is a word on the extent and borders of infor-mation science.

Focusing information science on the content-bearing properties of literature, and on associated techniques and systems dealing with providing effective access to and use of literature, provides a restriction for information science.

Thus, the field does not deal with great many other information systems, such as payroll, inventory, decision support systems, data processing, airline schedules, and a zillion others, nor does it deal with direct communication among and between persons. Information science is about a specific manifestation or type of information that defines its scope and its systems. Information science, as many other fields, also involves a professional component. Starting in 1950s, the profession of information science grew from research and applications in IR, to become a powerful component of the field, and in many ways a leading one in respect to innovation.

As in many other fields, there is an uneasy relation between the scientific or research-oriented component and the professi-onal or practice-oriented one. The profession is responding in its own way to needs of its users and organizations, and chartering its own technological applications, many times independently of research advances, and even in different directions. At present, the connection and feedback between profession and research in information science is not as well established as it is in older fields, such as engineering or medicine. This is a serious inhibitor for progress of both.

More Specific

A number of authors suggested a breakdown of specific areas of information science, beyond the structural analysis offered above. The breakdown among different authors is in significant agreement, although the labels differ somewhat. I will take the breakdown and labels provided by White and Mc Cain. They provided a factor analysis of co-cited authors and extracted 12 factors as specialties.

In descending order of how authors loaded, they labelled the specialties as:

* Experimental information retrieval (IR);
* Citation analysis;
* Practical retrieval;
* Bibliometrics;
* General library systems theory;
* Science communication;
* User studies and theory;
* OPACs;
* General imported ideas—other disciplines;
* Indexing theory;
* Citation theory; and
* Communication theory.

While one may quibble with some of the classes and labels, these specialties provide a fairly accurate picture of problem areas in which information scientists worked over the past quarter of a century.

Over time, there were shifts in emphasis and there were movements between specialties. Nothing is permanent. But these are the specialties of information science. New areas are clearly on the horizon.

For the 1990s, I would suggest that the major new areas include interaction studies; searching of the Internet; multimedia IR; multilanguage IR; and digital libraries.

These are prime examples of the new significant areas of concentration, not yet evident in the historical record. At the same time, the old area of experimental retrieval is blossoming like never before, courtesy of the *Text Retrieval Conference* (TREC), a government-sponsored mechanism for comparative evaluation of a variety of IR techniques and approaches that area of information science. Thus, a separate discussion of IR follows.

Information Retrieval

In the early and mid-1950s, a critical mass of scientists, engineers, librarians, and entrepreneurs started working enthusiastically on the problem and solution defined by Bush. By 1960s this became a large and relatively well-funded effort and organized activity. Often, there were heated arguments and controversies about the "best" solution, technique, or system.

These arguments brought on the tradition of evaluation, a major staple of IR research and development. What is now TREC started with Cranfield evaluations in the late 1950s and early 1960s. Remarkably, the basic evaluation principles developed then are still the underpinning of TREC today. Calvin Mooers, an active and highly visible pioneer of information science, coined the term information retrieval in 1951. The term took hold, and today is a part of the English language. At that time, Mooers not only coined the term, but also defined the problems to be addressed:

> *"Information retrieval embraces the intellectual aspects of the description of information and its specification for search, and also whatever systems, techniques or machines that are employed to carry out the operation.*

Today, we would add that IR also and particularly involves interaction in all of these, with all the contextual-cognitive, affective, situational—aspects that interaction embraces. An expanded Mooers' conception is still valid. As it advanced, IR produced a number of theoretical, empirical, and pragmatic concepts and constructs. Numerous IR systems were developed and successfully deployed. A great many historical examples can be given to illustrate the remarkable evolution of IR systems and techniques, adapting the ever-evolving information technology, from punch cards in the midcentury to the Internet at its close. Based on IR, an online information industry emerged in the 1970s, and grew through its own version of information explosion, as chronicled by Hahn. IR is one of the most widely spread applications of any information system worldwide. It has a proud history. Surely, information science is more than IR, but many of the problems raised by IR or derived from objects and phenomena involved in IR, are at its core.

Approaches and Paradigm Split

The approach taken by Mooers was to concentrate on the building of systems. This systems emphasis which was formulated early in the 1950s, was the sole approach to IR for some decades. It still predominates in a good part of IR research to this day.

Consequently, most of the IR research and practice concentrated on retrieval systems and processes. However, starting in the late 1970s and gaining steam in the 1980s, a different line of reasoning and research evolved-one that concentrates on the cognitive, interactive, and contextual end of the process. It addressed users, use, situations, context, and interaction with systems, rather than IR systems alone as a primary focus. The retrieval cluster started splitting into subclusters, as noted by White and McCain, and before by others such as Saracevic and Harter. We now have two distinct communities and approaches to research in the retrieval cluster. They became commonly known as systems-centred and user-centred. Both address retrieval, but from very different ends and perspectives. The split is not only conceptual, looking very differently at the same process, but also organizational. The systemscentered side is now mostly concentrated in the *Special Interest Group on Information Retrieval* (SIGIR) of the *Association for Computing Machinery* (ACM), while the user-centered cluster congregates around the *American Society for Information Science* (ASIS).

Each has its own communication outlets-journals, proceedings, and conferences. There is less and less overlap of authors and works between the two outlets. We have two camps, two islands, with, unfortunately, relatively little traffic in-between. The systems-centered approach is exemplified by work on algorithms and evaluation based on the traditional IR model, a model that does not consider the users or interaction. The massive research that evaluates a variety of IR algorithms and approaches within TREC is a culmination of this approach.

In contrast, cognitive, situational, and interactive studies and models, involving the use of retrieval systems exemplify the human-centered approach. Following that approach, interactive models, differing significantly from the traditional IR model, started to emerge. Even in TREC, a group of researchers started an interaction track, but so far have a hard time conceptually and methodologically, thus demonstrating the difficulty in merging the traditional and interactive models and approaches. Let me characterize, in a simplified way, the relationship between the two approaches or subclusters addressing different sides of retrieval.

On the one hand, the human-centred side was often highly critical of the systems side for ignoring users and use, and tried valiantly to establish humans as the proper center of IR work. The mantra of human-centred research is that the results have implications for systems design and practice.

Unfortunately, in most human-centered research, beyond suggestions, concrete design solutions were not delivered. On the other hand, the systems side, by and large, ignores the human side and user studies, and is even often completely ignorant of them. As to design, the stance is "tell us what to do and as suggested, do it." But nobody is really telling, or if telling, nobody is listening.

As a rule, in systems-oriented projects, people and users are absent. Thus, there are not many interactions between the two camps. Let me provide some examples. A rough analysis of the 1997 SIGIR proceedings found only 3 papers of some 34 that dealt in some way with people and users; in the ACM's Digital Libraries 1997 conference proceedings, of 25 papers only 3 mentioned people and users. If one reads authors such as Dervin and Nilan, and many of their successors, who champion the human centered approach, one gets the impression that there is a real conflict between the two sides and approaches, and that there is an alternative way to the "dreadful" systems approach.

In a way, this stance is a backlash caused by the excesses, failures, and blind spots of systems-centered approaches not only in IR, but also in great many other technological applica-tions. Unfortunately, sometimes the backlash is justified. All of us who work on the humancentered side are not that dismissive of the systems side. But the issue is not whether we should have systems-or humancentered approaches. The issue is even less of humanversus systems-centered. *The issue is how to make humanand systems-centered approaches work together.* In this sense, a number of works have addressed integrating usercentered and systems-centered approaches in IR, but this has been discussed mostly by researchers from the usercentered side.

Examples are works by:

* Bates,
* Belkin,
* Cool,

* Stein,
* Thiel,
* Fidel
* Efthimidiadis,
* Robertson and
* Beaulieu.

To reiterate, it is not one camp against the other but how can we incorporate the best features of both approaches and make them work jointly. The issue is how to deliver and incorporate the desired design features that will improve systems orientations towards users, integrate them with systems features, and use advantages provided by both, humans and technology. In other words, the issue is *putting the human in the loop* to build better algorithms and to exploit computational advantages. Real progress in information science, and by extension in IR, will come when we achieve this. Lately, the NSF has championed human-centered design involving an interdisciplinary approach to information systems. Hopefully, this will go beyond rhetoric. It is not easy to do. But, that is what research is for—to address difficult, not only easy problems.

Proprietary IR

By the 1980s, the commercial information industry based on IR became successful and profitable. Out of academe, grants, and government, IR became a money-making propo-sition. This, of course, is another and important sign of success. Not surprisingly, a number of former IR researchers, practitioners, and graduates of IR programmes ventured out to become IR entrepreneurs.

Sure enough, throughout information science history there were many entrepreneurs, and they were highly significant in development of the field. But this generation of entrepre-neurs was different. They ventured to develop and market a variety of IR procedures based on algorithms, applicable and scalable to large files, multiple applications, and/or various advanced technologies. It was knowledge industry at its purest. But, as in all commercial knowledge industries, the product was proprietary. While it was not that hard to guess the base of these various proprietary algorithms and how they worked—after all they were derived from publicly available knowledge and experiences, such as those that came from SMART experi-ments—they remain unpublished and "secret."

A new kind of IR evolved, separate from the rest, not communicating as to intellectual advances with the rest. None of these ventures became a high commercial success, as measured by Silicon Valley standards. But the World Wide Web, emerging in the first half of the 1990s, changed all this. The acceleration of the growth of the Web is an information explosion of the like never before seen in history. Not surprisingly then, the Web is a mess. No wonder that everybody is interested in some form of IR as a solution to fix it.

A number of academic-based efforts were initiated to develop mechanisms, search engines, "intelligent" agents, crawlers, and so forth, to help control the Web. Some of these were IR scaled, and adapted to the problem; others were a variety of extensions of IR. Many had few, if any original, developments, besides new packaging or labeling; and a good number were just the usual hype. The wheel was reinvented a number of times. But out of this, and fast, came commercial ventures, such as the pioneering Yahoo!, whose basic objective is to provide search mechanisms for finding something of relevance for users on demand.

And to make a lot of money. These enterprises pride themselves on having proprietary methods by which they are accomplishing the retrieval tasks. The connection to the information science community is tenuous, and almost nonexistent. The flow of knowledge, if any, is onesided, from IR research results into proprietary engines. The reverse contribution to public knowledge is zero. A number of evaluations of these search engines have been undertaken simply by comparing some results between them or comparing of their retrieval against some benchmarks.

Some evaluations were done within, others outside of information science. Results were not complimentary. The Web-based proprietary IR is expanding and flourishing outside of the field. It is addressing a vexing problem, the like we have not seen before. But as yet, the success is elusive and questionable.

Relevance

As information science pioneers developed IR processes and systems in the 1950s, they defined as the main objective retrieval of *relevant information*. Effectiveness was expressed in terms of relevance. From then to now, IR is explicitly geared not towards any old kind of information, but towards relevant information. Various IR approaches, algorithms, and practices were, and still are, evaluated in relation to relevance. Thus, relevance became a key notion in information science. It is also a complex phenomenon with a long and turbulent history in information science transcending IR, going back to early 1950s. Of course, there was a choice.

Relevance did not have to emerge as the key notion. Uncertainty was one choice suggested by a number of theorists to be the base of IR, and thus to reflect effectiveness. But it did not take. In contrast, uncertainty is the basic notion underlying expert systems. If the pioneers had not embraced relevance, but instead, let's say, uncertainty, as the base for IR, we would have today a very different IR, and probably not that successful. In general, relevance, according to Webster, means having significant bearing on matter at hand. As with many other concepts, relevance assumes related but more specific meaning in more specific contexts and applications.

In the context of information science, relevance is the attribute or criterion reflecting the effectiveness of exchange of information between people and IR systems in communi-cation contacts based on valuation by people. With relevance as the criterion, and human judgments of relevance of retrieved objects as the measuring instrument, the measures of precision and recall are widely used in evaluation of IR systems. The strength of these measures is that they involve people—users—as judges of effectiveness of performance. The weakness is the same: it involves judgment by people, with all the perils of subjectivity and variability. Relevance indicates a relation. For relevance, many relations have been investigated.

An consensus has emerged in information science that we can distinguish between several differing relations that account for different manifestations or types of relevance:

* System or Algorithmic Relevance: Relation between a query and information objects in the file of a system as retrieved, or as failed to be retrieved, by a given procedure or algorithm. Comparative effectiveness in inferring relevance is the criterion for system relevance.
* Topical or Subject Relevance: Relation between the subject or topic expressed in a query and topic or subject covered by retrieved texts, or, more broadly, by texts in the system file, or even in existence. Aboutness is the criterion by which topicality is inferred.
* Cognitive Relevance or Pertinence: Relation between the state of knowledge and cognitive information need of a user and texts retrieved, or in the file of a system, or even in existence. Cognitive correspondence, infor-mativeness, novelty, information quality, and the like are criteria by which cognitive relevance is inferred.
* Situational Relevance or Utility: Relation between the situation, task or problem at hand and texts retrieved by a system, or in the file of a system, or even in existence. Usefulness in decision making, appropriateness of information in resolution of a problem, reduction of uncertainty, and the like are criteria by which situational relevance is inferred.
* Motivational or Affective Relevance: Relation between the intents, goals, and motivations of a user and texts retrieved by a system, or in the file of a system, or even in existence. Satisfaction, success, accomplish-ment, and the like are the criteria for inferring motivational relevance.

Practically, IR systems assess systems relevance only-that is, they respond to queries-hoping that the objects retrieved may also be of cognitive relevance, and even more so of utility. However, a user may judge an object by any or all types of relevance-for a user they may interact dynamically. Difficulties arise when an object is of system relevance but not of cognitive relevance or utility, or conversely. If items are of cognitive relevance or utility, but were not reflected in the query, they are not and cannot be retrieved. At the bottom of IR research is a quest to align systems with other types of relevance. People all over have a strong intuitive understanding of relevance, thus, they intuitively understand, without manuals, what IR is all about. This makes IR systems generally understandable and acceptable-a critical attribute in their widespread application.

Disciplinary Relations

Two things introduced interdisciplinarity in information science. First and foremost, the problems addressed cannot be resolved with approaches and constructs from any single discipline-thus, intedisciplinarity is predetermined, as it is in many modern fields. Second, interdisciplinarity in information science was introduced and is being perpetuated to the present by the very differences in backgrounds of people addressing the described problems. Differences in background are many; they make for richness of the field and difficulties in communication and education. Clearly not every discipline in the background of people working on the problem made an equally relevant contri-bution, but the assortment was responsible for sustaining a strong interdisciplinary characteristic of information science. I will concentrate on interdisciplinary relations with two fields: librarianship and computer science. Obviously, other fields, most notably cognitive science and communication, have also interdisciplinary relations, but these are the most significant and developed ones.

Librarianship

Librarianship has a long and proud history devoted to organization, preservation, and use of graphic records and records in other media. This is done through libraries not only as a particular organization or type of information system, but even more so as an indispensable social, cultural, and educational institution whose value has been proven manifold throughout human history, and across all geographic and cultural boundaries.

Researcher defines the library as:

* ...Contributing to the total communication system in society... Though the library is an instrumentality created to maximize the utility of graphic records for the benefits of society, it achieves that goal by working with the individual and through the individual

it reaches society.

The common ground between library science and information science, which is a strong one, is in sharing of their social role and in their general concern with effective utilization of graphic and other records, particularly by individuals. But there are also very significant differences in several critical respects, among them:

* Selection of Problems Addressed and the Way they were Defined : A majority of the problems were not and are not addressed in library science;
* Theoretical Questions Asked and Frameworks Established: The theories and conceptual frameworks in librarian-ship have no counterpart in information science, and vice versa;
* The Nature and Degree of Experimentation and Empirical Development and the Resulting Practical Knowledge and Competencies Dderived: There is very little overlap in experimentation and development between the two, and professional requirements differ as well to a significant degree;
* Tools and Approaches Used: A most telling example is the very different approach undertaken in relation to utilization of technology in IR and in library automation; and
* The Nature and Strength of Interdisciplinary Relations Established and the Dependence of Progress on Inter-disciplinary Approaches : Librarianship is much more selfcontained.

All of these differences warrant a conclusion that librarianship and information science are two different fields in strong interdisciplinary relations, rather than one and the same field, or one being a special case of the other. This is not a matter of turf battles, or of one being better or worse than the other. Such arguments, while common between many fields, matter little to progress of either field. But differences in selection and/ or definition of problems addressed, agenda, paradigms, theoretical base, and practical solutions do matter. Thus the conclusion that librarianship and information science, while related, are different fields. The differences are most pronounced in the research agenda and directions.

Interestingly, research on OPACs, now that they are incorporating more and more IR features, is bringing the two fields in closer relation. Probably, so will the research in digital libraries, but at this time, it is too early to tell. The conclusion is not without heated controversy.

Among other authors, Vakkari contends on information science and librarianship being one and the same field, with the now commonly used name of "library and information science." Does it matter? Administratively yes, very much so, particularly in universities and professional societies.

Otherwise, no. The issue is, and always will be, in the problems addressed and solutions undertaken. I contend that they differ significantly.

Computer Science

The basis of relation between information science and computer science lies in the application of computers and computing in IR, and the associated products, services, and networks. In the last few years, this relation also involves research on the evolving digital libraries, with their strong technological base. To illustrate the connection, we use a definition by Denning:

> "The discipline of computing is the systematic study of algorithmic processes that describe and transfer information: their theory, analysis, design, efficiency, implementation, and application. The fundamental question underlying all of the computing is: "What can be automated?"

Computer science is about algorithms related to infor-mation interpreted in the first, whereas information science is about the very nature of information and its use by humans, interpreted in the third or broadest sense. Computer science is about symbol manipulation, whereas information science is about content manipulation, where symbol manipulation is the indispensable infrastructure. The two concerns are not in competition, they are complementary—they lead to different basic and applied agendas. Computer science is also many times larger than information science.

A number of computer scientists have been involved in research and development on information and its many spin-offs, to the point of being recognized leaders in information science.

Gerard Salton is a prime example. In addition, there are several streams of research and development in computer science that had no connection with the early evolution of information science, but have addressed information problems similar to those in information science. Among others, these include works on expert systems, knowledge bases, hypertext, and human-computer interaction.

More recently, this involves research and development on digital libraries, a "hot", financially heavily supported area by a host of government agencies in the U.S. and many other countries. Bolstered by heavy support, interest in digital library research exploded on the scene in 1990s, attracting the attention of computer scientists from a wide variety of streams, as well as people from many other disciplines.

These areas have a significant informational component that is associated with information representation, its intellectual organization, and linkages; meta-information, information seeking, searching, retrieving, and filtering; use, quality, value, and impact of information; evaluation of information systems from user and use perspective; and the like-all traditionally addressed in information science. Conversely, these streams of computer science research and development provide a different outlook, framework, and approach, and even a different paradigm, not only for information science research and development, but also for its academic and continuing education. Again, as with librarianship, the issue is not about turf.

It is about paradigms, theoretical foundations, and pragmatic solutions; and ultimately, it is about their appropriateness to human information problems.

Education

That education is critical for any field is a truism that hardly needs to be stated. In particular, research lives by education, it cannot be better than the education that researchers receive and then extend and plow back into education.

Unfortunately, education in information science has not received the attention that it deserves. This may explain the many difficulties in the field that I have discussed. Educational models that evolved differed to a degree or even substantially from country to country. I am concentrating here on the U.S. models only.

In the United States, two educational models evolved over time. I call them the Shera and Salton models, after those that pioneered them. Both have strengths and weaknesses. Jesse H. Shera was a legendary library school dean from the 1950s until the 1970s at Western Reserve University.

Among others, he was instrumental in starting the Center for Documentation and Communication Research in 1955. Shortly thereafter, the library school curriculum started to include courses such as "Machine Literature Searching" and several other more advanced courses and laboratories on the topics of research in the Centre.

The basic approach was to append those courses, mostly as electives, to the existing library school curriculum, without modifications of the curriculum as a whole, and particularly not the required core courses. Information science became one of the specialty areas of library science. The base or core courses that students were taking rested in the traditional library curriculum. Information science education was an appendage to independent degree and curriculum were not followed widely. But Shera's model was. Library schools in the U.S. and in many other countries imitated Shera's model. They used the same approach and started incorporating information science courses in their existing curriculum as a specialty. Out of this was borne the current designation "library and information science."

Shera's model is still the prevalent approach in schools of library and information science. The strength of the Shera model is that it posits education within a service framework, connects the education to professional practice and to a broader and user-oriented frame of a number of other information services, and relates it to a great diversity of information resources.

The weakness is a lack of a broader theoretical frame -work and a total lack of teaching of any formalism related to systems, such as development and understanding of algori-thms. The majority of researchers in the human-centered side, as I described earlier, came from or are associated with this educa-tional environment. Gerard Salton was first and foremost a scientist, a computer scientist, and the father of modern IR.

As such, he pioneered the incorporation into IR research a whole array of formal and experimental methods from science, as modified for algorithmic and other approaches used so successfully in computer science. His primary orientation was research.

For education, he took the time-honoured approach of a close involvement with research. Salton's model was a laboratory and research approach to education.

As Shera's model resulted in information science educa-tion being an appendage to library science education, Salton's model of IR education resulted in it being a specialty of and an appendage to computer science education. Computer science students that were already well-grounded in the discipline, got involved in SMART and other projects directed by Salton, worked and did research in the laboratory, completed their theses in areas related to IR, and participated in the legendary IR seminars.

They also published widely with Salton and with each other, and participated with high visibility in national and international conferences. From Harvard and Cornell, his students went to a number of computer science departments where they replicated Salton's model. Many other computer science departments in the U.S. and abroad took the same approach.

The strength of Salton's model is that it:

"Starts from a base of a firm grounding in formal mathematical and other methods, and in algorithms, and

* Relates directly to research. The weakness is in that it:
* Ignores the broader aspects of information science, as well as any other disciplines and approaches dealing with the human aspects that have great relevance to both the outcomes of IR research and the research itself, and

* Does not incorporate professional practice where these systems are realised and used. It loses users.

Consequently, this is a successful, but narrowly concen-trated education in IR as a specialty of computer science, rather then in information science.

Not surprisingly, the researchers in the systems-centred approach came out of this tradition. The two educational approaches are completely independent of each other. Neither is connected to the other. Neither reflects fully what is going on in the field. While in each model there is an increase in cognizance of the other, there is no educational integration of the systems-and usercentered approaches.

The evident strengths that are provided by Shera and Salton model are not put together. Their weaknesses are perpetuated. It is high time for communities from each model to try to integrate education for information science. It is an open question whether the human-and systems- centered approachcs can fruitfully work together as urged in all those calls for human-centered design until an educational inte-gration occurs.

While library education receives formal attention from the *American Library Association* (ALA), and education for computer science from ACM, no such formal attention is paid by any professional/scientific society to education for information science, or for IR in particular. Neither ASIS nor SIGIR, as primary homes for information science, have been involved to any great extent in educational matters, such as setting of standards or devising model curricula. Clearly, there is a need and an opportunity for more substantive involvement by both organizations in educational issues.

❐

2.

Library and Information Networks

The explosion in the amount of literature that is available, increases among the number of users and their different needs, and the application of electronic media are forcing libraries to construct and participate in networks. Magnetic tapes, floppy disks, and CD-ROMs provide enough data storage capacity. Retrieval through telecommunications networks and access to international databases are available for searching for information on various subjects. With the advent of networks, remote transmission of texts and graphics, video clips and animated clips are also possible.

Definitions:

- o A library network is broadly described as a group of libraries coming together with some agreement of understanding to help each other with a view to satisfying the information needs of their clientele.
- o UNISIST II working document defines Information Network as a set of interrelated information systems associated with communication facilities, which are cooperating through more or less formal agreements in order to implement information handling operations to offer better services to the users.
- o The National Commission on Libraries & Information Science in its National Programme Document (1975) defines a network as Two or more libraries engaged in a common pattern of information exchange, through communications for some functional purpose.

Objectives:

- o To promote and support adoption of standards in library operations. o To create databases for projects, specialists and institutions to provide online information services
- o To improve the efficiency of housekeeping operations for exchange of information and documents
- o To generate new services and to improve the efficiency of existing ones Network Development in India:
  Some factors that are responsible for the development of library and information networks in India are:
- o The report of the working group of the planning commission on modernization of library services and informatics for the seventh five year plan, 1985-90
- o The National Policy on Library & Information systems document (1986) accepted by the ministry of HRD, Government of India.
- o The report on national policy on university libraries prepared by the Association of Indian Universities (1987)
- o The UGC report on information systems for science and technology under the Department of Science & Industrial Research (DSIR) Government of India has been vigorously promoting an integrated approach to library automation and networking

Limitations in Network Development

A network may fail in the early stages if there is not proper planning or if adequate funds are not available. Moreover, a common memorandum of agreement signed by the participating libraries at the institutional level is essential for the success of a network venture.

On a more practical level, catalogue data must be in a standard, machine readable form for it to be shared and exchanged. And, finally, a continuous flow of external assistance is crucial for the network's survival.

LIBRARY AND INFORMATION SERVICES

" Impact Of Information Technology Vis-à-vis Free Library Services."

As you have just heard the reasons for charging "extra fee" for library & information services by Mr. Pramod Kumar, yes Indexing do agree with him to some extent, but not as a whole. Nobody can overlook the social aspects of it too. I am totally under the impression that it should be given "free" and for this I put forward my argument as follows:

Library Budget— Every library has a certain budget particularly to collection development & staff salary. As far as salary are concerned, we may here allocate certain budget for these services at the time of preparing expenditure keeping all factors in mind.

Development of the attitude of accessiveness—Due to the availability of almost all the document in the form of CD-ROM have a greater impact on the library services as it will certainly reduce the cost considerably, and the saving thus formed can be used to provide services.

Paper-based Publication—It provides far more comfortable reading, when one has to read continuously and in comfortable postures (in easy chair, sofa, bed, etc.) than any electronic or digital publication. So. The libraries designed with a view to accommodate more digital collections and expectedly fast decreasing paper-based collections will have problems in finding space for the paper-based collections.

Rapid change in IT—With the rapid change in IT, the CD-ROMs which are considered as "interim technologies" are likely to be replaced by DVDs (Digital Video Discs) in the near future, will become unusable as the drive for the CD-ROMs will go out of market. The heavy investments made in CD-ROM collections will have to be repeated for acquiring the new technology based collections.

Converting Problem—Converting the existing library collections into digital libraries will be a formidable task with the associated software, human skills and copyright problems.

Problem with INTERNET based publication—Using Internet based publications has two main problems. ONE, it is the lack of organization of the information published through Internet and so, one has to spend several hrs even for reasonably exhaustive information searches. The Internet may be compared to a large library without a catalogue, whose stock is unclassified and randomly shelved. Given Such chaos and the time needed to become familiar with its ever changing resources, academicians and researches even in advanced countries mostly prefer paper-based scholarly publications than their Internet editions, perhaps because of the convenience.

SECOND, a large part of the information available on Internet is not evaluated OR authentic and therefore cannot be relied upon for serious use. Such a situation can sometimes lead to the possibility that Internet became a vehicle for disinformation, ranging from conscious deception to inadvertent inaccuracies.

Infrastructural cost of IT—In the todays world, IT is enevitable and it reduces the cost. It is a one-time investment and being a major factor, it has been seen that in the subsequent year the cost of IT reduces, so there is at all no need to collect "extra fee". Infact on the other hand, its (IT) diverse functions & power is increasing day by day thus, reducing the cost of its installation as the competition in the market is very high.

Reduce Manpower—Due to the implementation of IT, it reduces the number of manpower to a great extent. Salary, being the most important factor may be saved and thus utilized for giving library services. Resource-Sharing = If the libraries form a network with the help of IT, then each and every library are not supposed to purchase every document in e-form, rather they can themselves make understanding that as per the requirement which library is going to purchase what document, and after that they will share it. Thus, it will empower their library facilities to a greater extent.

Making available the library facilities to outsiders—The library resources and facilities are at present made available to its own users in special & academic libraries. If the same facilities are offered to outsiders by charging, the resultant is generating finances. This is successfully practiced by many Library Information. Centres as " Indian Institute of Chemical Technology, Hyderabad", which is able to generate few lakhs of Rs. Per annum by providing their facilities to industrial houses.

Consultancy & Project work—Library & Information Centres can take the consultancy work for designing the databases, library automation etc. The senior and experienced staff can be assigned such consultancy projects. Successful completion of the consultancy projects generates the finances, which can be used for giving library services to the users. Internet facility= Internet being the household name, and the various services it offered, many of the information is available totally free of cost. Information available on the Net may not be a structured one.

A survey, published in the journal "Computers in libraries" in 1995, found that librarians usually took less time to provide information from library collections than from Internet. A paper published in " Communications of the ACM (1995) also advises, "IF YOU ARE IN A HURRY, GO TO LIBRARY NOT TO INTERNET." Searching on the Net is often more expeditious. This is not to say Internet is not useful for accessing information, but its contribution should not be overemphasized.

If Internet is going to be used by librarians, then a no. Of steps will have to be taken to make it more useful. For e.g. it will be necessary to develop and implement standards for organizing and evaluating information. One possible approach could be developing catalogues for the materials available on Internet in which case the feasibility for such cataloguing is to be worked out first. A problem with such an approach could be that different versions of a file may be accessed through different gophers, and files can disappear, be removed OR amended without warning. Thus, any library cataloguing information of its interest available on Internet has no control on such aspects.

Access point—By implementing IT in our libraries we can provide numerous services from one nodal point to the users, if we just increase the no. of access/ nodal points, we can't charge fee from the users, as initially we have already paid at the time of installation.

Keeping all the above mentioned factors in mind, I think it is not at all necessary to take " extra fee", but inspite of these if we are taking it, then it may create a problem, which in turn hamper the smooth functioning of the libraries. These may be summarized as follows:

(a) *Problem of Marketing*—They have decided to charge "fee", but they have no clue of the whereabouts of the marketing as the demand is not being studied carefully.

(b) *Constant Production*—In cyberspace, often works are constantly changing over time as electronic communities, together create information. In such an environment, at which point is something marked as an identifiable commodity? Similarly, many forms of Net are producing multiple manifestations at different points of time. The problem this raise for libraries is deciding which VERSION(s) of a text to acquire & what will be its cost, & atleast how to sale it, without knowing its users.

(c) *Problem of determining the needs and demand of information clients*—The libraries had not performed any "User Study" before implementing this idea, nor they had collected any data pertaining to it, creating a total collapse of it.

FUNCTIONS OF LIBRARY NETWORKS

Library Networks have been established with the main purpose of sharing resources so that unnecessary wastage of limited finance with them can be avoided. However, not all networks conform to the essential functions of library networks. It is noted that the essential functions should include the promotion of resource sharing, creation of resource sharing tools like union catalogues, rationalization of acquisitions and adoption of international standards for creation of records uniformly and delivery of documents. Keeping these things in view, functions of a typical library network might fall into the following three categories:

(i) Information services to users
(ii) Technical services to member libraries
(iii) Management service to the network administration

Information and technical services are goal-oriented, i.e. to fulfil the primary goal of the network. Functions that serve the users directly, i.e. information services to users are:

Information Services

- Inter-library loan service—it means that each member library may require to have the facility to photocopy for delivering the documents.
- Reference and Referral—each member library may require the facility of having dedicated telephone and/or E-mail service.
- Access to databases—to prepare retrospective bibliography for the purpose of browsing to know whether or not a document is available.

Technical Services

Functions that serve the libraries i.e. the technical services are:

- Cooperative collection development programme
- Technical processing involved in acquisition
- Cataloguing and other means of resources to identify and to locate documents
- Circulation control system

Management Services

The management services, i.e. functions that support the network administration are:

- Establish an operational system that implement the functions mentioned above
- Evaluation of the networks. This is done through
- collection of statistics
- analysis of performance of the network
- user studies
- Training activities. These are done through
- staff development programmes
- user oriented programmes
- Cost analysis

STRUCTURE OF NETWORKING

The earlier stated functions of a network can be implemented in different models of networks.

The structure of a network will depend upon the purpose for which libraries use it. A number of libraries should join the network that offers the facilities to make their functioning simpler, better and more cost effective. For instance, university libraries in a state may choose a model which is of totally decentralized type. However, the affiliated colleges in a university system can be linked to the respective university library, such a model may be known as distributed type. The public library system may choose a model of hierarchical type. Special libraries in a city may choose a model, which is of totally decentralized.

These are three basic anatomical structures, namely:

- Star network
- Hierarchical network
- Distributed network

Star Network

In a star network, one of the members maintains and operates a centralized bibliographical database. This database consists of all the bibliographical records of every member libraries. The node P holds all the bibliographical resources (databases) with all other members A, B, C, D, E utilizing these resources. It is the obligation of the node P to maintain and update the databases.

Hierarchical Network

Each member shares resources locally; each participating library at the lower level passes unsatisfied needs to the participating library which is at the higher level. The requests remaining unsatisfied are referred to the 'library of last resort' which may be obliged to check other centres to locate required materials. The configuration is:

Users of the network, members A1, A2, A3, A4 are mostly satisfied with the resources available in their respective libraries. Unsatisfied requests are passed on to the higher level resource centre B, finally the few remaining unsatisfied requests are referred to the library of last resort C which may be obliged to check other centres B2 and B3 to locate required materials.

Distributed Network

In a totally decentralized model, a type of distributed model, all network members hold in theory different resources which they may share with one another.

Here all members A, B, C, D, E, have different resources which they share with one another.

A modified model of a decentralized network looks like

Here A, B, C and D are themselves a network, either to star type or a hierarchical type.

NETWORK TECHNOLOGY: A BRIEF IDEA

The world over, library networks and consortia have developed technologies to facilitate the process of accessing databases, retrieval of information, processing of interlibrary loan requests and the delivery of documents. So we must have some idea about the network technology in general–various terms used in the context of networking, standards, protocols and the software that convert data from one format to another and the technology relevant to Information and information Service field in particular.

Basic Network Architecture/Topology

A network's architecture is the way the data flows within the network. The basic building blocks of a network are nodes, hubs and backbones

Hub—It is a device that accepts multiple connections. Nodes are connected to it. It, also known as concentrator, simplifies the wiring of the nodes to each other and routes signals between the nodes. There are many different types of hubs. Some are simple hardware devices that only accept connections called passive hubs; others are complicated electrical components that monitor and control the flow of information to various network locations called active hubs.

Ring Architecture

It arranges the nodes on the network in a circle. When one of the computers on the network sends a signal, it passes it to the next node on the network. If it is not addressed to that node, it is retransmitted to the next node and so on around the circle until it reaches the node it is addressed to. The connections between computers are not direct, instead, each computer attaches to a hub and the ring itself resides inside the hub.

Star Architecture

It has the nodes connected to a central, host, computer when one of the computers as the network sends a signal, the next routes it to the node it's addressed to. There are no direct connections between the nodes on the network except through the host computer.

Bus Architecture

Bus, or linear, architecture connects all nodes to a single bus much as the components are organized within the computer. A signal addressed to another node is sent to the bus. All other nodes on the network examine the signal to see if it is addressed to one of them. Typically, wires connect each node to the network's backbone, which is a fixed length of cable with terminator at both ends to stop reflections when signals hit the end.

Hardware Components of a Network

Servers—A server on a network is any computer that can shared by other computers working on the network. In many cases, the server has to be the most powerful computer on the network, because it is shared among so many users or clients. These clients (computers) depend on the server for programmes and data, or connection to other computers and devices.

File Server

It stores data files and some application programmes. It has large amounts of secondary storage in the form of hard disks, CD-ROM drives, tape drives and other storage dievices.

Print Server

It stores print jobs on a hard disk until the printer is ready to handle them.

Communication Server

It can be a fax or modem over which data from any other node can be sent. It can also be used as a gateway to the Internet.

Network Interface Card: It is the key component of the network workstation. It serves a number of purposes:

- It makes the physical connection or bridge between the computer and the network.
- It converts the parallel data on the computer's bus into serial data for the network.
- It boosts or amplifies the signal's strength so it can flow through the cables.

Cables—When signals are sent through a hard-wired network, they are sent along a common set of wires or cables, the network's circulation system. Three types of cables are used to connect the devices:–

(a) *Twisted Pair:* They are the least expensive way to connect computers because the wire is cheap and easy to install. However, they are relatively slow and have a tendency to pack up noise that can cause high error rates.

(b) *Coaxial:* It is the most common type of networking cable. It consists of inner wire surrounded by a layer of insulating material that is, in turn, surrounded by braided wire. They are more reliable and durable.

(c) *Fibre-optic:* It connects of the glass or plastic filament, protector by thick plastic padding and an external plastic sheets. It uses a pulse of laser light instead of an electronic frequency to transmit a signal. Fibre optic cables are fast and reliable, as well as small and light. They have an extremely wide bandwidth, so a large number of signals can be sent simultaneously.

Baseband Cable: A cable that transmits only one signal is called a baseband cable.

Broadband Cable: This can handle simultaneous transmission of different signals by sending them at different frequencies. Broadband cables are more expensive and require additional frequency modulating equipment.

Network Devices: When signals are sent through a network, they must be sent in the right direction, and they must also sometimes be amplified so they travel farther or converted so they can be transferred to a different network.

These are the roles of a series of hardware devices called repeaters, bridges, routers and gateways.

(a) *Repeaters (or Physical relays):* They connect segments of a network, and since signals get weaker and less distinct with distance, these small devices refresh and enhance them before sending them along. They are usually used to extend the network in effect joining two networks together by passing a cable signal between them.

(b) *Bridges (or Data Link Relays):* They connect networks, which use different physical links. For example, a network running on twisted pair wires is connected to one using coaxial cable with a bridge.

(c) *Routers:* They control where messages are sent on networks. The router keeps the addresses of other nodes in a table. If the address of a message sent through the router is on the network, the message is forwarded. If the address is not on the network, the router towards the message to another network by sending it to a gateway.

(d) *Gateways:* Gateways are used to connect different types of networks. Since two networks may not share a common protocol, these devices translate each network's protocol so the other network can understand the data.

RESOURCES SHARING NETWORK: MEANING, NEED AND SCOPE

Resources sharing is sharing of library resources such as document collection, staff members, technical facilities and mechanical aids among the participating libraries on the basic principle of cooperation, "All for one and one for all". In this respect it is possible to consolidate the document collection of participating libraries, exchange their technical capabilities and share their services. In this way it is possible to share the resources to provide on access to the vast amount of library and information sources to a larger user community at the least-cost. The objective of resource sharing is obviously to make the greatest amount of best information available to the most users at the reasonable cost.

Thus Resources sharing is a need-based concept founded on the sound principles of give and take. It is not the quantum of exchange but the real desire to do so, that is essential to become part and parcel of the important programme of resource sharing activities.

NETWORKED INFORMATION RESOURCES

Recently we presented a talk on electronic serials in the National Library in which we drew heavily on an electronic 'zine called *The Wollongong Pig-Breeders Gazette.*

For those of you who are unacquainted with the phenomenon of 'zines, perhaps we should explain that the term refers to popular magazines, produced at low cost and devoted to a particular theme, hence there are fanzines and sci-fi 'zines. In the Internet environment, there are increasing numbers of these to be found, usually produced by one individual and available at no cost. Having used the Wollongong Pig-Breeders Gazette last time, we sought another Australian 'zine around which to base today's talk.

We found one called the Grilled Pterodactyl. However, when we returned to it to select some quotations, the link had been broken and the fanzine had disappeared. There are two lessons to be learnt from this little tale, firstly that electronic networks are spawning new and different forms of publishing, and secondly, that these are likely to disappear at any moment. There is a third lesson here also which we will come back to later.

Like other libraries, the National Library is coming to terms with electronic publishing. Unlike other libraries, however, the National Library has a unique mandate which is expressed in its Act of 1960: *"to maintain and develop a national collection of library materials, including a comprehensive collection relating to Australia and Austratlians"*. This is the library has attempted to do by collecting a wide range of published materials in the form of books, newspapers, journals, ephemera, maps and music, and also unpublished manuscripts, pictorial materials and oral history tapes. These materials are not just collected, they are organised and recorded so that they can be readily located and made accessible, in both the short and the long term, to the Library's wide-ranging clientele. We would like to talk today about how these practices are being extended in a networked electronic environment and some of the issues which have arisen along the way.

Networked electronic publications are found primarily through the Internet. There are others as well, such as online newspapers and database services available through other networks but these at present constitute a minority. The Internet has now been available in Australia for five years and in that time its popularity as a publication medium has grown enormously. Initially, the universities and CSIRO were the major host sites. As Internet access has become more widespread, there are many more producers.

From an organisational point of view, the Internet is chaos in action. It lacks any kind of discernible order (because there is none) and it lacks comprehensive and reliable tools for discovering what is out there. From the point of view of a National Library with a responsibility for the national documentary heritage, it is proving very different to the print world. Several aspects of publishing in the networked environment are important in this regard:

- because anyone can be their own publisher, the quality of much of the material on offer is questionable and vanity publishing abounds
- there is little guarantee of continuity as items can move from one location to another or disappear without notice
- documents can be readily updated or changed making it difficult to know which version one is viewing
- many publications are not discrete entities because of their linkages to other documents hosted elsewhere which may in turn be linked to other documents, and so on. This makes long-term access problematical when links break.

The Library is attempting to bring some order to bear on Australian networked publishing. In doing so, the challenge is to develop mechanisms and standards which are globally applicable and which will enhance access to Internet resources while at the same time maintain the flexibility and spontaneity offered by it as a publication medium. At the time that the National Library Act was written in 1960, library materials were seen primarily as print and paper based and this is reflected in the provisions of the Copyright Act 1968 in regard to legal deposit. Legal deposit has played a significant role in enabling the Library to develop its collections. The Library and the National Film and Sound Archive have recently developed a joint submission to the Copyright Law Review Committee which endorses the principle of legal deposit as a means of "safeguarding the cultural memory of the nation".

The submission seeks extension of legal deposit to include "microforms, audio-visual materials of all kinds and electronic publications, both networked and artefactual (eg CD-ROM), and all formats yet to be developed". It recognises some of the specific issues associated with electronic materials in seeking to permit the reformatting of materials for preservation purposes. The fact that these two institutions are seeking deposit does not necessarily imply that they necessarily would take all technical responsibility for hosting them. Nor does it imply that they would wish to collect everything. The important issue here is that of getting recognition of the principle of legal deposit in the online environment.

In the absence of legal deposit legislation, the Library has already taken action to acquire electronic publications in forms such as CD-ROM and floppy disc. This has been done by development of a voluntary deposit scheme whereby producers agree to lodge copies of their publications with the Library. In return for this, the Library is able to record the existence of these materials for the *Australian National Bibliography* and so that bibliographic records are available through the Australian Bibliographic Network and through its own catalogue. The Library undertakes to ensure that materials are used in accordance with copyright. At a practical level, this means that products are made available to only one reader at a time, the Library ensures that readers are aware of copyright limitations in the copying of works and discourages undue downloading of copyright information. Anyone interested in seeking further details of the library's policy in this regard and the deed which depositors sign, can find the documents involved available on the Library's web server.

Library staff are currently drafting a deed to cover the deposit of Australian electronic journals published on Internet. This will enable the Library to copy the serials for storage and use inhouse and to use in other circumstances in accordance with the fair dealing provisions of the Copyright Act.

Probably the Library's most significant contribution to the handling of networked information to date has been through the establishment of government information on the 'net. A recent accomplishment has been the automatic indexing of all Australian government publishing sites using Harvest technology.

For those who may be wondering what all of this has to do with preservation, the answer is that the server is both publication and preservation tool The contents are regularly backed up as part of its maintenance programme and will stay there as long as required.

One important aspect of server developments has been the issue of metadata standards. Metadata refers to the data description which is embedded into a document. Metadata may include bibliographic elements, technical information and other information, such as whether the item has been quality assessed in some way. If all Australian networked publications used the same metadata standards, identification and description would be much easier.

On the whole the Library has found it easier to come to terms with electronic journals, than it has with the vast mass of other Internet materials which it is not appropriate to refer to as monographs but for which we have not been able to find a better term. E-journals usually come with some commitment to being available in the longer term and they have parallels with their paper-based cousins which make them relatively adaptable to handling in a library setting. The Library has a number of projects in hand which are designed to improve access to Australian electronic serials in both the shorter and longer term.

Firstly, the Library maintains a list of electronic journals on its world wide web server. The list is currently available as an alphabetical listing and will have subject access as well in the future. There are over 400 Australian electronic journals known about at present. The number keeps growing but some inevitably fall by the wayside, as print journals are apt to do also. Those which have disappeared now are gone forever as attempts to identify and preserve titles are only now starting to be made by the major collecting institutions. The Library is also cataloguing e-journals for inclusion on the National Bibliographic Database which is accessible through the Australian Bibliographic Network and inclusion in the Library's online catalogue. The list on the server is complete with links to the journals themselves, where this is possible. The Library proposes also to offer a similar linking facility through the World 1 service, which will replace the Australian Bibliographic Network and also through its online catalogue.

Two other test projects have been set up to facilitate access to electronic journals and to provide the Library with the opportunity to gain experience with the copyright and technology issues associated with collection and preservation.

The first is designed to test the possibility of using World 1 as an archiving platform. A number of journals have been selected for the project and copyright clearance has been obtained for each. This has not been a particular problem as all the titles are available at no cost. The next stage will involve transfer of the data files to World 1. A parallel proposal to host a group of electronic conference proceedings has proven much more complex because of the need to seek copyright clearance from each individual author.

The second project is intended to provide access to subscription electronic journals to inhouse clients. Unlike freely available titles, the Library is not able to simply provide a link to the site through the server for general access. Access to the journal site is usually via password, but there are logistical problems in supplying passwords for clients in a large reading room. One solution is to copy the journals for viewing inhouse only and this we are trying to do. A test group of ten titles has been identified for this trial, for most of which there is a charge.

One of the most importance issues which the Library has had to address in making decisions about the handling of Internet resources is that of lack of expertise. Because the issues involved cross so many areas, it has been important to bring together people from different backgrounds and encourage them to spend time exploring the Internet and gaining the confidence necessary to help them to contribute to decision making processes. Most of the projects mentioned today are experimental. Regardless of the results, the Library will have at the end of them a basis of experience on which to move further forward.

The issue of preservation is being directly addressed by a working group which has been set up specifically to determine a set of guidelines for identifying and selecting electronic publications which should be preserved in the national interest, either by the Library itself or by others in collaboration with the Library. In undertaking this task, the group recognises that the print world provides some useful principles which are also applicable in the electronic world. For example, a preliminary report states: It is neither feasible nor desirable to preserve everything which is published. In this regard, online electronic publications are no different to print publications.

The group also recognises that there are significant differences between the print and electronic worlds and that these will also have to be taken into consideration.

The group plans to concentrate on identifying resources and then examining each to determine whether it would be desirable for the Library to preserve it, whether it should be preserved by another body, or indeed not preserved at all. They will also look at how the item can best be described and whether it presents particular technical characteristics which might effect access.

Another small group is looking at access to Australian Internet resources from the perspective of providing an enhanced reference service to our clients.

This group is looking particularly at the selection of appropriate sites to which clients might be referred and how these can best be described.

They are developing a small database as part of the exercise and will conduct tests to compare ease of access through their own database and through other search tools such as Lycos. There is a cost-effectiveness issue here to be kept in mind and if indeed existing resource discovery tools are adequate, there is a need to consider what value can be added by manual identification and description.

Taming the chaos of the Internet is being tackled on a variety of levels. While undertaking the various projects we have spoken of today, the Library is keeping a watchful eye on developments elsewhere which we may be able to adapt to our advantage. At the same time, it is actively participating in a wide range of collaborative projects associated with electronic publishing and other developments in the communications area.

The time has come to return to the third lesson to be learned from my introduction to today's talk. This is that publications not only can disappear from this Internet but that they can equally unexpectedly reappear. This was the case with the Grilled Pterodactyl. So I would like to read a short excerpt from it to you, by courtesy of its writer and producer, David Grigg.

There is a major need for expert mediated virtual libraries (VLs) of well-selected and described links to scholarly and educational resources.

VLs are one important component in providing for the Internet resource- finding needs of the academic community.

Generalized commercial Web search engines, and even second generation engines such as Google, are often unable to produce consistently relevant results given their generalized focus, the immense amount of territory they cover, and the great number of audiences they serve. Other problems here include a lack of intelligible descriptive information contained in results displays, unobjective representation of search results (since site placement can be purchased), distracting messages and advertisements, and the possibility in the future of becoming fee-based at costs that academia might not be able to bear.

Expert-mediated, objective finding tools that describe and provide well organized, uniform, integrated access are needed because they make important scholarly and educational resources visible and of use to researchers and students.

The response to this need can be seen in the development over the last few years of virtual libraries of categorized links (i.e., Web directories, indexes, portals) of all sorts including the virtual libraries which are now augmenting and produced by, as of the last couple years, the general search engines themselves, such as AltaVista.

We believe that in providing a balanced effort that is positioned between labour intensive MARC cataloguing and traditional library catalogue approaches (1 to 1 hour per record created), generalized minimal indexing approaches of virtual libraries such as Yahoo! (1 minute per record) and the general search engines, academic virtual libraries, such as INFOMINE (25 minutes per record), have been providing an important finding tool service.

This service can be characterized, in most cases, by expert selected and described resources that cohere to various standards (new and traditional) in academic information organization and retrieval, while emphasizing efficient and streamlined approaches to content building.

The Web will continue to grow at an ever-accelerating pace. At their current levels of growth, the summed content of the community of academic virtual libraries will resultingly represent an increasingly smaller portion of the total number of worthwhile Internet resources. Obviously, there are many challenges that virtual library managers now face and need to meet in order to continue to sustain themselves while providing comprehensive, or even representative, coverage of useful research and educational resources.

Personal Area Network

A personal area network (PAN) is a computer network used for communication among computer devices, including telephones and personal digital assistants, in proximity to an individual's body. The devices may or may not belong to the person in question. The reach of a PAN is typically a few meters. PANs can be used for communication among the personal devices themselves (intrapersonal communication), or for connecting to a higher level network and the Internet (an uplink).

Personal area networks may be wired with computer buses such as USB and FireWire. A wireless personal area network (WPAN) can also be made possible with wireless network technologies such as IrDA, Bluetooth, UWB, Z-Wave and ZigBee.

Technology

A Bluetooth PAN is also called a piconet, and is composed of up to 8 active devices in a master-slave relationship (a very large number of devices can be connected in "parked" mode). The first Bluetooth device in the piconet is the master, and all other devices are slaves that communicate with the master. A piconet typically has a range of 10 metres (33 ft), although ranges of up to 100 metres (330 ft) can be reached under ideal circumstances.

Recent innovations in Bluetooth antennas have allowed these devices to greatly exceed the range for which they were originally designed. At DEF CON 12, a group of hackers known as "Flexilis" successfully connected two Bluetooth devices more than half a mile (800 m) away. They used an antenna with a scope and Yagi antenna, all attached to a rifle stock. A cable attached the antenna to a Bluetooth card in a computer. They later named the antenna "The BlueSniper." Skinplex, another PAN technology, transmits via the capacitive near field of human skin. Skinplex can detect and communicate up to 1 metre (3 ft 3 in) from a human body. It is already used for access control for door locks and jamming protection in convertible car roofs.

Wireless PAN

A WPAN (wireless personal area network) is a personal area network—a network for interconnecting devices centered around an individual person's workspace - in which the connections are wireless. Typically, a wireless personal area network uses some technology that permits communication within about 10 metres (33 ft) such as Bluetooth, which was used as the basis for a new standard, IEEE 802.15. A WPAN could serve to interconnect all the ordinary computing and communicating devices that many people have on their desk or carry with them today - or it could serve a more specialized purpose such as allowing the surgeon and other team members to communicate during an operation.

A key concept in WPAN technology is known as "plugging in". In the ideal scenario, when any two WPAN-equipped devices come into close proximity (within several meters of each other) or within a few kilometers of a central server, they can communicate as if connected by a cable.

Another important feature is the ability of each device to lock out other devices selectively, preventing needless interference or unauthorized access to information.

The technology for WPANs is in its infancy and is undergoing rapid development. Proposed operating frequencies are around 2.4 GHz in digital modes. The objective is to facilitate seamless operation among home or business devices and systems. Every device in a WPAN will be able to plug in to any other device in the same WPAN, provided they are within physical range of one another. In addition, WPANs worldwide will be interconnected. Thus, for example, an archeologist on site in Greece might use a PDA to directly access databases at the University of Minnesota in Minneapolis, and to transmit findings to that database.

Computer Networks and Internet Technology

Computer networks and Internet technology - This article gives a brief outline of foundation for networks, direct link networks, packet switching, internetworking, end-to-end protocols, resource allocation issues, and applications.

Computer Networks

When two or more computers are interconnected to each other via some kind of medium to share resources then the state is called computer network.

Connection Method

Computer networks can also be classified according to the hardware and software technology that is used to interconnect the individual devices in the network, such as Optical fiber, Ethernet, Wireless LAN, HomePNA, Power line communication or G.hn.

Ethernet uses physical wiring to connect devices.

Frequently deployed devices include hubs, network switches, network bridges and/or routers.

Wireless LAN technology is designed to connect devices without wiring. These devices use radio waves or infrared signals as a transmission medium. Ethernet over coax technology uses existing home wiring (coaxial cable, phone lines and power lines) to create a high-speed (up to 1 Gigabit/s) local area network.

Wired Technologies

Twisted pair—This is the most widely used medium for telecommunication. Twisted-pair wires are ordinary telephone wires which consist of two insulated copper wires twisted into pairs and are used for both voice and data transmission. The use of two wires twisted together helps to reduce crosstalk and electromagnetic induction. The transmission speed range from 2 million bits per second to 100 million bits per second.

Coaxial cable—These cables are widely used for cable television systems, office buildings, and other worksites for local area networks. The cables consist of copper or aluminum wire wrapped with insulating layer typically of a flexible material with a high dielectric constant, all of which are surrounded by a conductive layer. The layers of insulation help minimize interference and distortion. Transmission speed range from 200 million to more than 500 million bits per second.

Fiber optics—These cables consist of one or more thin filaments of glass fiber wrapped in a protective layer. It transmits light which can travel over long distance and higher bandwidths.

Fiber-optic cables are not affected by electromagnetic radiation. Transmission speed could go up to as high as trillions of bits per second. The speed of fiber optics is hundreds of times faster than coaxial cables and thousands of times faster than twisted-pair wire.

Wireless Technologies

Terrestrial microwave—Terrestrial microwaves use Earth-based transmitter and receiver. The equipment look similar to satellite dishes. Terrestrial microwaves use low-gigahertz range, which limits all communications to line-of-sight. Path between relay stations spaced approx. 30 miles apart. Microwave antennas are usually placed on top of buildings, towers, hills, and mountain peaks.

Communications satellites—The satellites use microwave radio as their telecommunications medium which are not deflected by the Earth's atmosphere. The satellites are stationed in space, typically 22,000 miles above the equator. These Earth-orbiting systems are capable of receiving and relaying voice, data, and TV signals.

Cellular and PCS Systems—Use several radio communications technologies. The systems are divided to different geographic area. Each area has low-power transmitter or radio relay antenna device to relay calls from one area to the next area.

Wireless LANs—Wireless local area network use a high-frequency radio technology similar to digital cellular and a low-frequency radio technology. Wireless LANS use spread spectrum technology to enable communication between multiple devices in a limited area. Example of open-standard wireless radio-wave technology is IEEE 802.11b.

Bluetooth—A short range wireless technology. Operate at approx. 1Mbps with range from 10 to 100 meters. Bluetooth is an open wireless protocol for data exchange over short distances.

The wireless Web—The wireless web refers to the use of the World Wide Web through equipments like cellular phones, pagers, PDAs, and other portable communication devices. The wireless web service offers anytime/ anywhere connection.

Scale

Networks are often classified as LAN, WAN, MAN, PAN, VPN, CAN, SAN, etc. depending on their scale, scope and purpose. Usage, trust levels and access rights often differ between these types of network - for example, LANs tend to be designed for internal use by an organization's internal systems and employees in individual physical locations (such as a building), while WANs may connect physically separate parts of an organization to each other and may include connections to third parties.

Functional Relationship (Network Architecture)

Computer networks may be classified according to the functional relationships which exist among the elements of the network, e.g., Active Networking, Client-server and Peer-to-peer (workgroup) architecture.

Network Topology

Computer networks may be classified according to the network topology upon which the network is based, such as bus network, star network, ring network, mesh network, star-bus network, tree or hierarchical topology network. Network topology signifies the way in which devices in the network see their logical relations to one another.

The use of the term "logical" here is significant. That is, network topology is independent of the "physical" layout of the network.

Even if networked computers are physically placed in a linear arrangement, if they are connected via a hub, the network has a Star topology, rather than a bus topology. In this regard the visual and operational characteristics of a network are distinct; the logical network topology is not necessarily the same as the physical layout. Networks may be classified based on the method of data used to convey the data, these include digital and analog networks.

OSI-ISO Model

The Open System Interconnection Reference Model (OSI Reference Model or OSI Model) is an abstract description for layered communications and computer network protocoldesign. It was developed as part of the Open Systems Interconnection (OSI) initiative.[1 In its most basic form, it divides network architecture into seven layers which, from top to bottom, are the Application, Presentation, Session, Transport, Network, Data- Link, and Physical Layers.

It is therefore often referred to as the OSI Seven Layer Model. A layer is a collection of conceptually similar functions that provide services to the layer above it and receives service from the layer below it. On each layer an instance provides services to the instances at the layer above and requests service from the layer below.

For example, a layer that provides error-free communications across a network provides the path needed by applications above it, while it calls the next lower layer to send and receive packets that make up the contents of the path. Conceptually two instances at one layer are connected by a horizontal protocol connection on that layer.

TELECOMMUNICATIONS AND NETWORKING

Telecommunication

Telecommunication is the transmission of information over significant distances to communicate. In earlier times, telecommunications involved the use of visual signals, such asbeacons, smoke signals, semaphore telegraphs, signal flags, and optical heliographs, or audio messages via coded drumbeats, lung-blown horns, or sent by loud whistles, for example. In the modern age of electricity and electronics, telecommunications now also includes the use of electrical devices such as the telegraph, telephone, and teleprinter, as well as the use of radio and microwave communications, as well as fibre optics and their associated electronics, plus the use of the orbiting satellites and the Internet.

A revolution in wireless telecommunications began in the first decade of the 20th century with pioneering developments in wireless radio communications by Nikola Tesla and Guglielmo Marconi. Marconi won the Nobel Prize in Physics in 1909 for his efforts. Other highly notable pioneering inventors and developers in the field of electrical and electronic telecommunications include Charles Wheatstone and Samuel Morse (telegraph), Alexander Graham Bell (telephone), Edwin Armstrong, and

Lee de Forest (radio), as well as John Logie Baird and Philo Farnsworth (television).

The world's effective capacity to exchange information through two-way telecommunication networks grew from 281 petabytes of (optimally compressed) information in 1986, to 471 petabytes in 1993, to 2.2 (optimally compressed) exabytes in 2000, and to 65 (optimally compressed) exabytes in 2007. This is the informational equivalent of 2 newspaper pages per person per day in 1986, and 6 entire newspapers per person per day by 2007. Given this growth, telecommunications play an increasingly important role in the world economy and the worldwide telecommunication industry's revenue was estimated to be $3.85 trillion in 2008. The service revenue of the global telecommunications industry was estimated to be $1.7 trillion in 2008, and is expected to touch $2.7 trillion by 2013.

Etymology

The word telecommunication was adapted from the French word telecommunication. It is a compound of the Greek prefix tele-meaning "far off", and the Latin communicare, meaning "to share". The French word telecommunication was first invented in the French Grande Ecole "Telecom ParisTech" formerly known as "Ecole nationale superieure des telecommunications" in 1904 by the French engineer and novelist Édouard Estaunié.

HISTORY

Ancient systems

Greek hydraulic semaphore systems were used as early as the 4th century BC. The hydraulic semaphores, which worked with water filled vessels and visual signals, functioned as optical telegraphs. However, they could only utilize a very limited range of pre-determined messages, and as with all such optical telegraphs could only be deployed during good visibility conditions.

During the Middle Ages, chains of beacons were commonly used on hilltops as a means of relaying a signal. Beacon chains suffered the drawback that they could only pass a single bit of information, so the meaning of the message such as "the enemy has been sighted" had to be agreed upon in advance. One notable instance of their use was during the Spanish Armada, when a beacon chain relayed a signal from Plymouth to London that signalled the arrival of the Spanish warships.

Systems since the Middle Ages

In 1792, Claude Chappe, a French engineer, built the first fixed visual telegraphy system (orsemaphore line) between Lille and Paris. However semaphore systems suffered from the need for skilled operators and the expensive towers at intervals of 10–30 kilometers (6–20 mi). As a result of competition from the electrical telegraph, Europe's last commercial semaphore line in Sweden was abandoned in 1880.

Telegraph and Telephone

The first commercial electrical telegraph was constructed by Sir Charles Wheatstone and SirWilliam Fothergill Cooke, and its use began on April 9, 1839. Both Wheatstone and Cooke viewed their device as "an improvement to the [already-existing, so-called] electromagnetic telegraph" not as a new device.

The businessman Samuel F.B. Morse and the physicist Joseph Henry of the United States developed their own, simpler version of the electrical telegraph, independently. Morse successfully demonstrated this system on September 2, 1837. Morse's most important technical contribution to this telegraph was the rather simple and highly efficient Morse Code, which was an important advance over Wheatstone's complicated and significantly more expensive telegraph system. The communications efficiency of the Morse Code anticipated that of the Huffman code in digital communications by over 100 years, but Morse and his associate Alfred Vail developed the code purely empirically, unlike Huffman, who gave a detailed theoretical explanation of how his method worked.

The first permanent transatlantic telegraph cable was successfully completed on 27 July 1866, allowing transatlantic electrical communication for the first time. An earlier transatlantic cable had operated for a few months in 1859, and among other things, it carried messages of greeting back and forth between President James Buchanan of the United States and Queen Victoria of the United Kingdom.

However, that transatlantic cable failed soon, and the project to lay a replacement line was delayed for five years by the American Civil War. Also, these transatlantic cables would have been completely incapable of carrying telephone calls even had the telephone already been invented. The first transatlantic telephone cable (which incorporated hundreds of electronic amplifiers) was not operational until 1956.

The conventional telephone now in use worldwide was first patented by Alexander Graham Bell in March 1876. That first patent by Bell was the master patent of the telephone, from which all other patents for electric telephone devices and features flowed. Credit for the invention of the electric telephone has been frequently disputed, and new controversies over the issue have arisen from time-to-time. As with other great inventions such as radio, television, the light bulb, and the digital computer, there were several inventors who did pioneering experimental work on voice transmission over a wire, and then they improved on each other's ideas. However, the key innovators were Alexander Graham Bell and Gardiner Greene Hubbard, who created the first telephone company, the Bell Telephone Company in the United States, which later evolved into American Telephone & Telegraph (AT&T).

The first commercial telephone services were set up in 1878 and 1879 on both sides of the Atlantic in the cities of New Haven, Connecticut, and London, England.

Radio and Television

In 1832, James Lindsay gave a classroom demonstration of wireless telegraphy via conductive water to his students. By 1854, he was able to demonstrate a transmission across the Firth of Tay from Dundee, Scotland, to Woodhaven, a distance of about two miles (3 km), again using water as the transmission medium. In December 1901, Guglielmo Marconi established wireless communication between St. John's, Newfoundland and Poldhu, Cornwall (England), earning him the Nobel Prize in Physics for 1909, one which he shared with Karl Braun. However small-scale radio communication had already been demonstrated in 1893 by Nikola Tesla in a presentation before the National Electric Light Association.

On March 25, 1925, John Logie Baird of Scotland was able to demonstrate the transmission of moving pictures at the Selfridge's department store in London, England. Baird's system relied upon the fast- rotating Nipkow disk, and thus it became known as the mechanical television. It formed the basis of experimental broadcasts done by the British Broadcasting Corporation beginning September 30, 1929. However, for most of the 20th century, television systems were designed around the cathode ray tube, invented by Karl Braun. The first version of such anelectronic television to show promise was produced by Philo Farnsworth of the United States, and it was demonstrated to his family in Idahoon September 7, 1927.

Television, however, is not solely a technology, limited to its basic and practical application. It functions both as an appliance, and also as a means for social story telling and message dissemination. It is a cultural tool that provides a communal experience of receiving information and experiencing fantasy. It acts as a "window to the world" by bridging audiences from all over through programming of stories, triumphs, and tragedies that are outside of personal experiences.

Computer Networks and the Internet

On 11 September 1940, George Stibitz was able to transmit problems using teleprinter to his Complex Number Calculator in New York and receive the computed results back at Dartmouth College in New Hampshire. This configuration of a centralized computer or mainframe computer with remote "dumb terminals" remained popular throughout the 1950s and into the 60's.

However, it was not until the 1960s that researchers started to investigate packet switching — a technology that allows chunks of data to be sent between different computers without first passing through a centralized mainframe. A four-node network emerged on December 5, 1969. This network soon became the ARPANET, which by 1981 would consist of 213 nodes.

ARPANET's development centred around the Request for Comment process and on 7 April 1969, RFC 1 was published. This process is important for the reason that ARPANET would eventually merge with other networks to form the Internet, and many of the communication protocols that the Internet relies upon today were specified through the Request for Comment process. In September 1981, RFC 791 introduced the Internet Protocol version 4 (IPv4) and RFC 793 introduced the Transmission Control Protocol (TCP) — thus creating the TCP/IP protocol that much of the Internet relies upon today.

However, not all important developments were made through the Request for Comment process. Two popular link protocols for local area networks (LANs) also appeared in the 1970s. A patent for the token ring protocol was filed by Olof Soderblom on October 29, 1974, and a paper on the Ethernet protocol was published by Robert Metcalfe and David Boggs in the July 1976 issue of Communications of the ACM. The Ethernet protocol had been inspired by the ALOHAnet protocol which had been developed by electrical engineering researchers at the University of Hawaii.

NETWORK SECURITY

In the field of networking, the area of network security consists of the provisions and policies adopted by the network administrator to prevent and monitor unauthorized access, misuse, modification, or denial of the computer network and network-accessible resources. Network security is the authorization of access to data in a network, which is controlled by the network administrator. Users are assigned an ID and password that allows them access to information and programs within their authority. Network Security covers a variety of computer networks, both public and private that are used in everyday jobs conducting transactions and communications among businesses, government agencies & individuals.

NETWORK RESILIENCE

In computer networking: "Resilience is the ability to provide and maintain an acceptable level of service in the face of faults and challenges to normal operation."

Views of Networks

Users and network administrators typically have different views of their networks. Users can share printers and some servers from a workgroup, which usually means they are in the same geographic location and are on the same LAN, whereas a Network Administrator is responsible to keep that network up and running.

Network administrators can see networks from both physical and logical perspectives. The physical perspective involves geographic locations, physical cabling, and the network elements (e.g., routers, bridges and application layer gateways) that interconnect the physical media. Logical networks, called, in the TCP/IP architecture, subnets, map onto one or more physical media. For example, a common practice in a campus of buildings is to make a set of LAN cables in each building appear to be a common subnet, using virtual LAN (VLAN) technology. Both users and administrators will be aware, to varying extents, of the trust and scope characteristics of a network. Intranets do not have to be connected to the Internet, but generally have a limited connection. Anextranet is an extension of an intranet that allows secure communications to users outside of the intranet (e.g. business partners, customers).

Unofficially, the Internet is the set of users, enterprises, and content providers that are interconnected by Internet Service Providers (ISP). From an engineering viewpoint, the Internet is the set of subnets, and aggregates of subnets, which share the registered IP address space and exchange information about the reachability of those IP addresses using the Border Gateway Protocol. Typically, the human-readablenames of servers are translated to IP addresses, transparently to users, via the directory function of the Domain Name System (DNS). Over the Internet, there can be business-to-business (B2B), business-to-consumer (B2C) and consumer-to-consumer (C2C) communications. Especially when money or sensitive information is exchanged, the communications are apt to be secured by some form of communications security mechanism. Intranets and extranets can be securely superimposed onto the Internet, without any access by general Internet users and administrators, using secure Virtual Private Network (VPN) technology.

❐

3

Software Uses in University Libraries

University libraries are complex entities, having large collections and serving a huge clientele. To carry out various operations in a library effectively, there is a need for automation.

Computer and communication technologies have brought revolutionary changes in the information acquisition, processing, storage, retrieval and dissemination. Keeping in view the latest trends in Information Technology (IT), INFLIBNET Centre has developed a Windows based Library Management Software "SOUL", which provides total solution for Library Automation.

SOUL is designed using Client-Server Architecture which imparts extra strength to storage capacity, multiple access to single database, various levels of security, back up and storage facilities etc. This software has been designed after a comprehensive study of different library related functions practiced in university libraries. It has MS-SQL Server 6.5 RDBMS as the back end. This user-friendly software is quite easy to work with. The software comprises following modules:

- Acquisition
- Catalogue
- Circulation
- OPAC
- Serial Control
- Administration

The in-built network feature of the software will allow multiple libraries of the same university to function together as well as access to the distributed databases installed at various university libraries and union catalogue mounted at INFLIBNET using VSAT network.

MANAGEMENT INFORMATION SYSTEMS IN LIBRARIES

The contemporary approach casts academic librarians as managers within the higher education system. What academic librarians need, now much more than ever before, is the information which will allow them to plan properly, to know whether or not the library service is meeting the needs of the academic community.

The introduction of computers into academic libraries was largely a response to the problem of dealing with increased workloads with fewer staff, and they are now able easily to handle most of the routine and repetitive work of the library staff. In addition, they have the capability to enhance the provision of management information, since automated data processing is able to present reports more accurately and much faster than manual systems.

Nonetheless, most librarians claim that they would now like to install decision support systems, even though they see the expense as a problem. Living in an age of such information explosion, Management Information Systems (MIS) have emerged as a solution to this capacity expansion requirement of Academic Libraries. The MIS's function is to provide library Staff and Readers with data, information, analysis and tools that enhance the effectiveness and efficiency of library services and assist in the decision- making process.

The objectives of an MIS are to assist staff with the daily decision making process, to maintain better accountability and control of resources, to monitor budget allocations, to improve overall library effectiveness by focusing on outcomes to generate internal and external reports to improve long-term planning and to facilitate performance measures activities. Further, the MIS intervention offers utility to Readers too by means of a wider bibliographic database through e-resources. The present study is therefore an attempt to propose collaborative partnership with neighboring university libraries of Chhattisgarh in order to make better use of common resources and to improve services to Readers.

A management information system (MIS) is a subset of the overall internal controls covering the application of people, documents, technologies, and procedures. According to McClure (1990), Management information systems are tools designed to improve management decisions. The terms MIS and information system are often confused. Information systems include systems that are not intended for decision making. The expansionary momentum of the 1960s and 1970s was followed by pressure for efficiency and economies. The 1980s was not a period in which academic libraries prospered. The four main objectives for Management Information systems have been defined as: (1) to facilitate the decision making process in the library by providing the managers with accurate, timely, and selective information that assists them in determining a specific course of action.

(2) to provide for the objective performance measurement and assessment of selected relevant areas of the library. The areas are to be determined during strategic planning. (3) to provide pertinent information about the library's internal and external environment and, (4) to provide information on alternative strategies and contingency plans.

In recent years, data processing for management information systems in business and industry has increasingly been undertaken by computers. In libraries, in contrast, the development of the use of computer has been modular, in the sense that it is based on a single library operation such as acquisitions, serials, control or cataloguing. The more general applications of management information lay hidden, as it is often seen only as a departmental resource. Technological changes have helped to ease this problem. As opposed to the use of mainframe and mini-computers, the advent of the microcomputer now provides an alternative to the dependence on large-scale centralized computer systems.

Data Analysis and Interpretation

The present study is intended to investigate about Library Effectiveness by maintaining Library Automation in the University Libraries of Chhattisgarh. Using appropriate statistical tables, common reference of F-ratio was applied to test the significance of differences for verification of various hypotheses. Scores for all the scales collected from all the samples were analysed separately. The study further uses a three- dimensional (3 x 2 x 8) ANOVA technique at SPSS to analyze the data whereby numerical values were assigned for various independent variables of the study. Three levels of Library Automations were studied as low, moderate and high respectively. For the dimension of Readers, the two categories were Teachers and Students respectively. For the dimension of Universities, the eight University Libraries of Chhattisgarh were studied.

Finally, Library Effectiveness was observed as the dependent variable. For the first problem, results reveal the overall mean score of 129.62 making a favorable indication that Library Automations positively effects the Library Effectiveness perception of Readers. Further, for the effects of various levels of Library Automations on Library Effectiveness, the mean scores of 66.89, 130.33 and 191.64 respectively at the low, moderate and higher levels of Library Automation make it clearly evident that higher the Library Automation more will be the Library Effectiveness perception of the Readers. For the second problem, the respective mean scores of Teachers and Students as 148.36 and 110.87 proved that the Teachers of all libraries perceived their library as more effective compared to their students.

Significant main effect value (F = 20.148, p=.000) was found thus there remained no two ways to accept the first hypothesis that Library Automations strongly affect the Library Effectiveness. Significant main effect value (F = 16.52, p=.001) exhibited that there are significant differences between perceptions of Teachers and Students for the overall Library Effectiveness perceptions higher Library Automations in their University Library.

The third main effect, 'Libraries' i.e. the eight University Libraries of Chhattisgarh, studies the different levels of Automation in subjected Libraries and its effect on the perception of the Readers over its Effectiveness state. According to the study, again the significant main effect value (F = 24.15, p=.0001), indicated that the Libraries in the present study vary with their levels of Automation and resulting in a varying reader perception over their Effectiveness status.

All three first-order interactions were found to have significant results. Significant results as (F = 19.74, p =.000) for Level of Library Automation and Reader; (F = 19.21, p =.001) for Level of Library Automation and Libraries; (F = 27.168, p =.002) for Readers and Libraries.

Pandit Ravishankar Shukla University Library scored highest at all levels, followed by Guru Ghasidas University, Indira Gandhi Krishi Vishwavidyalaya, Indira Kala Sangeet Vishwavidyalaya, Hidayatullah National Law University, Chhattisgarh Swami Vivekanand Technical University, Pandit Sundarlal Sharma (Open) University and lastly Kushabhau Thakre Patrakarita Avam Jansanchar Vishwavidyalaya. The second-order interaction giving the combined effect of Level of Library Automation,Readers and, Libraries with the dependent variable Library Effectiveness were also studied. Significant F-value for this second-order interaction (F = 14.114, p=.000) was obtained for this joint interaction indicating a significant interaction of all the independent variables together with the dependent variable 'Library Effectiveness'

The fact that some libraries claimed to have only 'informal' or 'partial' management information systems or to have no management information systems does not mean that they had no collection of external and internal data. They do collect and use information for establishing library objectives and priorities or for resources allocation, but they have not formalized their management information systems, typically because their institutions had not required them to do so. Organizational commitment therefore stands as major prerequisite for successful implementation of MIS in university libraries.

WEB SERVICE SOFTWARE FACTORY

The Web Service Software Factory (also known as the Service Factory) is an integrated collection of tools, patterns, source code and prescriptive guidance. It is designed to help you quickly and consistently construct Web services that adhere to well known architecture and design patterns.

If you are an architect or developer responsible for building service-based applications, the patterns & practices team would like to invite you to learn how the Service Factory can help your future service development activities.

The Service Factory provides guidance that addresses many of the challenges associated with building ASP.NET (ASMX) and Windows Communication Foundation (WCF) Web services and the components of a distributed application. These challenges include:

- Designing ASMX and WCF messages and service interfaces.
- Applying exception shielding and exception handling.
- Designing business entities in the domain model.
- Translating messages to and from business entities.
- Designing, building, and invoking the data access layer.
- Validating the conformance of service implementation, configuration, and security using code analysis.
- Planning for the migration to WCF.
- Applying security to WCF services.
- Applying message validation.

Use the following information to determine whether Service Factory is right for you, your team, and the services you are building.

What is the Service Factory?

Generally speaking, software factories represent a collection of guidance that helps architects and developers build a specific kind of application. Therefore, the Service Factory helps developers and architects build Web service applications. Web service applications are more than just the technologies that send and receive SOAP messages and expose WSDL contracts—they also include the functionality that is needed to fulfil the service's behaviour. Figure illustrates the parts of the application, and their relationship with one another, the Service Factory will help you build.

In addition to the challenges listed in the "Summary" section, the reality is that technologies are constantly evolving. Another challenge that should be addressed is how to build XML Web services using the. NET Framework 2.0 (ASP.NET and Web Services Enhancements (WSE)) so they can be migrated in the near future to the.NET Framework 3.0 (WCF, Windows Workflow (WF), and CardSpace™). The Service Factory helps build services on currently shipping technologies that have a path to future technologies. It does this by introducing concepts that are closely related to the next generation technologies and providing design guidance that minimizes the amount of future change. If you are already building services using WCF, the Service Factory also helps you build and secure those services.

Service Factory guidance is available in three basic forms:

- Written documentation. In addition to detailed How-to topics and the printable patterns enabled through the use of the Service Factory, there are several architecture-related topics that explore the finer details and rationale of the guidance. For example:
- Web Service Application Architecture
- Message Design in Service-Oriented Applications
- Exception Handling in Service-Oriented Applications
- Planning for and Migrating to WCF
- Guidance packages. Using the Guidance Automation Extensions with guidance packages, developers can have a "conversation" with Visual Studio 2005 through the use of wizards and shortcut menus. The conversation results in the generation of source code and configuration that adhere to proven practices. Two guidance packages are included in the Service Factory:
- ASMX guidance package. This guidance package helps build the service interface, the messages the service will expose and consume, and the translators that map these messages to domain model entities.
- Data Access guidance package. This guidance package helps build business entities from and existing data model, build stored procedures from a data model, and generate the repository classes and factories that comprise the data access logic.
- WCF guidance package. This guidance package helps build the service interface, the messages and data contracts the service will expose and consume, and the translators that map these messages to domain model entities.
- WCF Security guidance package. This guidance package helps secure WCF services using X.509, Kerberos, and direct authentication approaches by generating the necessary configuration sections.
- Reference implementation. Global Bank is a fictitious organization whose requirements are addressed by this solution. The solution was built using the preceding guidance packages and can be used as an example of how to apply additional functionality, such as logging and exception management, to a service.

The Service Factory provides the following benefits:

- Increased quality. It provides tested and accepted reusable assets, guidance, and examples that address common scenarios and challenges. It is based on patterns derived from proven industry and Microsoft practices.
- Increased predictability. The patterns & practices team works closely with the development teams responsible for building current and future generations of service and data access technologies. All services built with the Service Factory will be built in a predictable way, arrive at a predictable result, and will enable a predictable migration path to future technologies.
- Increased productivity. It includes automated code and configuration file generation for Visual Studio 2005. With this automation, developers can easily apply guidance in consistent and repeatable ways. Developers can also effectively use the.NET Framework without having to devote significant time to learning the necessary APIs.
- Increased flexibility. The Service Factory is carefully designed according to proven practices, but it is also open and highly customizable. Architects and development leads can customize the factory to include the conventions, policies, and practices specific to a team or organization.

Intended Audience

Based on the target audience, the Service Factory will provide various levels of value. This target audience can be defined by the role of the person using it, and the type of application being built:

- *Architects.* If you are an architect with a focus on service orientation, it is likely the Service Factory was designed with you in mind because of the responsibilities of your role.
- *Developers on a team.* If you are a developer on a team and your responsibilities do not span all of the layers in Figure, the guidance packages can be installed separately to help you build the part of the application you are responsible for. Development of these various layers can often occur simultaneously. Also, the Service Factory should help larger teams realize larger productivity gains.
- *Single developer.* If you are a developer who is responsible for building the entire service, the Service Factory includes detailed guidance about how and when to perform the activities necessary to construct each layer. During this process, you will also have

the confidence that you are adhering to established patterns and proven practices.

- *Service types.* This release of the Service Factory helps with the following services:
- *Entity services.* These services provide access to data entities that provide a business-oriented view of the information managed and manipulated by an organization's processes while encapsulating the details of their persistence strategy. An example operation might be "Get Customer Details."
- Activity services. These services deliver repeatable encapsulated business value and may require the consumption of entity services to fulfil the request. An example operation might be "RetrieveCreditScore."

Future releases of the Service Factory will also help with the following services:

- Process services. These services manage long-running business processes. These services are controlled by an organization's workflows, and they often orchestrate the use of other services. An example operation might be "Process Insurance Claim."
- Utility services. These services provide infrastructure functionality, such as logging, content routing, security, and publish/subscribe capabilities. These services may operate on the headers or body of the message, and they may have to comply with specifications, such as WS-Security.

The patterns & practices team expects individuals and organizations to standardize on the use of Service Factory for the development of their services. This will ensure consistency across services and provide predictability for future technology evolutions.

Getting Started

The best way to get familiar with the Service Factory is to view the webcast listed in the "Summary" section. This introduction tells you why the Service Factory was built and demonstrates the guidance automation experience in Visual Studio. Toward the end of the webcast, there is a demonstration that applies security to a WCF service using the next release of the Service Factory.

The best way to begin your evaluation of the Service Factory is to download the hands-on lab listed in the "Summary" section. This lab introduces you to many of the activities that will be performed during the construction of an ASP.NET service in C# for the fictitious Coho Winery:

- Exercise 1: Create solution structure
- Exercise 2: Create data types
- Exercise 3: Create message types
- Exercise 4: Create service operations
- Exercise 5: Create business entities
- Exercise 6: Translate between messages and business entities
- Exercise 7: Create CRUD stored procedures
- Exercise 8: Create data repository classes
- Exercise 9: Invoke data access layer
- Exercise 10: Wire up client and test service

The lab has been put together in such a way that the exercises can be completed in order, but you can also start at any point and perform the exercises in any order that is appropriate for your learning.

If there are specific areas you would like to know more about, you can use the "Exploring the Service Factory" topic in the documentation.

System Requirements

To view and run the Service Factory assets in your development environment, you need the following software installed on your computers:

- Microsoft Windows 2000, Windows XP Professional, Windows Server 2003, or Windows Vista operating system
- Microsoft.NET Framework 3.0
- Microsoft Visual Studio 2005 (with the exception of the Express edition)
- Microsoft SQL Server 2005 Express Edition or SQL Server 2005
- Guidance Automation Extensions Technology Preview (February 2007 Release for Visual Studio 2005)

In addition, you may want to install the following software:

- If you will be modifying the Web Service Software Factory guidance package, you must install the Guidance Automation Toolkit Technology Preview (February 2007 Release for Visual Studio 2005) in addition to the Guidance Automation Extensions.
- If you want to use the Enterprise Library Configuration Tool—for example, to modify the settings in the Data Access Application Block that is being used in the reference implementation—you will need to install Enterprise Library.
- To run the Visual Studio Team System (VSTS) unit tests, you must have Visual Studio Team System version 2005 installed.
- To run the NUnit tests, you must have NUnit version 2.2.7.0 installed. You can download NUnit from the NUnit Web site.

Future Plans

The good news is that this is not the last version of the Web Service Software Factory. The next version of the Service Factory is expected to be released toward the end of the 2007 calendar year and will focus primarily on service modelling, additional automated guidance, and composing various parts of the application's architecture. Planning for these releases is in the very early stages, but the key areas of focus are likely to include the following:

- Service modelling
- Data access

Service Modelling

Adding support for modelling Web services using a Domain Specific Language (DSL) is a major theme for the next release of Service Factory. The details of exactly how this will be implemented have not yet been finalized.

Data Access

This release of the Service Factory includes guidance to help developers adhere to proven practices while building business-entity based data access layers with ADO.NET 2.0.

The next release of Visual Studio will include additional features designed to simplify the process of designing and implementing data-driven.NET Framework applications, in the form of.NET Language Integrated Query (LINQ). LINQ to ADO.NET will enable the LINQ programming model to work with the Microsoft managed code data access platform. As these new technologies become available, the recommended practices for building data-driven applications will be updated.

The initial releases of the Service Factory target ADO.NET 2.0, but the suggested patterns and approaches for building data access layers and entities are designed to simplify migration to the LINQ to ADO. NET technologies in the future. To demonstrate this migration, the patterns & practices team will release migration guidance and reference implementations that show how the Service Factory architecture applies these new technologies. The Service Factory will also be updated to fully support these technologies when they are officially released.

Known Issues

For information about known issues with the Service Factory, read the KnownIssues.htm file. To view this file, click Start on the taskbar, point to All Programmes, point to Microsoft patterns & practices, point to Web Service Software Factory, and then click Known Issues.

Feedback and Support

To provide feedback about this guidance, or to get help with any problems, visit the Web Service Software Factory Community Web site. The message board on the community workspace is the preferred feedback and support channel because it allows you to share your ideas, questions, and solutions with the entire community.

Note It is very important you understand that all the releases on the community workspace are NOT final in any way. They have not yet undergone the complete array of performance and security tests, so patterns & practices team recommends that you treat downloads from the community as beta guidance.

Authors and Contributors

The Service Factory was produced by the following individuals:

- *Programme and Product Management:* Don Smith, Dmitri Ossipov, Jason Hogg, Sanjeev Garg, and Tom Hollander (Microsoft Corporation)
- *Architect:* Dragos Manolescu, Wojtek Kozaczynski, and Edward Jezierski (Microsoft Corporation)
- *Development:* Chris Tavares (Microsoft Corporation); Hernan de Lahitte (Digit Factory); Pablo Galiano, Juan Wajnerman, José Escrich (Clarius Consulting); and Brian Button (Asynchrony Solutions, Inc.)
- *Test:* Larry Brader and Carlos Farre (Microsoft Corporation); Tushar More, Mani Krishnaswami, Manickavasagam Shanmugasundaram, Arunkumar Sundararajan, Sajjad Nasir Imran, Meenakshi Krishnamoorthi, Muralidharan C Narayanan, Manu Agarwal, Bhavin Raichura, Vinod Kumar S, Venkata Reddy Donthireddy, and Lalitha Sundaram (Infosys Technologies Ltd)
- *Documentation:* Nelly Delgado and RoAnn Corbisier (Microsoft Corporation); Lonnie Wall (RDA Corporation); William French (Linda Werner & Associates, Inc.); Paul Slater (Wadeware LLC); Tim Osborn (Ascentium Corporation); Tina Burden McGrayne (TinaTech, Inc.); and Claudette Siroky (CI Design Studio)

Many thanks to the Microsoft Practice team at CGI's Quebec City office who contributed to the development of the Service Factory and who were entrusted with its conversion to Visual Basic.NET. A leading IT and business process services provider with approximately 25,000 professionals operating in more than 100 offices worldwide, CGI works on behalf of its clients to evolve Service Factory and other patterns & practices offerings. To learn more about CGI's Microsoft solutions, visit the CGI corporate Web site.

Many thanks to the following advisors who provided invaluable assistance:

- Edward Bakker and René Schrieken (LogicaCMG); Aaron Skonnard (Pluralsight); Gabriel Gilabert and Patrick Johnston (Thomson Financial); Norman Headlam (Fidelity Investments); Brandon Bohling (Intel Corporation); Alejandro G. Jack (Southworks); Christian Weyer (Thinktecture); Daniel Cazzulino (Clarius Consulting); Steve Millet, Jan Alexander, Andy Gordon, Mark Fussell, Ford McKinstry, Steve Maine, Eugene Osovetsky, Daniel Roth, Jezz Santos, Beat Schwegler, Shy Cohen, Serena Yeoh, Vajira Weerasekera, Sam Keall, Jason McConnell, Pablo Castro, Sanjay Mishra, and Umachandar Jayachandran (Microsoft Corporation)

INFORMATION ARCHITECTURE

The term information architecture describes a specialized skill set which relates to the interpretation of information and expression of distinctions between signs and systems of signs. It has some degree of origin in the library sciences. Many schools with library and information science departments teach information architecture.

Information architecture (IA) is the art of expressing a model or concept of information used in activities that require explicit details of complex systems. Among these activities are library systems, Content Management Systems, web development, user interactions, database development, programming, technical writing, enterprise architecture, and critical system software design. Information architecture has somewhat different meanings in these different branches of IS or IT architecture. Most definitions have common qualities: a structural design of shared environments, methods of organizing and labelling websites, intranets, and online communities, and ways of bringing the principles of design and architecture to the digital landscape. Historically the term "information architect" is attributed to Richard Saul Wurman. Wurman sees architecture as "used in the words architect of foreign policy. I mean architect as in the creating of systemic, structural, and orderly principles to make something work—the thoughtful making of either artifact, or idea, or policy that informs because it is clear."

In the context of information systems design information architecture refers to the analysis and design of the data stored by information systems, concentrating on entities, their attributes, and their interrelationships. It refers to the modelling of data for an individual database and to the corporate data models an enterprise uses to coordinate the definition of data in several (perhaps scores or hundreds) of distinct databases. The "canonical data model" is applied to integration technologies as a definition for specific data passed between the systems of an enterprise. At a higher level of abstraction it may also refer to the definition of data stores.

Information architecture is defined by the R.I.P.O.S.E. technique, developed in 1989 as:

1. The conceptual structure and logical organization of the intelligence of a person or group of people (organizations). Note: In this case the term intelligence is used to the effect of "knowledge used to inform".

Information architecture is defined by the Information Architecture Institute as:

1. The structural design of shared information environments.
2. The art and science of organizing and labelling web sites, intranets, online communities, and software to support findability and usability.
3. An emerging community of practice focused on bringing principles of design and architecture to the digital landscape.

It is worth mentioning that the term Information Architecture has been criticized, as the term "architecture" is primarily used for habitable physical structures and imply that information systems are static like habitable physical structures or buildings. Information systems are "living systems", which frequently get updated, altered, and morphed, both by author and users. In some cases, information systems dynamically adapt to specific actions and context of users. Since the discipline of architecture ("habitable physical structures") increasingly uses materials and solutions that are less static, this criticism may be unjustified.

User-Centred Information Designers analyse cognitive, behavioral, and emotional processes of users and define User-Centred Information Systems and taxonomies. Furthermore, some activities involved in the creation of information systems can be similar to activities involved in the creation of taxonomies. Some have suggested that the term information architecture is analogous with taxonomy.

Others contend that the activities involved in the creation of a taxonomy are a subset of the activities involved in developing an information architecture, since this typically also involves articulating the objectives of the information, and understanding the intended audience. Some practicing information architects specialize in developing taxonomies, as part of their IA "toolkit," along with deliverables like site maps, flow diagrams, and screen-level design prototypes to represent the structure of a Web site or interactive application.

Further, because information architecture practices and techniques became popularized with the advent of the World Wide Web, some information architects may lack experience designing systems that are not web-based where browsing is less relevant. Users of enterprise systems and business systems typically have different goals from users of web-based systems. Business systems within the enterprise, for example, provide users with tools to expedite required business tasks. In contrast, commerce sites, social sites, and news sites invite users to explore and browse information in many cases to support their business model. It is important for Information Architects to understand the specific business and user requirements rather than apply the same techniques to shape every system's information. Finally, with the ever increasing integration of applications within the enterprise, neither websites nor corporate data models and master data systems can any longer be considered in isolation. Information Architecture will be challenged to evolve to include the entire spectrum of both structured and unstructured data, ranging from transactional systems to ad hoc usage.

Publishing has a crucial place in the librarian's ethos. To the outsider the book trade has never been easy to understand. As the structure is now being modified it is even less comprehensible and not noticeably more rational. One of the difficulties has been that traditionally the trade, or at least the publishing part of it, has been conscious of a cultural role and responsibilities, and has insisted that the publisher is not like other businessmen or manufacturers, but is concerned with other values as well as profit. This claim is not without some justification, but it has produced an ambivalence which has always affected the relationships of publishers with authors, or even librarians.

Quite apart from the publishers' ideals or pretensions, it is true that there are unique features of the book trade which made analysis difficult. Books are 'different', not only because of their essential cultural role, but because a book is not a commodity in the usual economic sense, and each title is unique. One book costing £I is unlikely to be comparable in any other way as a product to another book costing the same amount. If one compares book publishing with the other communications industries, the special characteristics of the former are apparent. Unlike broadcasting or newspaper publishing, expensive plant is not required, so that small firms can enter the business. Advertising resources for each book (product) are limited by the short production runs—short in comparison to a mass circulation periodical or newspaper. Books are not necessarily mass media and quite small editions can be produced economically. The contents of books are not influenced by a dual role of advertising media, as are periodicals and newspapers.

Lastly, because of their usually compact physical form and the absence of auxiliary equipment for their use, books have several practical advantages over other media. These characteristics make it possible for publishers to respond to demands for a wide variety of different material; book publishing is, therefore, a fairly flexible industry which includes many different types of activity in the act of presenting communication.

ONLINE ACCESS TO THE UNION DATABASES

All the databases have been mounted on different servers at INFLIBNET. Librarians and scholar community can access these databases. There is no restriction for access. Keeping in view the current trends in information technology and web based access to information, INFLIBNET has developed web interface for online access to all the union databases in 1998 itself, thereby providing access over the INTERNET

SEARCHING DATABASES

To search the databases hosted by INFLIBNET, one has to have one's computer connected to the Internet with access to WWW and GUI based browser running on it viz. Netscape Communicator or Internet Explorer. With this, log on to the the INFLIBNET site at URL: http://www.inflibnet.ac.in.On reaching the home page on the site, one needs to follow the below given steps:

- First, choose the database. To carry out the search, select the desired database from the front page
- Read carefully the description and example given on the first page of each database.
- Select the access point to retrieve the data.
- Type in correctly search term(s) or phrase in given search box.
- After you complete typing, press return key or click the mouse button on search.
- Then results of the query are displayed with brief detail at first level.
- To see further details click on fields appearing in blue colour in the respective records.

b) Off-line/E-mail Access to INFLIBNET Databases : INFLIBNET Centre has mounted a variety of bibliographic databases on the Internet. Persons having Internet connectivity can access these databases on-line by logging on to INFLIBNET's web site at URL http://www.inflibnet.ac.in. On the other hand, persons having only e-mail facility could till now only send their queries through e-mail to INFLIBNET, which were manually processed at the Centre and replies were sent back through e-mail. This was a time consuming exercise. Now, INFLIBNET Centre has developed a software tool called SEWAK, which automatically processes queries received through e-mail and sends back replies. This mode of search scores over the on-line search in view of:

Reduced Internet Access Time: A user simply shoots a query and relaxes. He/she need not spend large amount of Internet time on searching through the databases to get the results. SEWAK does the searching on behalf of the user, saving his/her time and money.

Multiple Queries: A user can send multiple queries at a time through e-mail. SEWAK conducts the needful searches and sends back results to the user. This is not possible in on-line searches.

Multiple Users: A number of users in a particular location having only one e-mail address can send their respective queries and receive individual results.

Thus SEWAK truly serves the users, saving their precious time and money.

c) ***CD-ROM Database :*** INFLIBNET Centre has been subscribing to quite a few Bibliographic Databases in CD-ROM/Floppies covering different subjects. These have been subscribed with a view to provide Bibliographic Information Service on the topics of interest to the faculty members and researchers working in the universities and colleges. List of such databases currently available with INFLIBNET is given below.

To make an effective use of these databases, it has been decided to promote this service to the faculty members and researchers at the national level.

To begin with, this service is provided free of cost. Interested users may send in their requests in a prescribed format through the Librarian.

The search output will be provided in a floppy or through Email wherever possible.

List of Databases subscribed at INFLIBNET:

- Current Content on Diskette:Social and behavioural Sciences
- Dissertation Abstracts International: Humanities & Social Sciences
- EconLit: Economic Literature
- EMBASE Drugs & Pharmacology CD
- ERIC: Education and Research Centre
- IICD: Inside Information
- Inside Science

- Inside Social Science
- ISSN Compact: The ISSN register on CD-ROM
- LISA: Library and Information Science Abstract
- NUCSSI: National Union Catalogue of Scientific Serials in India
- Philosopher's Index
- PsycLit: Psychological Literature
- SSCI: Social Science Citation Index
- Sociofile: Sociological Abstracts
- Ulrich's On Disc: International Periodicals Directory

Following CD-ROM based databases are also available at INFLIBNET, which are being frequently used for database creation work.

- BNB: British National Bibliography, Current file, 1986 to 1999
- OCLC: Recent Books 1999
- OCLC: Old Books 1999
- OCLC: Serials 1999
- OCLC: Authority file 1999
- CDMARC: Subject Heading 1996
- CDMARC: Names 1996
- CDMARC: Holdings 1996

These can also be used for providing the required information to the Universities.

d) ***COPSAT Service (Contents of Periodicals in Science and Technology):*** The Contents of Periodicals in Science and Technology is a service provided by INFLIBNET in collaboration with National Centre for Science Information (NCSI), Indian Institute of Science, Bangalore. It is basically a Current Awareness Service provided every month covering more than 4000 top ranking journals in the area of life sciences, physical sciences, chemical and earth sciences, engineering, computing technology, agricultural and environmental sciences. Besides contents, most of the journals covered by this service also contain author abstracts. This service allows one to select upto 40 (depending upon the output medium opted) titles from wide range of 4000 journals and subscribe as one set at an affordable price. One can subscribe to more than one set and it is open for both individuals and institutions for academic and research purposes.

e) ***OCLC's First Search:*** The On-line Computer Library Centre Inc. is a not-for-profit largest leading network and bibliographic utility for libraries in the world, linking more than 26,000 libraries from 64 countries. The OCLC offers number of services to its member users over the network. The prominent and highly used ones are union catalogues, ILL and First Search Service. In the recent past, OCLC has introduced number of new services over the Internet, making available services cheaper, faster and widely available.

First Search is an economically priced on-line bibliographic service that offers a comprehensive collection of over 85 databases and includes links to the WWW. It offers online full text, document delivery, library holdings and Inter-Library-Loan services. There is no charge for database connect time, record displays, record printing or record delivery by email. The databases covered are the ones that are highly used and important ones from the academic and research point of view. These 85 databases represent all major areas.

The INFLIBNET which aims to supplement the existing information services in the country in a cost-effective manner, has recently started helping universities by subscribing to OCLC's FirstSearch Service. This service enables INFLIBNET to provide the FirstSearch Service to all its funded universities, to begin with in an off-line mode. The user of library will have to send the request for literature search along with keywords etc. to the INFLIBNET. INFLIBNET will access the databases, conduct the search and download the records and send it to the requested libraries. Only requests routed through the libraries will be accepted. Charges are borne by INFLIBNET to begin with. It may please be noted that, only bibliographical information will be provided under this service and will be restricted to the databases covered through this service. This service is launched on an experimental basis by the INFLIBNET.

DOCUMENT DELIVERY SERVICE

Due to ever increasing subscription cost of learned journals, decreasing value of the Indian rupees against major foreign currencies and the stagnant library budgets, INFLIBNET has launched the Document Delivery Service to make optimum use of the existing collection of some of our resourceful libraries in support of academic and research work in the universities in the country. The Document Delivery Service is a new service initiated by INFLIBNET in collaboration with the following six university libraries which are well known for their strong collection base and commitment to provide timely service.

- Banaras Hindu University, Varanasi
- University of Hyderabad, Hyderabad
- Indian Institute of Science, Bangalore
- Jawaharlal Nehru University, New Delhi
- Punjab University, Chandigarh
- Tata Institute of Social Science, Mumbai

Under this service, the above mentioned six university libraries will serve as Document Delivery Centres and deliver, on demand, the copies of papers from learned journals, conference proceedings and other materials available in their collection at nominal cost. The role of INFLIBNET here is mainly to act as a catalyst in promoting this service to the academic and research community in India.

Other Activities

Publications: INFLIBNET centre has been bringing out the following publications on regular basis.

- CALIBER Proceedings
- Union Catalogue of Secondary Serials(including Bibliographic database on CD-ROMs)
- Guidelines for Data Capturing: A User manual
- Newsletters (A Quarterly Publication of Information and Library Network Centre, UGC)

CALIBER Proceedings

Topics covered in these proceedings are contemporary, covering major areas of librarianship viz. Library Automation, Library Networking, Database Management, Impact of Information Technology to library and Information Centres, Changing role of Library professionals and future role of libraries in INTERNET environment. These volumes will be valuable resource for library professionals who would like to keep up to date with recent development in the field

Union Catalogue of Secondary Serials

This union catalogue of Secondary Serials is the first publication in the series of publications been brought out by INFLIBNET Centre. This covers 337 unique titles which includes 99 CD-ROM based Secondary Serials titles. This data has been contributed by 106 universities, covering for the period of 1998. The catalogue provides list of titles along with minimum bibliographic information and library codes. The same is being updated for 1999.

Guidelines for Data Capturing (a user manual)

To maintain consistency and quality in databases prepared by the libraries and INFLIBNET, INFLIBNET Centre had constituted a taskforce consistency experts in this area. This task force has brought out a 100 pages documents entitled GUIDELINES FOR DATA CAPTURING: A USER MANUAL. This document is prepared based on Common Communication Format (CCF), 1992 edition and same has been given to participating libraries for adoption. The task force also studied other standards required for this activity and accordingly recommended that the following

- Anglo American Catalogue Rules. Edition 2nd revised
- Library of Congress Subject Headings may also be used

Disussion Forum: INFLIBNET Centre proposes to start a Discussion Forum on the network for various subjects. The first Disussion Forum already started is regarding the SOUL Software developed by INFLIBNET Centre and installed at a number of Universities. The users of SOUL or anyone else interested in SOUL can make use of this Forum to seek clarifications on SOUL.

Installation of SOUL at 27 Universities by INFLIBNET: Library Management software SOUL, developed by INFLIBNET Centre, has been installed at 27 University Libraries. Teams of INFLIBNET visited these universities for installation of SOUL and for providing online training.

Launching of Electronic Document Delivery Service by INFLIBNET: INFLIBNET has taken a new initiative by launching an innovative service called Electronic Document Delivery Service. This service was launched in the month of July 2000, simultaneously by following six university libraries, which are identified to serve as Document Delivery Centres.

- Banaras Hindu University, Varanasi
- University of Hyderabad, Hyderabad
- Indian Institute of Science, Bangalore
- Javaharlal Nehru University, New Delhi
- Panjab University, Chandigarh
- Tata Institute of Social Science, Mumbai

Under this service the above Document Delivery Centres will provide copies of research papers appearing in learned journals, conference proceedings etc. from their available collection to academic and research community at an affordable cost. This service is preferably going to be delivered using Internet. The required infrastructure viz. Computer connected to Internet, scanner, printer, fax, etc. are being set up at each Centre.

The end users and libraries using e-mails can request for the research papers. The service is primarily targeted at the academic and research communities in the country who currently have very limited access to the information available in very few select libraries. All these libraries have been provided with a minimum grant to support the infrastructure facilities. With this service, it would be possible to optimally use available resources in the country.

Retro-Conversion of Five Major Libraries by INFLIBNET: The Retrospective conversion of five major library catalogues has been launched under the INFLIBNET Programme from June 2000. This is a new project initiated by INFLIBNET to minimize the effort & cost involved in retrospective conversion work of its member libraries. Under this project, following five libraries, who have the largest and unique collection, have started creating a qualitative database. This work of Retro-Conversion is expected to be completed in two years. The data will be provided to all other universities on CD-ROMs for directly downloading the records. This will avoid need for entry and reduce overall cost and improve quality of the data.

1. Banaras Hindu University, Varanasi
2. Indian Institute of Science, Bangalore
3. Jawaharlal Nehru University, New Delhi
4. University of Madras, Chennnai
5. University of Mumbai, Mumbai

All these five libraries have been given extra funding to take up this mammoth task of creating records of their holdings as per the standards recommenced by INFLIBNET. This funding is basically restricted to creation of records in electronic form only. The infrastructure cost will be borne by the respective libraries. The bibliographic records contributed by five libraries will be hosted on INFLIBNET Servers for online access. INFLIBNET proposes to use this data for retrospective conversion and shared cataloguing of all its member libraries and large number of college libraries thereby minimizing duplication of effort and cost involved.

Organizing Seminars, Workshops, Conferences, etc.: INFLIBNET has also been engaged, from time to time, in organizing seminars, symposia, workshops and conferences for the benefit of Library staff and Information Professionals. A 10 days intensive workshop on "Bibliographic Standards and Formats for Retro-Conversion: Tools and Techniques" was organized at INFLIBNET from May 15, 2000.

Membership

- Primary
- Secondary.

Primary membership: The University Libraries entitled to receive from UGC will become primary members immediatly on receipt of the initial grant under the INFLIBNET programme.

At present, there are 13 Central Universities. The UGC is assisting 19 deemed universities at present, out of the 38 universities for plan grants. The UGC is providing development grants to 108 State Universities. Currently, 142 universities and other institutes have been covered under the INFLIBNET programme.

Associate membership: The libraries who are not entitled to receive the grants from the UGC but are public funded academic and research organizations, Govt. departments, Non-profit making organizations can have the associate membership of INFLIBNET by signing an MOU and by paying the requisite fees.

MALIBNET

MALIBNET has been conceived to overcome the problem of resource crunch in the libraries and to provide information at a low cost to the users in and around Chennai. As a universal phenomenon, libraries in the region are facing two major problems:

- Knowledge explosion and the consequent information explosion and
- Price escalation of library documents.

These problems have forced the information specialists to cut down the number of journals they procured to manage the situation within the available resources. In order to find a solution to these pressing problems, the concept of automation and cooperation are proved much effective.

The need for interconnecting libraries and information centres in Chennai was visualized by Indian National Scientific Documentation Centre (INSDOC) in 1991. INSDOC undertook a feasibility study, which was completed in March 1992. MALIBNET was registered as a society in Chennai in February 1993. The nucleus of MALIBNET, the Network Service Centre (NSC) for MALIBNET is located at INSDOC Regional Centre, CSIR, CSIR, Madras Complex, Tharamani, Chennai.Presently, nearly 50 libraries in Madras are contributing actively to the creation of various databases on MALIBNET. With the help of communication links and sophisticated information technology, the resources of the member libraries are shared and made available to the users.

Aims and Objectives

The main aim of MALIBNET is to facilitate resource sharing and information dissemination by establishing network of libraries, and thus helps fostering growth in the field of Information science and Technology. Following are the main objectives of MALIBNET:

- To encourage cooperation among libraries, documentation centres and information centres in Chennai so that the resources can be pooled for the benefit of helping the weaker resource centres by the stronger ones.
- To evolve a network, interconnecting various libraries and information centres to improve capability in information handling and services.
- To provide reliable access to document collection of libraries by creating a union catalogue of library holdings and housing it in a centralized host system of the network.

- To provide better access to bibliographic information through access to national and international databases.
- To optimize information resource utilization through shared cataloguing, and inter library loan services and avoiding duplication in acquisition to the extent possible.
- To centrally acquire information, specially the contents and abstracts from all the journals and then disseminate information as and when required, thus avoiding duplication in journal acquisition and reducing the expenditure of individual libraries.
- To organize conferences, lectures, workshops and seminars.
- To undertake scientific research in the field of library & documentation.

Activities/Services

MALIBNET provides the following services

I. *Services:* General
   - Access to list of current serials subscribed in 50 libraries
   - Full journal holdings of these libraries
   - Access to specialized database giving article index with abstracts
   - Door delivery system for document copies
   - Access to International databases through INSDOC
   - Contents, Abstracts & Photocopies from about 1200 important journals under CAPS service
   - Contents information of journals supplied as per user's choice
   - Each subscription covering 20 journals
   - Contents data suppiled in hard copy form, through E-mail or in diskette with retrieval software
   - 12 despatches under one subscription
   - Standing order based/Demand based Abstract service from journals
   - Full text of journal articles from member libraries supplied within 48 hours
   - Creation of specialised databases at user's request
   - Library automation
   - Training courses
   - Consultancy in networking and computerization

II. Services available free of cost to members
   - Electronic Mail (E-mail)
   - Free exchange through E-mail among all member libraries and Network Service Centre

- MALIB Card
- Enables card holder to consult member libraries
- Provides free access to MALIBNET resource centres
- Online Access
- Free online access to all the MALIBNET databases
- Free CAPS service
- Free dispatch of contents information of journals through E- mail

III. Databases Information services MALIBNET has following databases

- Directory Database of Current Serials:
- Contents Database:
- Specialized database for Automotive Industries:
- NUCSSI(National Union Catalogues of Scientific Serials in India):
- Medicinal and Aromatic Plants Abstracts (MAPA):
- Patents Database:
- Polymer Science Database:

Databases' Updates

- Directory Database of Current Serials includes 2720 unique titles from 46 libraries.
- Contents Database has information from 371 journals and 45746 records for the current year.
- Automotive Industry Database has information from 16 journals and 12567 records.
- Current Journal Holdings Data collected from 30 libraries.

MALIBNET Freeware

MALIBNET's worldwide database information services can be utilized by users around the world by placing their orders through the cost effective mechanism of E-mail. In order to place their orders, users may request for MALIBNET freeware software customized to run on Dos, Windows & Unix platforms. For this purpose, they have to send an email to MALIBNET.

Users will receive two emails from MALIBNET. One is a 'readme' mail and the other is the freeware software in encoded form. The 'readme' email provides all the necessary instructions required to decode and get an executable version of the freeware software. Freeware software can be executed on the system (DOS/Windows/UNIX) at the user end to avail MALIBNET services. The Freeware software contains:

- Information on MALIBNET
- Member Institutions of MALIBNET
- Services Offered on MALIBNET
- Malibnet Registration Form
- Fee Structure For Members & Non Members
- Order Registration Forms

IV. Network based Information Services

MALIBNET offers five network based services to its users all over the world.

- Contents Search
- Keyword Based Literature Search
- Document Procurement Service
- Access to International Databases
- Access to Internet Service

Content Search Service

This allows a search on the contents database existing at MALIBNET. It contains nearly 500 online journals. The journal list is provided to the user in the Freeware software. This database is searchable through journal title, year, volume & issue. Results are sent back to the user through E-mail. Requests for availing these services can be made by filling up the data entry forms for these services provided in the MALIBNET freeware software supplied to the user. Users can start availing MALIBNET services after they become registered users of the MALIBNET. On registration, each user is given an unique code number & password.

Literature Search Service

This is a keyword based search service on four MALIBNET databases namely Contents, Autoabst, Polymer Science & Patents. Users can specify the keywords to include and keywords to exclude as well as specify the period to be covered in the search. Users can also specify the maximum number of references needed. Contents database holds article index of approximately 500 journals. Autoabst (a Specialized Database for Automotive Industries) is very useful for research professionals and industrialists. This database covers valuable national and international journals and currently has 10,000 records. The Patents database covers around 40,000 records and the keyword based search can give details like the inventor, country code, patent number, international classification code etc. The Polymer Science Database is a database on polymer science and related scientific areas.

Document Procurement Service

MALIBNET provides full text of articles from S & T journals. To avail this service, users are expected to provide the details of journals, year, volume, & issue along with page numbers.

The charges for this service is very nominal. Requests for availing these services can be made by filling up the data entry forms for these services provided in the MALIBNET freeware software supplied to the user. Users can start availing MALIBNET services after they become registered users of the MALIBNET. On registration, each user is given an unique code number & password.

Uses of MARC

MARC tapes are being used for various purposes. Following are some of their important uses:

1. A centrally prepared catalogue can be distributed to the receiving libraries in a machine-readable form.
2. In spite of increasing acquisitions, the catalogue can be kept up-to-date without employing additional staff.
3. The MARC tapes can be utilised for acquisition functions i.e., selecting, ordering and claiming unsupplied books without any additional cost. They can be used to produced spine labels, book pockets etc.
4. The MARC tapes can be used for producing conventional card catalogue by the subscribing libraries, as demonstrated by the University of Toronto.
5. The production cost of card catalogue on the computer (MARC System) is lesser than that of purchasing the Library of Congress catalogue cards.
6. The MARC data can also be used for producing book catalogues as demonstrated by the Washington State Library.
7. It automatically performs resource-sharing functions.
8. The MARC tapes can be used for computerised SDI service.

Mini or Microcomputer-based MARC is commercially based cataloguing system. Practically a microcomputer is housed in the Library and a set of floppy disks is provided which contains the entire MARC database. It is then quickly retrieved and edited as needed. (J. Rice). Within the United States, the terms MARC, LC MARC and USMARC are interchangeable. The term do have slightly different meanings such as follow:

1. MARC is a generic term applied to the universe of MARC formats, including UKMARC, CANMARC, InterMARC, and so on;

2. LC MARC refers to the set of options and content designation called "MARC II";
3. USMARC is a new name of LC MARC, introduced in the Underlying Principles document in 1983. There is no sharp distinction in content between LC MARC and USMARC. The term USMARC or MARC are also applied to MARC extensions, formats such as OCLC MARC and RLIN MARC that include data in addition to USMARC data.

MARC I

MARC I pilot project began in April, 1966 in which sixteen libraries participated. By the year 1968, the Library of Congress had distributed over fifty thousand English language monographs records. The purpose of MARC I was the automation of cataloguing, indexing, searching and retrieval functions.

The participating libraries made better use of the MARC tapes distributed by L.C., in a variety of ways in producing catalogue cards, book form of union catalogues, specialised lists of materials under subjects, lists for acquisition on purposes and the like. The LC MARC database-the accumulation of Library of Congress cataloguing data in machine-readable form-now contains more than 2.5 million records.

MARC II

The MARC I format was based entirely on the structure of the L.C. catalogue cards and covered monographs only. Encouraged by the success of MARC I, staff of the L.C. started redesigning the procedures and programmes to cover material in other forms, and developed character set to include all the major Roman alphabet language as well as Romanised forms. Meanwhile the British National Bibliography (BNB) showed interest in the UK MARC Pilot Project. Similarly interest was also shown by many foreign libraries to design a standard communication format suitable for interchanging bibliographic data not only from one source organisation, the L.C., to many participating libraries, but also for exchanging information on cooperative basis among libraries at the international level. The US, the UK and other countries wanted a machine-readable catalogue format that would be a common one for international exchange of cataloguing and bibliographic data. Such an interchangeable record format was designed and was called MARC II. It was a one-format structure on the machine-readable medium capable of containing bibliographic data of all forms of library materials, such as books, monographs, serials, maps, music etc., and related records.

The structure or the physical representation of the machine-readable medium; the content designators, such as tags, indicators, and subfields codes used to identify the data elements; and the content or the data itself such as author, title and bibliographic descriptions are the three components of the LC MARC format. MARC II officially began in March, 1968. Distribution began for all English Language material providing a weekly magnetic tape of zonal 1000 records.

Thereafter, other documentation begain to be issued, including formats for other materials over the period 1970-73. In 1972 films records were distributed, by 1973 records for serials, maps and French books, by 1975

German Spanish and Portuguese materials. MARC II is a subscription service. By subscribing to this service a library can acquire, in machine readable form cataloguing data for American and other foreign publications as described above.

In fact the Library of Congress catalogues the documents i.e., books and non-book materials, records the data on magnetic tape and supplies copies of the tapes to various interested libraries. The libraries which get the copy of magnetic tape, can then produce printed catalogues of their collections entries on cards and various kinds of bibliographies (author or subject etc.) by using a computer. Most libraries obtain access to MARC data, through products and services developed by publishers computer system developers, timesharing services and other intermediaries. MARCFICHE is the earliest of MARC-derivate products. At present a growing number of vendor supply the MARC database, on CD-ROM disks or digital optical videodiscs accompanied by software which supports the retrieval of specific cataloguing records and the printing of card sets.

Limitations

George Piternick points out the following few limitations of the Machine- Readable catalogue systems:

1. The MARC record for any title is almost similar to the conventional bibliographic record, as such it inherits all its limitations.
2. The MARC format will be limited, at least for the next few years, to the English language books because the MARC character set is severally limited in respect of special characters and diacritical marks.
3. Expenditure on account of machine time by the participating libraries will go on increasing in view of the weekly shipment of about 1,200 records or about 62,000 records annually requiring 15,000 feet of magnetic tape.
4. The time gap between the creation of MARC record and a catalogue record copy by the participating library, which is inherent at present in the existing card production methods of

the Library of Congress, will not be removed until and unless both the cards and tapes are prepared from the same machine-readable record.

MARC records are no longer created only, by L.C. but also by many other agencies, and are available through bibliographic utilities and from commercial services.

Retrospective Conversion (RECON) in MARC

The MARC Distribution Service was enlarged and proved to be efficient in making conversion of all current intake into the machine-readable catalogue.

But all these were for the current holdings of libraries only. Librarians were interested to the preparation of machine-readable catalogue of their older holdings and to replace their card catalogues with machine readable catalogues. But it was realised that uncoordinated activities by individual libraries would entail expensive repetition of work in converting the existing catalogue into the machine-readable form.

Personalised efforts would also be devoid of uniformity in headings and forms. RECON Pilot Project was initiated in August 1969. It continued for two years and approximately 58000 records were converte. The most significant technical achievement of this project was the development and implementation of the format recognition process.

UNI MARC

The implementation of US MARC, UK MARC and ISBD, the increasing number of national MARC formats etc. created an environment for international cooperation in interchanging bibliographic data. The IFLA Working group discussed some of the problems encountered in the area of universal standardisation and agreement on content designators in machine-readable format.

The concept of SUPER MARC as an international system for exchange of information was agreed upon in principle. A draft of the international

MARC format was made in 1975 for universal use. Finally, for international exchange of MARC records, a new machine-readable format was designed and is known as UNI MARC. It has been envisaged that the national organisations producing MARC records will produce them in the national standards for use within the country and will reformat them according to the UNI MARC format for international exchange. The international and universal MARC has become a reality.

UNIVERSITY INFORMATION SYSTEM

INFLIBNET has created home pages for a number of Universities, giving entire information about each university with focus on academic and research activities. These are Developed by INFLIBNET CENTRE based on the data sent by the respective Universities :

Networking of University Libraries: Currently libraries funded under the programme are advised to subscribe to one of the following networks, depending on the availability in the respective locations:

- ERNET
- VSNL
- NICNET
- Other ISPs

Wide Area Network

- It is planned to setup a Wide Area Network "UGCNET" linking more than 170 universities and other academic institutes in the country.

Local Area Network

- INFLIBNET Centre has suggested all the funded universities to set up LANs using HUB/SWITCH and CAT V cables within their libraries for successful installation of SOUL software. Since SOUL is based on client/server architecture, It is essential that the server and all other nodes be connected by LAN.
- INFLIBNET Centre desires that each university should establish a LAN in it's campus linking all the departments including library. This LAN in turn will be connected to the WAN.

Human Resources Development

Following training courses are conducted to enhance the skills of University Library staff for implementation of INFLIBNET Programme:

- *One month Training Programme:* This is mainly meant for operational staff of libraries. They are given exhaustive training on application of computers to library and information services. Eighteen such programmes were held covering most of the universities, and around 350 persons have been trained.
- *On-site Training:* Staff from INFLIBNET Centre visited 31 universities, and conducted training for the library staff members for a week initiating automation process.
- *ILMS Training:* Ten Librarians from different universities spent a week at INFLIBNET to solve their problems in using ILMS.

- *SOUL Training:* Soul was installed at 15 University Libraries and onsite training of one week to the library staff was provided at each site.
- *CALIBER:* It is an annual convention held every year in collaboration with a university in different region on a theme related to library automation. Seven such conventions have been held so far.
- *Workshops:* Six workshops for senior level staff viz, University Librarians and Deputy Librarians were conducted.

❒

4

Technological Advances in Library Automation

Technological advances in recent years have enabled researchers to exchange ideas from almost any location on the globe. This possibility, and the availability of remote databases, has heightened the need for information to be in machine readable form.

For machine readable information to be exchanged internationally it must be formatted in accord with accepted standards. In Korea the development of such standards must be accomplished in the context of a national information policy.

Henriette D. Avram has stressed the importance of standards in organizing information for resource sharing:

We should not loose sight of the importance of the organization of information and the critical role that standards play in this organization. Indeed, it is the information organization function of technical processing that underpins and makes possible research and reference. This will not change with the development of NREN, no matter how sophisticated it becomes.

A successful automated library system requires adherence to a variety of standards: library–specific standards for creating and formatting machine readable records; structures for communicating machine readable records; and data communication standards for the transmission of information between systems. Content standards are rules for the creation of records.

Cataloguing rules, subject analysis rules for subject headings or descriptors, and classification rules for DDC or LCC are examples. Encoding standards are used to put bibliographic and authority records into machine readable form; they are the foundation for any automated library system. MARC of various types, BISAC and SISAC for computerized ordering, interlibrary loan data elements, common command language, and ISBN are examples. Networking standards establish interfaces, for various functions, among local systems and other automated systems.

A good example is the LSP (Linked System Project) and its concomitant Z39.50. Encoding standards and networking standards are referred to as technical standards. They are explicitly defined and, if carefully implemented, lead to predictable and consistent results. Technical standards include format structure, character sets, and code lists standards.

The purpose of this paper is to examine the status and prospects of automation standards in Korea. At present, development of standards in Korea is uneven. A number of library and industrial organizations are promoting standardization for information exchange; their activities are discussed: Certain solutions are proposed in regard to issues of standardization for shared cataloguing and databases in the context of a national network.

INFORMATION TECHNOLOGY

Information technology (IT) is playing a crucial role in contemporary society. It has transformed the whole world into a global village with a global economy, which is increasingly dependant on the creative management and distribution of information. Globalization of world economies has greatly enhanced the values of information to business organizations and has offered new business opportunities.

Today, IT provides the communication and analytical power that organizations need for conducting trade and managing business at global level with much ease. To coordinate their worldwide network of suppliers, distributors and consumers, organizations have developed global information systems that can track orders, deliveries, and payments round the clock.

This has been possible because of the development of IT in its present form. In the broadest sense, information technology refers to both the hardware and software that are used to store, retrieve, and manipulate information. At the lowest level you have the servers each with an operating system. Installed on these servers are things like database and web serving software. The servers are connected to each other and to users via a network infrastructure. And the users accessing these servers have their own hardware, operating systems, and software tools.

Definition of Terms Used

UNESCO defines IT as, "Scientific technological and engineering disciplines and the management techniques used in information handling and processing information, their interaction with man and machine and associated social, economic and cultural matters".

Librarian's Glossary defines IT as," a development of information sources handled by computers and communication by electronic channels; database can thus be accessed telephone and television links and computer output can be transmitted in an electronic format directly to a remote receiver".

Glossary of Academic Information Technology Terms, San Diego State University

Information Technology includes matters concerned with the furtherance of computer science and technology, design, development, installation and implementation of information systems and applications.

Kathleen Guinee wrote, "By information technology, I mean the tools we use to perform calculations, to store and manipulate text, and to communicate. Some of these twentieth century tools include: the adding machine, slide rule, and calculator for performing calculations, the typewriter and word processor for processing text, and the telephone, radio, and television for communicating."

Components of Information Technology

Also known as information and communication technology (ICT), IT is defined as the technology required for information processing. In particular, the use of computer and computer software to convert, store, process, transmit, and retrieve information. In Information technology we primarily concentrate on the following technologies:

Computer Hardware Technologies: These technologies include microcomputers, midsize servers and large mainframe systems, and the input, output and storage devices that support them.

Computer Software Technologies: These technologies include operating system software, web browsers, software productivity suits and software for business applications.

Telecommunication and Network Technologies: These technologies include telecommunications media, processors and software needed to provide wire-based and wireless access and support for Internet and other networks.

Data Resource Management Technologies: These technologies include database management system software for the development, access and maintenance of the databases of an organization.

Emergence of an Information Society

The information society has passed through four transformational stages of development, the most radical stage starting at the tail end of the twentieth century. This stage has brought a never-ending revolution, particularly with the introduction of information and communication technologies.

During this period, there have been unprecedented developments, profoundly affecting the social structure – the decline of manufacturing sector as compared to the prospering information-rich service sector is one example of such developments. India is moving fast towards becoming an information society as the Government of India is paying due attention to the use of information technology (IT).

The Prime Minister of India constituted a National Task Force on IT and Software Development in May 1998 with the purpose of formulating a long-term National IT Policy to convert India into an IT software superpower. These steps are helping India to shift from an "economy of goods" to a "knowledge economy" or "knowledge driven economy". The beginning of the knowledge society has been made through creation of parks and corridors, and the Prime Minister has given a mission of converting India into a "knowledge society" by the year 2008. Today, India is one of the largest exporters of knowledge workers.

Impact of Information Technology on Societal Development

A society can also refer specifically to any group of people, other animals and/or plants and the interactions within that group. This can be anything from a small neighbourhood to the entire global community. Religion, ethnicity, interests, political opinions or other relating factors may help form a group of people. Society can be defined as "a community, nation, or broad grouping of people having common traditions, institutions, and collective activities and interests." Technological developments which have occurred in information technology have influenced a "broad grouping of people" in their "common traditions, institutions and/or collective activities". This broad grouping of people primarily occurs in the industrialized world of where "information technology" is commonly available.

We shall use the common traditions, institutions and collective activities and interests as the basis for our examination of the impact information technology has had on society. We shall also integrate this examination with the impact of how information technology has changed the "way we work". This integration will occur in two areas of the analysis of society, first the institutions and second the collective activities of the society.

Common Traditions

In the context of this report it is helpful to highlight a difference between "traditions" and "activities/interests". Tradition can be defined as the following:

> *"An inherited, established, or customary pattern of thought, action, or behaviour (as a religious practice or a social custom). Cultural continuity in social attitudes, customs, and institutions."*

The influence of information technology on religious practices has mainly been to the effect of making information about them more accessible. The most relevant question though is whether the developments in information technologies have influenced the continuity of social attitudes, customs or institutions.

Cultural Continuity

Social attitudes have changed in that citizens of a society now expect the various elements of that society to be better informed than previously. They also expect to be able to access more information about a specific product, service or organization so that they can make informed decisions with regard to their interactions with that entity.

Institutions

The word institutions can incorporate a wide variety of organizations. For the purposes of this report the institutions we will examine will be:

- Governments,
- Commercial businesses,
- News & media organizations,
- Educational organizations.

The focus is on how information technology development has improved the processes by which these institutions accomplish their tasks or goals.

Governments

The government of a nation is comprised of many varied institutions. However developments in information technology have helped governments to improve their "service" to their citizens.

Information technology has also had a major impact on the defense capabilities of governments. This covers both a government's capability to wage war and their intelligence gathering capability. Advances in weapons technology and weapons design have increased the effectiveness of various governments' armed forces. For example it would have been impossible to design aero planes such as the B2 Bomber if it were not for the advances made in information technology.

The B2 bomber relies on a "continuous curvature" design to minimize radar signature. It would have been impossible to design or build this machine without the development of computer modelling techniques.

Governments also have had to become more careful with their sensitive information. The proliferation of Internet technologies has led to stories such as:

"The Web becomes the focal point of British politics as a list of MI6 agents is released on a UK Web site. Though forced to remove the list from the site, it was too late as the list had already been replicated across the net. (15 May 1999)"

The governments data protection act Web Site gives the following eight rules regarding personal information:

1. It must be fairly and lawfully processed;
2. Processed for limited purposes;
3. Adequate, relevant and not excessive;
4. Accurate;
5. Not kept longer than necessary;
6. Processed in accordance with the data subject's rights;
7. Secure;
8. Not transferred to countries without adequate protection.

Commercial Businesses

The advances in information technology have heavily influenced commercial businesses in several areas. The most important role of information technology in a commercial business, however, is to provide a commercial advantage.

Advances such as computer-aided design, relational database technologies, spreadsheets and word processing software provide a commercial benefit to the business, as does automation of manufacturing processes (which Sara-Lee did in 1964). Advances in information technology over the last thirty years have lead to the television, for example, being more widely used today than thirty years ago (e.g. the introduction of transistor-based televisions reduced costs while increasing reliability).

News & Media Organizations

Due to the nature of news and media organizations, information technologies have particular relevance to them. As noted earlier, "Information technology is the technology used to store, manipulate, distribute or create information". News and media organizations are intimately acquainted with each of these elements of information technology. This report focuses on the distribution and creation of information.

Educational Organizations

The developments that have occurred in information technology have had many influences on educational establishments. The distribution of information is not the only concern of educational establishments.

For example, one of the aims of universities is to create information. This creation is often done by research. Information technologies have enabled researchers to access a wider source of information than previously available through such technologies as the Internet.

The original Arpanet was set up primarily to assist research. The Internet and other related technologies, such as electronic mail, enable collaborative projects to be undertaken between geographically distant groups.

Collective Activities and Interests

One of the aims of the report is to analyze the influence of information technology on the collective activities and interests of a broad range of people. The phrase "collective activities and institutions" has a wide scope which can be divided into two main areas:

1. Work processes,
2. Social.

THE NEW TECHNOLOGY GROUP

Remarkably, parallel with the establishment of some of these projects, especially the remote access and document storage ones which have been running for quite some time, since 1975, the Research and Development Department felt the need to set up a special committee to investigate new technology and how it could be applied to library and information problems. The department had become aware that developments were taking place in somewhat esoteric research environments, and perhaps in other application areas, the results of which could directly benefit the library and information world, if they could be caught and trapped.

A forum was therefore established of scientists and information professionals to bridge the gap. It looks at existing and emerging technology to see whether the technologies are developing in such a way that the needs of library and information are catered for — and suggests projects where this can be encouraged. It looks at developing existing new technology to see how it can be used to benefit existing or new services and it is also concerning itself with the idea that existing professional staff need some educating so that they can make use of the emergent new technology when it becomes available, and are discouraged from the more unfruitful areas. Two areas that the Group particularly singled out of the new technologies that should have an impact in the library and information communities in the near future are novel input technologies and novel forms of storage.

The latter I have touched on earlier in the form of Dr. Barrett's interest in mass stores (microfiche and now videodiscs). We had a brief flirtation with holography last year, but it's future is unclear at present due to internal rearrangements at Plessey (who are doing the research in the UK) and the possibility that for some applications holography has been overtaken by events — the introduction of videodiscs.

However, mass storage, the technical developments and the reduction in costs over time will have an impact on library and information work in the provision of media to permit the economic storage of full text and graphics. Novel input technology has two themes. On the one hand, some devices like the hand print input device, and voice input when available are attempts to overcome the lack of user-friendliness of keyboards which are fine for those who can type, but no little deterrent for those that cannot.

Advances here include a pair of devices, that allow users to print on paper overlaying a sensitive pad. The movements of the pen are used to recognise the characters being printed — and the code for the character can then be passed to the computer or wherever. To the computer the device behaves like an ordinary keyboard. There are other devices also, like the Microwriter, with five keys. Combinations of keys are depressed to form the desired characters. The combinations of keys have been selected so as to mimic the shape of the characters to provide a simple aid to memory.

Devices of this nature continue the theme of a trend towards more user-friendly systems. The other feature that new forms of input bring is of course the possibility of inputting material other than text. Tablets have been developed that permit the input of graphics drawn on the them which have found applications already in the computerisation of maps, etc. The British Library has been supporting, since the autumn of last year, a research project based at Cambridge University Library under Mr. A. Tucker to look at the integration of Chinese and Roman script in automated library catalogues. Roman scripts have traditionally been input into library catalogue systems using keyboards, and Chinese and non-Roman scripts coped with by the usage of romanisations and transliterations. The development of the Ideographic Encoder at the Faculty of Oriental Studies and Cable and Wireless (a commercial company) has enabled the input of Chinese in its ideographic form.

The device consists of a drum over which is laid a matrix of Chinese characters. To input a character, it is located by rotating the drum and positioning the curser over the character—being identified by its row and column co-ordinates. These can then be manipulated in the way analogous to the way a code could be for a Roman character. Developments in COM have resulted in devices that are capable of the right definition and resolution to display these characters at the size required. These two developments paved the way for the Cambridge project which includes the further development of the Encoder to cope with a full character set; the selection and arrangement of the characters at the drum to suit non-native Chinese speakers the development of all the necessary interfacing required to handle the character sets with input facilities for Chinese Telegraphic code and all the official romanisations; the solution of problems of sorting and filing the Chinese characters; and the integration of this project with developments in the standards areas and the construction of a library catalogue containing part of the record in Chinese and part in, say English. Another interest the New Technology Group had was to negotiate with the appropriate bodies some test bed facilities, to have available for usage with suitable projects. The negotiation of specialised computing facilities always takes time, and the proposer of a project requiring computing or other complex facilities may not easily have access to them.

So far these include batch, parallel processing and novel input testing facilities. Predictions of the impact of new technology on the user are always difficult since there is generally a time lag between the technical feasibility of an operation and it being adopted on a large scale, due to financial assessment and organisational changes that are required for their further implementation. Some tentative effects can be predicted, as having some impact in the near future.

The user will observe a trend towards multi-purpose and integrated technology. Multi-purpose editing terminals, that will permit access to computers, to Prestel, and to other remote stores, that will have facilities for receiving traditional print-out and facsimiles. Perhaps with voice and other sound capabilities. This approach would favour the naive user, the person without the time or the inclination to ascertain which piece of technology to obtain to access specific information sources; the larger markets that would ensure would also favour the user allowing potential reduction in cost. The necessary equipment and telecommunication sub-structures are gradually being developed and will emerge in the light of needs and market forces. The trend towards cheaper storage will allow users to computerise and automate new or larger data bases. The changing economic will be such that in the future, the storage of full text will become an economic proposition should it be desired rather than merely the bibliographic surrogates common at present. These developments, together with improved input devices will enable people to consider the establishment of data bases of graphics and other non-textual material, hitherto decidedly uneconomic, except perhaps on microfiche.

Users' needs will increasingly come under consideration. The effect of market forces attempting to reach a wider audience outside the traditional market for computerised products, and economic forces causing users to consider very carefully the efficiency with which such devices are being used will result in an emphasis on fitting the device to the user rather than expecting the user to conform to the rigours of the machine. This change will greatly affect the ease with which users take up the new technology and greatly affect the new uses to which it can be put. These will favour the trend towards electronic dissemination of information and people feeling as happy to communicate via a terminal as perhaps they do by telephone today.

The researchers in some organisations will find that his reports and papers are being prepared increasingly on word processor equipment. He will see the benefits in increased freedom to create, amend and change his work. The use of retrieval software, either in the word processor or in the computer to which copies of documents could be passed, can be used to enable the researcher to manage more efficiently reports created by him, or other colleagues. Increasingly, the user may find himself disseminating his research results via electronic means, benefiting from the speed that electronic communication can generate. The form of the journal article favoured by this medium and the type of communication may well differ from the traditional form. As far as those concerned with the humanities are concerned; perhaps the most important thing is a ready understanding of the needs of the group is essential, so as to be able to influence the evolution of the new technology to take account of the undoubted special needs of the humanities researcher and his information needs. Education of future users should be a serious consideration so that they can see the benefits (or otherwise) of the changing technology, can adjust to the changing scene, and accept the changing role of the information centre as more and more information becomes available.

The economic situation is changing rapidly too, so it is as well to keep this factor under consideration also so as to be able to determine at what point it is best to introduce technological change.

In fact, the need for facsimile transmission from remote access storage facilities was discussed. Its importance was questioned, when fiche can easily be transmitted by post. A central storage facility was seen as having the advantage of facilitating up-dating. It was stressed that decisions did not to be made between new technology and existing technology. There is a need for a mix and to select the technology most appropriate to the needs of a given situation. For instance, some fiche might be required on hand while some might be placed in remote storage. In the context of the use of technology to facilitate up-dating, it was suggested that there might be a need to freeze up-dating in order to obtain a snapshot view. There was some discussion of the drawbacks of facsimile transmission, particularly the time taken for scanning. It was suggested that the implementation of facsimile transmission would depend on the economic climate, which affects the balance between central and local storage. Developments in word processing and its applications to libraries were discussed.

The National Reprographic Centre for Documentation at Hatfield Polytechnic is evaluating the use of a Word Processor, not simply for preparing reports, but also in terms of exploiting the accompanying software supplied by the manufacturers, with particular reference to the capacity to take over traditional library functions. Concern was expressed about the long-term conservation aspects of new technology.

It was admitted that while information is available concerning microfiche, less is known about videodiscs, which are currently mainly used for entertainment purposes in the United States. Questions of copyright and security were raised. Not all the copyright issues have been resolved. It was questioned whether humanists are less willing than natural scientists to share there current thinking. It was pointed out that there are means of providing electronic locks for personal files. One of the problems of technology was seen to be that it is moving so rapidly that ideas may not be exploited commercially because they might be overtaken.

Generally, Librarians have often demonstrated a pre-recorded online search. The search dealt with the history of violent crime in the eighteenth century. A number of different data bases were used, on two systems, Blaise and Lockheed Information Services. The recording was done using the Mediatron, a device which enables real searches to be stored, together with voice-over and cued slides. The search was presented on a V.D.U. and a monitor.

As an example, the bibliography of a classic book, "The making of the English Working Class" by E.P. Thompson, published in 1965, was cited.

Thompson lists papers found in the Public Record Office, in London, in the Manuscript Room at the British Museum and in the Sheffield Reference Library. He also consulted the Radcliffe papers at a private country mansion, at Rudding Park, Harrogate. It was pointed out that students engaged in work for a PhD need to look in depth at a narrow field and so inevitably need primary materials. Very few primary materials are recorded in machine-readable form, and the demonstration was concerned with improving access to secondary sources, in order that time thus freed could be devoted to teaching and thought.

HISTORY OF LIBRARY AUTOMATION

Concerns about library automation in Korea emerged in the mid–1970s. The first major attempt was the Serials Control System of the Korea Scientific and Technological Information Centre (KORSTIC), in 1976. In the following year, the Western Monographs Retrieval System was developed by the Korea International Economic Institute. Since then broader scale projects have been pursued by several types of libraries.

Special Libraries

Most library computer applications in Korea have occurred in special libraries. The Korea Atomic Energy Institute developed a technical report retrieval system, and the Korea Standard Research Institute developed a standards information retrieval system and a cataloguing system using CD150; ROMs. Many other libraries created retrieval or management information systems. Particularly noteworthy is the work of the Korea Institute of Industry and Technology Information (KINITI) in providing domestic and foreign databases.

In 1983 the government requested KINITI to create databases that could be used by small and medium industries to access Korean technology information, in addition to foreign technology information. KINITI initiated its databases for Korean patents in 1984. It now operates 13 databases that present domestic scientific and technological information. Access is through leased lines or dial–up lines, or DACOM–NET (Korean Data Communications Company Network), a nationwide packet–switched component of the Korea Data Communication Company Network. It was decided to develop these systems locally, instead of through outside contractors.

While most of the basic systems are fully operational, some sub–modules related to serials control are still being tested. DACOM also links users to foreign databanks such as DIALOG, and to domestic databases of such vendors as the Chunlian I, II.

Public Libraries and School Libraries

Automation in these libraries lags far behind what is found in other types of library. When the systems of the National Central Library and the National Congress Library are completed, they may stimulate automation in public libraries, which may become local nodes of nationwide information communication.

And as concerns increase about the need for computer education at the primary school level, prospects for automation of school libraries will be stimulated. Both public and school libraries are handicapped by scarce resources and lack of trained personnel. The main hope for improvement is in the government plan mentioned earlier, for education and research networks.

Standards Organizations

Standards activity has not been emphasized until recently, but concerns are increasing. Several organizations are prominent. As the only library association in Korea that represents all types of library and professional activity, KLA's role in standards is critical. A committee on standards has produced cataloguing rules for Korean publications. KLA has contributed to the work of KORMARC through participation in the KORMARC Administration Council.

National Libraries

The National Central Library, one of the national libraries in Korea, developed the KORMARC format and Korean MARC databases in the early 1980s. The other national library, the National Congress Library, began to produce the Domestic Periodicals Articles Index and the Domestic Doctoral and Master Dissertation Catalogue databases in 1986.

Both of these national libraries are developing total library systems, composed of subsystems to support various library functions, such as cataloguing, acquisitions, circulation, and serials control. The cataloguing and serials controls subsystems are now operational.

Academic Libraries

Most of the innovations in library automation among academic libraries have come from newer institutions that are not burdened by the need for retrospective conversion of manual catalogues. A typical example is the Pohang Science and Technology Institute system. The institute created a system called PLASMA, using MUMPS, in 1986. Initially, batch processing of LC MARC and KORMARC tapes was carried out. The practice was discontinued because of inefficient processing and low hit rates, and the CD–ROM version of LC MARC, provided by the BiblioFile, was contracted for use of copy cataloguing of Western language materials— a first in Korea.

However, there was no alternative to original cataloguing for Korean publications. At the same time, BACS (Bibliographic Access and Control System) of Washington University School of Medicine was adopted for the automation of basic library operations. BACS was updated and modified, and its serial control component PHILSOM was merged with the existing PLASMA system. CD–ROM products are used for information management and services, and a CD–ROM LAN is in operation. At roughly the same time, the Korea Institute of Technology developed an in–house system called KITLAS, but they use a self–developed MARC format and do original cataloguing as well.

More recently, many prestigious old universities like the Ewha Women's University, the Inha University, and the Seoul National University have created their own systems. For instance, the locally developed integrated total system of Ewha Women's University incorporates diverse languages— in particular Korean, Chinese, and Japanese— in its cataloguing, circulation, serials, and other subsystems.

In a different vein, other libraries have adopted software packages or turnkey systems. For example, Yonsei University has an integrated total library system based on a modification of DOBIS (a turnkey system used worldwide); it has a classified catalogue to accommodate the various languages in its collection. Both circulation and cataloguing modules are operational, and retrospective conversion of books received since 1990 has been completed. In contrast, the Seoul National University began library automation in 1991, the largest and most ambitious programme in Korea. Its system is intended to be the backbone network for resource sharing among all national academic libraries.

It has been almost 20 years since automated library systems emerged in Korea, but in spite of high interest among librarians the success stories have been few. The primary obstacles have been the uneven computer resources, absence of standards implementation, and lack of trained personnel.

The National University Librarians Council reported in 1990 that there was not one national university library with a dedicated mainframe computer. The libraries have terminals connected to university mainframes, but do not enjoy priority access. Consequently no national university has a total library system in place. (There are four private university libraries with operational integrated total library systems.) However, a recent government plan for five national computer networks includes the automation of libraries as part of the education network and the research network, so the situation will be enhanced.

Industrial Advancement Administration (IAA)

As part of the Korea Ministry of Trade and Industry, IAA works to enhance scientific and technological progress and to further the public interest. It is engaged in research and testing, and it provides services to the government as well as to industry. IAA has created a number of Korean Standards (KS), such as KS–C–5601, the standard of the two–byte letter code for computer processing.

KINITI, a government–sponsored organization, succeeded the Korea Science and Technological Information Centre (KORSTIC), which had been established in 1962 for the collection and dissemination of foreign scientific information. In working toward complete automation, KINITI is engaged in many kinds of research. One project is standardization, with present attention to establishment of a national interchangeable standard code acceptable to a wide range of users; and to standardization of data creation, retrieval systems, and dissemination of networks.

KORMAC: The National Central Library formulated KORMARC in 1981, beginning with a format for monographs. Data input began at the library and by 1983 printed card distribution was available. The KORMARC Administration Council was organized to further efficient management.

The Council influenced the revision of KORMARC to facilitate the sharing of data, and a 1984 standard format for monographs that partially adopted UNIMARC. This is the domestic format for input of Korean literature, following the KORMARC description rules that are based on ISBD. The adoption of ISBD instead of the Korean cataloguing rules has created a problem in respect to uniformity of bibliographic description. The structure follows ISO 2709, so it is convertible with LC MARC. ASCII is used for character representation of alphanumeric data, and 5,000 Chinese characters are represented through the converting methods of Hangul–Hanja, i.e., Korean alphabet into Chinese characters.

Although 10 years have passed since the system began distributing cards, dissemination of KORMARC output is not yet widespread in Korea. Only a small number of libraries participate in the card and tape distribution services, and the system has not been enhanced.

It is rare to see a national MARC system anywhere that is as underutilized as KORMARC. However, a recent survey indicated that many libraries want to adopt the KORMARC format for their cataloguing standard and will do so if it is improved.

There is an urgency for other KORMARC formats to handle other nonbook library materials, and that address related needs in authority control, classification, holdings, etc.

There are five major problems faced by KORMARC. The first is low quality cataloguing in the system, because not many librarians are able to process materials correctly. (The reasons for this are that public and national librarians are poorly paid and have inferior work conditions.) Cataloguing information in KORMARC is not regarded with much confidence.

The second problem is the general lack of cooperation among libraries of different types. Most of the automated libraries use their own MARC formats rather than the KORMARC format, which they find too cumbersome and complicated for easy local use. Satisfying local automation needs takes priority over the potential and less tangible benefits of information exchange among libraries.

The third problem is the absence of a unique identification number for each record in KORMARC, similar to the LCCN of LC MARC, or the ISBN. There is a control number that identifies each KORMARC record, but it is not found in the Korean national bibliography and is not included on the verso of the title page of a Korean publication. Therefore it is difficult to match bibliographic information in KORMARC with local materials to be catalogued.

The fourth problem comes from the difficulty of dealing with the Korean language, for example in the consistent spacing of words. The technology used for computer processing of documents in oriental languages is still underdeveloped. Finally, the fifth problem is the low hit rate in searching. This low rate is primarily caused by the fact that KORMARC covers only a portion of current publications. For all these reasons, original cataloguing is frequently more efficient that copy cataloguing of KORMARC.

LIBRARY AUTOMATION: A BUYING GUIDE

For some time school districts have relied on library automation systems to catalogue and circulate their book collections. In the past few years, however, this software has played an even larger role in supporting teaching and learning. No longer just automating processes once done by hand, library systems have morphed into full-search resource portals. The latest offerings typically let school librarians index Web sites, add related Web links to book records, provide patrons with home access to the library catalogue, and many other features that secure the position of the library media centre as the research hub of any school. When shopping for a new library automation system, there are many considerations. Each system may do its job well, but there are significant features that might make one system better for your district's situation than another. Here are some questions to ask and the rationale for asking them.

Key Considerations

Does the System Use Standardized Formats for Importing and Exporting Data?: There are two important reasons for having a standardized data format (such as comma-separated values). First, it often makes it much easier for libraries to convert their current digital records to work with a new system. Second, it reduces redundant data entry, allowing schools to populate their patron database with CSV data from their student information system, or conversely export data to a third- party application to create booklists, inventory sheets, and more.

Is it SIF-Compliant?: A particularly exciting development in library automation is the move by some vendors to make their systems SIF-compliant. The Schools Interoperability Framework is an industry initiative to develop an open specification that allows different types of software to "talk" to each other. This means, for example, your current student information system, the library automation system, and any other legacy system can easily and automatically share and update any information they have in common (e.g., student names and home addresses).

What Type of Database Is Used?: In the past, library automation software used proprietary databases for storing data. This closed environment made it difficult for schools to move to another system and, in some cases, precluded features such as just-in-time support. The system you're considering should be built using newer, open-standards technologies such as SQL, ColdFusion, or XML.

How Does Data Conversion Work?: This aspect of converting your current library data to a new system can get expensive and may take some time to complete. In addition to ensuring you can still use the current barcodes on your books, find out if the vendor bills a flat-rate or per record charge for conversion. If it's a per record charge, do a thorough weed of your collection and delete any unwanted records from your current system before sending the data to be converted. It's also a good idea to have the new system up and running on a server while the old data is being converted. This way, you can add any incoming materials to the new system.

Can Other Applications Besides Library Software Run on the Workstations: There are times when you'd like your 10 public catalogue stations to function as writing stations, and there are other times when you'd like the writing stations to become public catalogues. The library automation software you select should make it easy to switch between the public catalogue and the third-party software residing on the public access terminal computers. In addition, students and staff should be able to log-in and log-off on their own.

Can the Online Public Access Catalogue Be Accessed from Other Computers in the School?: With the advent of schoolwide networks, the answer to this question should be yes. Library automation systems should allow a simple icon to be installed on remote desktops to allow classroom access to the Online Public Access Catalogue or allow access to the system via a Web browser. This feature cuts down traffic to the library media centre for simple availability queries.

Feature Cheat Sheet: Your next library automation system should offer the following attributes:

- SIF-compliant system that uses standardized data formats
- Database built on open-standards technologies such as SQL, ColdFusion, or XML
- Online public access catalogue available on computers outside the library; users can search the OPAC and the Web simultaneously
- Standardized and customizable reporting capabilities
- Hands-on training and flexible support options
- Manual hand scanner for check-out if system goes offline.

What Reports Does the Software Generate?: All library automation systems allow users to generate standard reports, including collection size, circulation statistics, inventories, overdue notices, and booklists sorted by call number, author, title, or subject. However, a helpful feature is the ability to create your own specialized reports to meet the needs of your students, teachers, or administration-for example, reports that target certain subjects and publication dates, or a list of hardware that's catalogued within the system.

Can You Metasearch Both the OPAC and the Web with a Single Search? Many automation systems also catalogue Web sites in addition to the print and nonprint materials available in the library media centre. These Web sites are added by the library media specialist manually. It follows, then, that many systems allow patrons to search the OPAC and the Web simultaneously using a keyword search-a very helpful feature for students conducting research.

What Types of Support Agreements Are Available? As with any large, complex software package, there should be a menu of choices for support ranging from simple telephone support to on-site visits and automatic Web-based updates to the software. The technology infrastructure in your school may preclude certain options, so make sure your district IT specialist is part of this discussion. Also, remember to check the hours of operation for telephone and Web-based support-sometimes time zone differences can cause problems.

What Type of Training is Offered? Training for a new system should be either offered on-site, at a training centre, or at a school nearby that already has the system. The training should be conducted by a company-trained representative, be hands-on, and accompanied by easy-to-follow supporting print materials.

What Are the Technical and Infrastructure Set-ups? Discussing with a vendor operating systems, various computer platforms, wireless connectivity, routers and switches, the types of servers already existing in the network, the addition of new servers, and setting permissions for users can quickly escalate into a geek-speak session. Therefore, the IT people at your school or district, if available, should be the ones to speak to the vendor's IT people. Before he or she does that, however, the library media specialist should first create an overview of how the new system needs to work to effectively meet the needs of students and teachers. Parameters might include classroom access to the OPAC and the ability to use workstations as computer terminals.

Can the System Be Accessed from Outside of the Firewall? This question is important for two reasons. First, the technical support from the library automation system company may want to take control of your system from their site to install upgrades, patches, or simply to help you out with a particular function. In addition, many of the systems have the ability to be accessed from computers outside of the school walls via a Web browser, and this can only work if the firewall can be set to accept users from the outside or the library server is outside of the firewall.

Is There a Power-out Feature Included? If your network or server is down, you want to make sure that your library media centre can still function. There should be a manual hand scanner available to check materials in and out that can easily be connected to the system computer once it's back up and running. This hand scanner also can be used for remote check-out of books or in-the-stacks inventory data collection.

What's the Total Price of the System? This is a hard question to answer in a straightforward manner. Most library automation packages come in modules. For example, you can buy just the circulation component. Or you decide to purchase circulation and cataloguing modules, plus retrospective conversion of your data. Once you have a good feel for the type of things that you need, draw up your specifications and submit them to each vendor you're considering. That way you'll be comparing apples and apples for your bottom-line costs.

LIBRARY AUTOMATION DEVELOPMENT

Library automation has developed rapidly in recent years and as a result has become vital to the function of library services. Advances in computer and other technology have allowed library automation to meet patron needs more effectively.

History: Library automation evolved from the card catalogue in the early 1960s when computer systems became readily available for library use. The Internet advanced library automation even further as libraries were able to automate services and connect with other databases.

Function: Library automation systems can be tailored to meet each library's needs. Most use an automated system to streamline the process of creating item records and use these records to check items in and out. Automation systems also allow patrons to access an online catalogue where they can search records online from home.

Features: Library automation systems can have a variety of features beyond the ability to track items being checked in and out of the library. Commonly used systems allow patrons to search for items, check item availability and place holds on desired items.

Considerations: Library automation has made great advancements over its history of more than 50 years. With the advent of digital music and eBook borrowing, libraries are again redefining how library automation systems can be used.

HOW TO PREPARE A LIBRARY AUTOMATION COLLECTION

Using the Web is one stage of preparing a library automation collection. The issues involved in library automation are numerous and highly complex. According to Library Fact Sheet Number 21 of the American Library Association (ALA), these issues include "creating a technology plan, selecting automation systems, soliciting information from vendors, training staff, using MARC records and maintaining databases." To navigate these issues wisely, seek guidance from experts. While some information is available on the Internet, much of the professional literature is only available in books.

Instructions: Decide what you need in the collection. You may decide that you are interested in books that are devoted to a specific library system, such as the Aleph system of Ex Libris or the Millennium system of Innovative Interfaces. Alternatively, you may decide that you are interested in books that are devoted to a specific library function, such as cataloguing, acquisitions or circulation. You may even want to have a few books that are devoted to the history or development of library automation.

Research websites for specific titles, focusing on websites that are dedicated to library automation. The ALA has an online store with a comprehensive selection of titles relating to specific library functions, such as acquisitions and cataloguing.

The Library and Information Technology Association (LITA), a division of the ALA that is dedicated to information technology in libraries, has a website with a useful list of publications. Another valuable resource is the website of Library Technology Guides, which "aims to provide comprehensive and objective information related to the field of library automation."

Note the price of each book and consider your budgetary constraints. You will undoubtedly need to tailor your "wish list" to the realities of the budget available to you.

Order the books, ideally using the automated library system that you have selected. The acquisitions module of the system will allow you to place the orders and to record the arrival of the orders. There are two advantages to doing it this way. It will give you practice in using the system, and it will publicize the on-order status of these books to your patrons.

Catalogue and end-process the books. Ideally, catalogue the books using the automated library system that you have selected. The cataloguing module of the system will allow you to create the cataloguing record and to add the appropriate call number. There are two advantages to cataloguing the books using your system of choice. It will give you practice in using the system, and it will publicize the availability of the books to your patrons.

After each book has been cataloged in the automated system, forward it for the usual end-processing steps, which include affixing a label with the call number and stamping the library's stamp on the book.

CHECK-OUT SYSTEMS FOR LIBRARIES

A library catalogue is an index of all the information a library has in its collection. Library card catalogues were the preferred means libraries used to make this information available to the public for generations.

As computers became more and more popular, libraries have switched from the card catalogue method of indexing their collections to more modern, computer-automated library check-out systems.

- Libraries were originally organized alphabetically by manuscript or folio lists. This method slowly evolved into the catalogue system. In the year 800, the first catalogue of books organized by genre was created. It wasn't until the late 1500s that the first dictionary catalogue—a catalogue in which author, title, subject, series, etc. are all interfiled and arranged alphabetically—was printed. The dictionary catalogue set the foundation for current cataloguing systems. The first card catalogues didn't appear until the 19th century. When computer technology caught on in the 1970s and 1980s, libraries began automating their card catalogues. Automation allowed libraries to make their collection easily assessable to patrons on the computer and online through online public access catalogues (OPACs). OPACs are more user friendly and more efficient than card catalogues and are available both on site and online, allowing patrons 24-hour, 7-day-a-week access to a library's holdings.

Significance

- OPACs have significantly enhanced the usability of catalogues in the library environment. In the 1960s, the creation and adoption of Machine-Readable Cataloguing (MARC), a uniform computer language librarians use to catalogue their library records, helped set the foundation for standardization of library catalogues in the U.S. and abroad.

Function

- Automated catalogues in libraries have many functions. First, they provide one central location to store and display a library's complete holdings. Second, they are standardized and user-friendly making it so that most libraries in the U.S. catalogue their items by the same standards. If a patron knows how to use one library's catalogue, he has the skill set to use any library catalogue in the U.S. even if they are not exactly the same. Third, they provide key word and subject search, allowing a patron to search for a book even if she is not sure of the title or author.

Types

- There are as many types of library check-out systems as there are libraries. The type of automated system a library chooses for their collection will depend on the size of a library's collection, the types of materials they have in their collection, the size of their user base, circulation statistics and the features that are important to the unique library environment the check-out system will be used in. Some systems allow librarian access only, while other systems allow patrons to check out books themselves.

Benefits

- While automated library systems are commonplace in today's libraries, not every library has one. There are many federal grants available to help libraries update their card catalogues to automated library systems. Automated check-out systems benefit everyone. They make a librarian's job regarding circulation and statistics collection much easier. They also make it easier for patrons to find the material they are looking for themselves, making them more self-sufficient.

LIST OF LIBRARY AUTOMATION SOFTWARE

Libraries are seeking ways to cut costs while maintaining excellent service for their patrons. Library automation software offers solutions that benefit both the libraries and their communities, including its youngest members. Patrons can come in, browse through the books and media, and check out on the library's computers. Thanks to this technology, librarians now have an easier way to track down overdue books or search for an author.

Atriuum

Atriuum is a Web-based library automation solution. It has several supplemental modules, services and programs. Examples include managing print subscriptions and acquisitions orders, and importing patron data in a variety of formats.

Librarians have access to a variety of customizable reports that will help them run their library more efficiently. Patrons save time by searching for books on the computer in a variety of ways, and then checking them out through the self-checkout system. A module called KidZviZ allows children from Pre-K through the 3rd grade to explore the library system through a kid-friendly interface.

Apollo

Apollo is Web-based, so there are no system requirements other than possessing a reasonably modern Internet browser and connection. Apollo has a slew of features for the library and its patrons. The library staff no longer has to keep track of overdue notifications. The single catalogue interface gives a sense of consistency to the patrons, who may reserve books from home. Apollo can be set up as a network across several branches.

EOS.Web Express

EOS.Web Express is for small to medium-sized libraries that do not require full-bodied enterprise systems. It is a Web-based system that is built for speed and efficiency. Libraries may customize their system to include whatever modules they need.

Polaris ILS

Plolaris ILS automates your cataloguing, circulation, acquisitions, serials control and PAC functions. It works well with your existing products and services so that you do not have to reinstall or redo anything.

Resource Mate

ResourceMate is a library automation system for small to medium-sized libraries. The software has a variety of features, including patron search and free Library of Congress data import. Librarians can also generate reports that will help them find books or track overdue items. Demos are available for the Standard and Museum ResourceMate. You may also download the Info Pack if you need more information, and try out the search demo on the site.

LIBRARY AUTOMATION, NETWORKING, AND OTHER ONLINE

Over the past twenty years, academic libraries have changed considerably as bibliographic utilities, online catalogues, automated circulation systems, and other new technologies have been implemented in a majority of library operations and services. These changes have created rising costs for libraries in a time of tight fiscal constraints, particularly in the area of telecommunications, buildings, furniture, and electronic equipment. For the medium and larger sized academic libraries, it is not uncommon for computer costs associated with implementing online catalogues, circulation/reserve, acquisitions accounting, and serials control systems - including retrospective conversion of paper records into machine-readable forms - to require $5 million plus. Annual maintenance, licensing agreements, software, and hardware requirements will exceed an additional $250,000 to $350,000 per year.

The increased access to electronic information systems not held locally and to other new technologies such as CD-ROM, laser technologies, interactive multimedia packages, OCR (optical character recognition) and imaging systems, satellite communication and teleconferencing, laptop computers, packet telephone switches, and cellular telephones have also been making an impact in a few libraries along with LANs (local area networks) and WANs (wide area networks) for interconnecting local computing resources.

The impact has not been only on more technologically oriented methods of operations and services; new information and instructional technologies have placed tremendous pressures on outdated cabling and wiring. Expanded budgets are required for such things as asbestos abatement in ceiling and floor tiling as well as utility tunnels; installation of fibre optics and additional connective wiring and cabling within and among buildings; and equipment (hardware and soft ware) for both staff and public access. Additional funding is needed for online network memberships and connections to local, state, regional, national, and international networks. These network relationships require new and expanded licensing agreements with updated copyright procedures and related issues. New formats and access tools require revamped policies and procedures, rules, and regulations. Expanded training (of staff and users) and continuing education require increased travel budgets for participation in new professional associations and continuing education and training opportunities. Employment of new types of personnel to handle technological problems (including troubleshooting of hardware/ software problems), programming, and maintenance and repair work, plus retooling of existing staff and enhanced hiring requirements when keyboarding skill (i.e., typing) becomes more important at all levels. The new equipment can focus stuff demands for installation of ergonomic furniture and security devices. There are increased costs in HVAC (heating, air conditioning, circulation, and humidity) and other utilities costs (telephone, telefacsimile, electrical power, security and control of equipment, software, building access, and other costs associated with telecommunications and online networking). Reconfiguration and reconstruction of physical facilities both within and outside of library buildings is often necessary. Special consultants to assist with strategic planning, selection of systems, technological issues, and related problems are often hidden costs. The emphasis on equipment increases the need for analysis of depreciation and replacement costs associated with many aspects of new technologies.

In addition to all the new budget-impacting workloads, much greater interaction, collaboration, and cooperation have been required among librarians, their primary clientele, computer centre personnel, physical plant operations, university administration, and others related to telecommunications planning and budgeting of all aspects of informational and instructional technologies.

Fund-raising has become far more commonplace in all types of academic libraries (public and private) than ever before in history - and not just through state and federal granting agencies but through approaches to foundations and corporations, as well as individual benefactors. Priorities have changed; funding methodologies have expanded; resources (budget, personnel, space, equipment, responsibilities) have had to be re-examined and reallocated. All of this requires that far more personnel time be devoted to both short- and long-range planning within libraries, across campus, and often within consortia of a local, state, regional, and even national nature.

The new technologies have required not only different expertise and training requirements for personnel but have required new types of personnel and more personnel, even though shifts in existing personnel could be made to meet new demands when the newer technologies made some activities obsolete and others less labour intensive.

Gaddis (1989) notes that libraries have had to become more involved in soliciting bids, writing specifications, identifying potential vendors, evaluating systems and services, and preparing RFPs (request for proposals). These RFPs have to ensure that future activities be accommodated by the systems selected for use and that these are also documented (i.e., systems must be sized to meet potential for growth and development as well as strategically developed to support linking capabilities among systems and to allow similar connections to other multimedia resources). Systems costs, Gaddis notes, include central processing units, disk and/or tape storage/ drives, printers, freight and installation, and maintenance. Costs must be included for terminals for staff and users, wands or laser readers, and furniture for equipment. There are obvious software costs (for the operating system, application programs or modules, maintenance, customizing to accommodate local systems), interfaces to other systems, and backup systems.

There is site preparation (space, air conditioning, raised floors, dedicated electrical power, power protection, fire extinguishing systems, grounded electrical outlets, individual surge protectors, antistatic materials, cleaning kits for terminals, and cabling throughout buildings).

There are conversion costs (bibliographic with authority control; copy level conversion and barcoding; patron file creation; and creation of patron identification cards). There are implementation costs (time for planning, including staff line reporting, and developing policies and procedures), installation, training, publicity, and public relations in an environment where there is also operational disruption for barcoding of collections, structural modifications, rewiring, and so on.

At the end, there is staff recognition for all of the implementation activity. And always there are ongoing operational costs (including bringing systems up and taking them down), doing file saves; ongoing staffing needs for troubleshooting problems with peripherals and software operations; for coordinating vendor maintenance performance; for preparing documentation of hardware operations as they are handled locally, including emergency procedures; for performing day-end processes, including generation of reports and notices; ceaseless needs for funding initiatives to cover purchase costs for enhancements; membership in user groups (membership fees, navel costs, and staff time to attend meetings); and other developmental service components that grow from a successful library management system.

Another, even more important, benefit is discussed by Tyckoson (1989): "[Automation] allows users to access and share information by methods that could not be achieved with more traditional formats". Many libraries have already begun planning and implementing other benefits of the new technologies, including coordinated collection development; speedy document delivery of full-text information; ability to digitize special collections unique to a particular library; linkages and interfaces with other information agencies, vendors, and libraries for data that are not held locally; improved and enhanced access to visual and sound collections; and expanded capabilities to use all the new technologies and, often, even the more traditional formats in an interactive multimedia way in wired classrooms around the world with real face-to-face online collaborative research and study going on among students, faculty, researchers, and scholars.

Other benefits include, Rush (1986) notes, "expanded service to the public, decreased backlogs, more timely processing, increased productivity, reduced space requirements, or other improvements". Joan Frye Williams adds another benefit: "an automated system contains staff costs by accommodating workload increases".

Funding priorities today must also include assisting with standardization of databases, communication and access protocols, and simplified entry from one system or personal computer into other systems, regardless of location, type of system and network, and computer (mainframe, personal computer, or other). Funding priorities must provide for continuing innovation and creativity to enhance access to all information resources - print and nonprint, electronic, and so on.

Juergens (1990) notes that, "there are at most 1,400 library employees in all of the nation's technology-based networks, as opposed to 340,000 library employees in the country in 1987, according to the American Library Association". Of those 340,000 library employees, it would be interesting to discover how many of them use automation daily and at what level.

Juergens also states that "bibliographic networks (e.g., OCLC, WLN, RLN) cost 1-2.8% of a library's annual expense budget". Hunter (1988) notes that, "the amount of recorded literature doubles every 15 to 17 years". The amount of that literature in electronic format is still a minimal part of information dealt with by libraries, but it is growing dramatically each day. Hunter (1988) also notes that "we are already technically capable of doing far more than our budgets will ever allow" and that "scholarly publishers and research librarians cannot afford all of the things which new technology makes possible - we will have to make choices". Gupta (1991) states that, "the investment in information systems, if used effectively, will lead to improved information systems performance, and therefore will result in better organisational decision making which may enhance the overall performance of the organisation".

Malinconico (1992) quotes David Bishop saying that "revenues earned by the electronic database industry are already near $11 billion and are expected to grow 20% per year for the next 5 years, reaching more than $22 billion by 1995". Malinconico (1992) also notes that database growth is about 25 percent per year with CD-ROM database growth about 60 percent per year. In addition, he notes the growth of electronic journals, specialized networks - such as NASA's Mission to Planet Earth - campuswide networks, electronic imaging and virtual libraries, and national network development - such as the NREN (National Research Education Network).

As he points out, "the new information services simultaneously increase user need for the assistance of information specialists and reduce the contact they have with them". Susan Baerg Epstein (1990) expands this to note that with the new technologies we have "improved services and limited increases in number of staff needed to meet greater demands" and that "existing staff can [now] be more productive".

Many libraries have found new, or adapted old, methods to increase their fiscal resources. These include, as Rush notes, sharing costs across consortia; distributing operating costs over a broader base; improving resource sharing through state and federal grants and through proposals to foundations; obtaining legislation for funding; gaining funds from wealthy and influential citizens/ benefactors; and offering revenue-producing services to businesses. Williams (1986) adds "allocating available operational funds more wisely using management reports generated by automated systems, transferring financial resources now supporting repetitive clerical tasks to other parts of the budget in order to improve direct user services". Williams also suggests that a library should "deposit one seventh of the system's original price in a special interest-bearing replacement account" each year, or consideration of funding strategies such as "commercial lease-purchase agreement, Municipal Leasing Corporation (MLC) Lease Purchase Agreements, and Limited Partnerships with investors". At least one academic library (Southern Methodist University Libraries, Dallas, Texas) received a $500,000 endowment for library automation and new technologies.

Strategic planning for electronic systems, most library administrators will agree, is an absolute necessity. Mann (1986) suggests "intensive long- range planning and budgeting programs that include start-up, performance, utilization, enhancement, and replacement criteria for each component of the system". He also urges preparation of "financial feasibility studies before the library initiates investments in technology, preparing strategies, and projections to relate investments in technology to financial benefits such as the avoidance and/or recovery of costs as a result of reduced operating expenses, and use of ratios and other analyses to identify trends in the financial health of the library, and comparison of the results with trends at peer libraries". Future technologies will continue to change libraries and the ways in which they operate. Bazillion (1992) focuses on the new "notebook computers of increasing power and portability" which he feels will "reduce valuable space [required] for banks of conventional pcs [personal computers]" and which "will not need the same noise reduction" considerations. But what will they need in the availability of active telecommunications ports to connect to the local library system? What will that flexibility cost? He also predicts that "CD-ROM will diminish as library computers become more powerful, and software more sophisticated...", and that "libraries will be regional research centres which must provide enough communications ports for convenient dial-in access".

FUTURE OF LIBRARY AUTOMATION

Vendor announced they will be dropping support for C Client Sirsi/ Dynix, the vendor for the INFOhio library automation software, has announced they will no longer support the current client we are using after the GL3.2 software upgrade targeted for release in Summer 08. Hence, it is necessary for INFOhio to begin migrating all users across the State off the current client and onto the new Java Client being released.

INFOhio has begun a pilot phase for the migration and has already migrated some schools in the State to the beta version of the new Java client. LACA will not be migrating our schools to the new client until the pilot phase has been completed and the final "Gold" release of the client is made available.

Today's Future

There are times that lend themselves to speculation about the future, and this seems to be one of those times. The future library is being referred to as "Library 2.0," although there is little agreement on what that new library will look like: Walt Crawford claims to have found as many as sixty- two views and seven definitions of the term. If nothing else, there is plenty of fodder for a lively discussion.

There are hints of change on the horizon and the potential change agents in libraries today are numerous. Library cataloguing practice, one of the more stable elements of library activity, has been challenged by the theory of Functional Requirements for Bibliographic Records, or FRBR. New cataloguing rules (Resource Description and Access, or RDA) are being discussed that would incorporate that theory. In the area of technology, the desire to work seamlessly with web services and to integrate the library catalogue into the larger networked information universe is causing some questioning of the functionality of the catalogue and the assumptions behind the Integrated Library System.

Before delving into our future, it might be instructive to look at some of the futures that preceded us. There may be lessons that can help us in our own divination process. I have taken some predictions covering the years 1949 to 1984 to inform this investigation.

These are not by any means the entirety of relevant works on the future of libraries. If you are interested in this topic I suggest the almost 300-page annotated bibliography by Gregg Sapp. The earliest of the predictions come on the cusp of the computer revolution, and those, not surprisingly, see stunning changes taking place. Later authors, especially those in the library field, are struggling more to see beyond the existing systems, and are closer in their views of the future to today's library futurists.

What Most Got Right

There were certain predictions regarding technologies and libraries that many of the authors got right. These may seem obvious to us today, but the authors, and especially the earliest authors, were working from a very different perspective than ours. What nearly all of our past futurists seem to have agreed on was that it would be possible to interact with the library from a remote location. Users would access the library catalogue from home or from other locations around town. Most authors correctly predicted online access to the library catalogue, access to databases of information, and even direct access to full text. Although there was not yet talk about the computer making some experiences "virtual," Taylor may have been the first to coin the expression "library without walls" in his 1975 article in which he envisioned remote access to the library and to various information resources provided by the library.

Nearly all of the authors predicted that new technologies would reduce the storage requirements for information, an important use of the technology since there was usual agreement that the increase in the amount of information is one of the great challenges of our electronic world. Vannevar Bush, the creator of the "memex" concept, predicted the miniaturization of documents through micro-reprographics: "The Encyclopedia Britannica could be reduced to the volume of a matchbox." He can be forgiven for missing the seemingly obvious computerization of documents since he was writing in 1949. Griffin in 1962 boldly stated that computers would "Take over the storage problem." Of course, working for IBM might have influenced her viewpoint. Interestingly, Branscomb, a computer scientist, is the one who appears to have coined the measure of information based on the number of characters in all of the books in the Library of Congress (which he estimated as 70 trillion bits).

Although Lancaster is often derided for his prediction of "paperless" information systems, a careful reading shows that he was not proposing that there would be no more use of printed documents, but that it would be possible to create and exchange documents in digital form. He successfully predicted everything from word processing and email to markup of documents by reviewers. His concern was the need for greater efficiency, a concern shared by others in this roundup.

Various authors went into great descriptions of this future technology and how people would interact with it, such as:

"When I press a key, a code goes into the system, and the system then sends back a code [that] activates the marking unit."

"[The memex] consists of a desk… On the top are slanting translucent screens, on which material can be projected for convenient reading. There is a keyboard, and sets of buttons and levels."

Although their exact details look somewhat silly today, conceptually they were on the right path with networks delivering information resources and technology that allowed the creation of research documents using machines to take on some of the mundane aspects of that work.

It is interesting that as early as 1962, Griffin predicted that there would be regional catalogues, and that these would facilitate inter-library loan. The expansion of the geographical scope of the catalogue became a common theme as soon as the existence of online catalogues was in sight.

Like the prediction of an "always open" library, the ability of networks to remove geographical boundaries caught the imagination of our futurists. Griffin also predicted that it would be possible to automate the launching of an ILL request whenever an item was not found in the local catalogue. A form of this is realized today as patron initiated interlibrary loan.

It is particularly impressive that in 1949 Bush essentially describes hypertext links, social tagging and peer-to-peer networks, at least if you interpret his ideas generously. He saw researchers creating associative maps between documents and exchanging these with each other in an early form of social tagging. Kilgour has the advantage of speaking in 1984, but he did declare that the 1990's would bring a new information culture. Unfortunately, he thought that the focus of that culture would be the online public access catalogue when in fact the focus was the World Wide Web.

Wishful Thinking

Early thinkers on the future of libraries had what we would consider rather generous ideas about the capabilities of computers. That makes sense, of course. They hadn't had enough experience with these modern machines to have witnessed their limitations. Some of them fell into the trap of seeing the computer as a thinking machine. Griffin predicted that computers would be answering reference questions and guiding users through their research. Kilgour and Branscomb expected actual speech to be the interface between computers and humans, implying that computers would answer questions posed by library users or would guide them through the research process.

The division of labour between computers and humans varies in these visions of the future. Licklider anticipated a working relation between men and computers in which the computer would be relegated the repetitious work and humans would do the intellectual work. He referred to his idea as a "pro-cognitive system" where machines aid humans in the cognitive function. Griffin sees computers taking over the cataloguing of information and acting as reference librarians, while Licklider anticipates a one hour interview (!) between a researcher adding a paper to the store of knowledge and a human indexer who will make the necessary connections between this document and ones already indexed. Egeland saw a relief from routine tasks: "... machines, not librarians, should be ordering and cataloguing materials, checking in serials, checking out books, and compiling bibliographies."

Both Lancaster and Garfield saw a glowing future for librarians, if not for libraries themselves. They anticipated a new role as information consultant for those with library skills. Kilgour saw the utility of librarians growing, although he was not so optimistic about the future of libraries themselves: "Libraries as we now know them will diminish in usefulness. The functions of librarians, as distinct from libraries, will, however, almost certainly enlarge intellectually as well as usefully."

There was some optimism about the economics of automation. Egeland took the position that computers would free up the time of librarians, thus leaving more time for patron service, and Auerbach stated that libraries in usual would be less expensive and hence more special libraries would be created. Bauer recognized that a future generation of librarians would appear with specialties in library automation, although it is still a matter of debate in some institutions whether management of the technology is a role for librarians or if it is best assigned to non-library staff with technology skills.

Cautions

Futurists tend to be an optimistic bunch when describing the world to come. In addition, in professional literature it is probably considered unseemly to predict dire outcomes for your colleagues and their institutions. Some of the authors did have cautions to offer, however. Egeland warned that there would be more opportunities for libraries, but only if libraries could move from the passive "caretaker" role to a more active role in disseminating information. She saw the main barrier to be the reluctance of the profession to make changes, and warned that such change would take a number of years. Kilgour chided his audience that although librarians have used computers to improve the efficiency of certain management operations like circulation and serials control, they hadn't yet used the computer for radical change in the management of information delivery. Today's work with web services may finally be fulfilling Kilgour's vision.

Branscomb acknowledged the difficulties of using computers for truly intellectual work. He provides many calculations relating to the growing power of computers but admits that no computer has come near the capability of the human brain to make associations. He also had the insight to state that it is relatively easy to store data in a computer, but much harder to retrieve that data.

Misses

There are some predictions that are nearly universally missing from the future scenarios of these authors. With the exception of Branscomb, who made a brief mention of copyright law ("If we can solve the problem of protection of intellectual property... there will be an effective market for knowledge in itself, since distribution to the consumer will be easy and direct and very inexpensive."), no one anticipated the difficulties that would arise over intellectual property in this new digital age. Griffin stated: "The library of tomorrow will have eliminated the overdue notice.

A permanent copy of any document will be available at a small cost to a reader." There was mention by others of the delivery of copies of documents to researchers, both electronically and in a print-on-demand format, but the legal aspects of this were not examined.

Disintermediation and user independence was also missed by many of the authors. Garfield went so far as to say: "I cannot envision information retrieval as being entirely self service!" Although not one hundred percent self service, the migration of library users to web sites and search engines was no where in the vision of librarians in our past.

Of course, any prediction of a specific technology is unlikely to survive the actual passage of time. Bauer, in 1980, saw great potential for videodiscs both for home entertainment and for information storage. The videodisc had a brief heyday in the early 1980's but was surpassed by the DVD format in short order. Many of the authors thought the home access and display device would be the television set. Although still in existence, WebTV does not appear to have made significant inroads into the market despite the fact that televisions are still vastly more numerous in homes than personal computers. The personal computer hit the public consciousness in the early 1980's (in January, 1983 the computer became Time Magazine's "Person of the Year"), but it wasn't a common home appliance for another decade.

The key "miss" on the part of the librarians mentioned here was to totally ignore the burgeoning computer industry and hence to assume that information access would remain the purview of libraries. Perhaps the greatest lesson for us in these writings is that we have to look beyond libraries in our long range planning. The future of libraries is inherently integrated with the future of a larger context: economics, technologies, social developments.

❐

5

Library Cataloguing and Internet

LIBRARY CATALOGUE

A library catalogue is a register of all bibliographic items found in a particular library or group of libraries, such as those belonging to a university system spread out over several geographic locations. A bibliographic item can be any information entity (e.g., books, computer files, graphics, realia, cartographic materials, etc.), that is considered library material (e.g., a single novel in an anthology), or a group of library materials (e.g., a trilogy), or linked from the catalogue (e.g., a webpage) as far as it is relevant to the catalogue and to the users (patrons) of the library.

The card catalogue was a familiar sight to library users for generations, but it has been effectively replaced by the Online Public Access Catalogue (OPAC). Some still refer to the online catalogue as a "card catalogue", but this is incorrect.

Some libraries with OPAC access still have card catalogues on site, but these are now strictly a secondary resource and are seldom updated. Many of the libraries that have retained their physical card catalogue post a sign advising the last year that the card catalogue was updated. Some libraries have eliminated their card catalogue in favour of the OPAC for the purpose of saving space for other use, such as additional shelving.

CATALOGUING RULES

Cataloguing (or cataloguing) rules have been defined to allow for consistent cataloguing of various library materials across several persons of a cataloguing team and across time. Users can use them to clarify how to find an entry and how to interpret the data in an entry. Cataloguing rules prescribe

- which information from a bibliographic item is included in the entry;
- how this information is presented on a catalogue card or in a cataloguing record;
- how the entries should be sorted in the catalogue.

The larger a collection, the more elaborate cataloguing rules are needed. Users cannot and do not want to examine hundreds of catalogue entries or even dozens of library items to find the one item they need. Currently, most cataloguing rules are similar to, or even based on, the International Standard Bibliographic Description (ISBD), a set of rules produced by the International Federation of Library Associations (IFLA) to describe a wide range of library materials. These rules organize the bibliographic description of an item in the following areas: title and statement of responsibility (author or editor), edition, material-dependent information (for example, the scale of a map), publication and distribution, physical description (for example, number of pages), series, note, and standard number (ISBN).

The most commonly used set of cataloguing rules in the English speaking world are the Anglo-American Cataloguing Rules, 2nd Edition, or AACR2 for short. In the German-speaking world there exists the Regeln für alphabetische Katalogisierung, abbreviated RAK. AACR2 has been translated into many languages, however, for use around the world. AACR2 provides rules for descriptive cataloguing only and does not touch upon subject cataloguing. Library items that are written in a foreign script are, in some cases, transliterated to the script of the catalogue.

Sorting

In a title catalogue, one can distinguish two sort orders:

- In the *grammatic* sort order (used mainly in older catalogues), the most important word of the title is the first sort term. The importance of a word is measured by grammatic rules; for example, the first noun may be defined to be the most important word.
- In the mechanic sort order, the first word of the title is the first sort term. Most new catalogues use this scheme, but still include a trace of the grammatic sort order: they neglect an article (The, A, etc.) at the beginning of the title.

The grammatic sort order has the advantage that often, the most important word of the title is also a good keyword (question 3), and it is the word most users remember first when their memory is incomplete.

However, it has the disadvantage that many elaborate grammatic rules are needed, so that only expert users may be able to search the catalogue without help from a librarian. In some catalogues, person's names are standardized, i.e., the name of the person is always (catalogued and) sorted in a standard form, even if it appears differently in the library material. This standardization is achieved by a process called authority control. An advantage of the authority control is that it is easier to answer question 2 (which works of some author does the library have?). On the other hand, it may be more difficult to answer question 1 (does the library have some specific material?) if the material spells the author in a peculiar variant. For the cataloguer, it may incur (too) much work to check whether *Smith, J.* is *Smith, John* or *Smith, Jack.*

For some works, even the title can be standardized. The technical term for this is *uniform title.* For example, translations and reeditions are sometimes sorted under their original title. In many catalogues, parts of the Bible are sorted under the standard name of the book(s) they contain. The plays of William Shakespeare are another frequently cited example of the role played by a *uniform title* in the library catalogue. Many complications about alphabetic sorting of entries arise. Some examples:

- Some languages know sorting conventions that differ from the language of the catalogue. For example, some Dutch catalogues sort IJ as Y. Should an English catalogue follow this suit? And should a Dutch catalogue sort non-Dutch words the same way?
- Some titles contain numbers, for example 2001: A Space Odyssey. Should they be sorted as numbers, or spelled out as Two thousand and one?
- de Balzac, Honouré or Balzac, Honouré de? Ortega y Gasset, Joséor Gasset, José Ortega y?

In a subject catalogue, one has to decide on which classification system to use. The cataloguer will select appropriate subject headings for the bibliographic item and a unique classification number (sometimes known as a "call number") which is used not only for identification but also for the purposes of shelving, placing items with similar subjects near one another, which aids in browsing by library users, who are thus often able to take advantage of serendipity in their search process.

Online Catalogues

Online cataloguing has greatly enhanced the usability of catalogues, thanks to the rise of MAchine Readable Cataloguing = MARC standards in the 1960s. Rules governing the creation of catalogue MARC records include not only formal cataloguing rules like AACR2 but also special rules specific to MARC, available from the Library of Congress and also OCLC. MARC was originally used to automate the creation of physical catalogue cards; Now the MARC computer files are accessed directly in the search process. OPACs have enhanced usability over traditional card formats because:

1. The online catalogue does not need to be sorted statically; the user can choose author, title, keyword, or systematic order dynamically.
2. Most online catalogues offer a search facility for any word of the title; the goal of the grammatic word order (provide an entry on the word that most users would look for) is reached even better.
3. Many online catalogues allow links between several variants of an author name. So, authors can be found both under the original and the standardised name (if entered properly by the cataloguer).

Searching with an OPAC

As noted above, the acronym OPAC means Online Public Access Catalogue.

Many libraries have their catalogue accessible via Internet; some of them can be queried using a simple browser, other using a special version of browser (with Javascript and CSS features), some others using Z39.50 clients.

If you are looking for a book or another item, you can access to the OPAC of your nearest library and search for it there. If you cannot find a particular book in the catalogue, it may be obtainable through interlibrary loan, also known to librarians as I.L.L. Ask the nearest Reference librarian for assistance.

If you want to look if a book exists and you have few elements to identify it, you can use a meta-searcher: you can fill the query form once and spread you search over many library catalogues. A service such as MultiOpac does this task for you.

Another option is to use a union catalogue, in which many libraries have combined their entire holdings into one database. The largest union catalogue is OCLC's WorldCat.

CATALOGUING THEORY AND PRACTICE

Modern descriptive cataloguing theory and practice has developed over the past 150 years as a means of organising information for retrieval in libraries. Library catalogues typically consist of a collection of bibliographic records that describe published materials, usually-as the name implies-in the form of printed books but also including cartographic materials, music scores and manuscripts. The standards and cataloguing codes originally developed to support this activity have expanded to include a range of newer publishing media, typically: sound recordings, microforms, video recordings, films and computer files. In response to the current widespread (and increasing) use of computer networks-primarily the Internet-for publishing, bibliographic standards and the formats associated with them have also been adapted to describe this type of material.

However, the increasing use of the Internet as a publishing medium has led to a reassessment of the usefulness or validity of the traditional cataloguing approach in this new environment. In 1995, Vianne T. Sha outlined three broad approaches to Internet resource discovery .

1. The development of search services using robot-based search engines to index Web pages, an approach exemplified by services like Lycos andAltaVista.
2. The "manual subject guides" approach where human intelligence is utilised to identify and evaluate Internet resources. These are typically subject-based guides that take the form of HTML lists. Examples include the various WWW Virtual Library sites and the subject-guides listed by the Argus Clearinghouse .
3. The library cataloguing method, creating bibliographic records for Internet resources in library catalogues. The classic example of this approach is OCLC's InterCat project .

Sha favours the third, traditional, approach where bibliographic records for Internet resources are catalogued using existing library standard formats, primarily MARC.

Researchers will then need to go to only one place-the local library-to access all formats of information resources. Cataloguing records of the resources also give detailed descriptive information to help the researchers identify whether the resources are what they really need, saving the researchers a tremendous amount of time wandering on the Internet to browse through the information. This is a laudable aim, but one could sensibly wonder whether the relatively heavyweight codes developed for traditional library cataloguing are really suitable for the mobile and ephemeral resource that is the Internet? Perhaps better solutions would not involve the use of traditional cataloguing codes or formats at all but would combine information professionals' expertise of selecting and evaluating resources with a resource discovery system that makes use of a relatively simple metadata format. Internet resources can be adequately described, for example, using the fifteen elements in the Dublin Core metadata element set . Another relatively simple approach is embodied by the subject-based gateways that use the software developed by the eLib funded ROADS project . These services use information specialists to evaluate and select Internet resources and to create a metadata record for each resource using a ROADS template, a simple metadata format that uses attribute-value pairs.

This chapter will attempt to compare traditional library cataloguing practices with the approach taken by subject-based gateways using SOSIG (the Social Science Information Gateway) as a particular example.

TECHNICAL SUPPORT

Technical support or tech support refers to a range of services by which enterprises provide assistance to users of technology products such as mobile phones, televisions, computers, software products or other electronic or mechanical goods. In general, technical support services attempt to help the user solve specific problems with a product—rather than providing training, customization, or other support services. Most companies offer technical support for the products they sell, either freely available or for a fee. Technical support may be delivered over the telephone or online by e-mail or a website or a tool where users can log a call/incident. Larger organizations frequently have internal technical support available to their staff for computer related problems. The internet is also a good source for freely available tech support, where experienced users may provide advice and assistance with problems. In addition, some fee-based service companies charge for premium technical support services.

Coverage of Support

Technical support may be delivered by different technologies depending on the situation. For example, direct questions can be addressed using telephone calls, SMS, Online chat, Support Forums, E-mail or Fax; basic software problems can be addressed over the telephone or, increasingly, by using remote access repair services; while more complicated problems with hardware may need to be dealt with in person.

Types of Technical Support

This type of technical support has been very common in the services industry. It is also known as "Break-Fix" IT Support. The concept behind this type of support is that the customer pays for the materials (Hard Drive, Memory, Computer, etc.) as well as pays the technician based on their pre-negotiated rate when they have a problem.

Block Hours

Block Hours is basically a way to purchase a bunch of hours upfront to pay a reduced hourly rate. The premise behind this type of support is that the customer has negotiated a discounted rate and a fixed number of hours to use either per month or year. This allows them the flexibility to use the hours as they please without doing the paperwork and the hassle of paying multiple bills.

Managed Services

Managed Services means a company will receive a list of well-defined services on an ongoing basis, with well-defined "response and resolution times" for a fixed rate or a flat fee. This can include things like 24/7

Monitoring of Servers, 24/7 Help desk for your daily computer issues and On-site visits by a technician when issues cannot be resolved remotely. Some companies also offer additional services like Project Management and Vendor management in the monthly price.

Outsourcing Technical Support

With the increasing use of technology in modern times, there is a growing requirement to provide technical support. Many organizations locate their technical support departments or call centers in countries with lower costs. There has also been a growth in companies specializing in providing technical support to other organizations. These are often referred to as MSP's (Managed Service Providers).

For businesses needing to provide technical support, outsourcing allows them to maintain a high availability of service. Such need may result from peaks in call volumes during the day, periods of high activity due to introduction of new products or maintenance service packs, or the requirement to provide customers with a high level of service at a low cost to the business. For businesses needing technical support assets, outsourcing enables their core employees to focus more on their work in order to maintain productivity. It also enables them to utilize specialized personnel whose technical knowledge base and experience may exceed the scope of the business, thus providing a higher level of technical support to their employees.

Multi-tiered Technical Support

Technical support is often subdivided into tiers, or levels, in order to better serve a business or customer base. The number of levels a business uses to organize their technical support group is dependent on a business' need, want, or desire as it revolves around their ability to sufficiently serve their customers or users. The reason for providing a multi-tiered support system instead of one general support group is to provide the best possible service in the most efficient possible manner. Success of the organizational structure is dependent on the technicians' understanding of their level of responsibility and commitments, their customer response time commitments, and when to appropriately escalate an issue and to which level. A common support structure revolves around a three-tiered technical support system.

Tier/Level 1(T1/L1)

This is the initial support level responsible for basic customer issues. It is synonymous with first-line support, level 1 support, front-end support, support line 1, and various other headings denoting basic level technical support functions. The first job of a Tier I specialist is to gather the customer's information and to determine the customer's issue by analysing the symptoms and figuring out the underlying problem. When analysing the symptoms, it is important for the technician to identify what the customer is trying to accomplish so that time is not wasted on "attempting to solve a symptom instead of a problem." Once identification of the underlying problem is established, the specialist can begin sorting through the possible solutions available. Technical support specialists in this group typically handle straightforward and simple problems while "possibly using some kind of knowledge management tool." This includes troubleshooting methods such as verifying physical layer issues, resolving username and password problems, uninstalling/reinstalling basic software applications, verification of proper hardware and software set up, and assistance with navigating around application menus. Personnel at this level have a basic to general understanding of the product or service and may not always contain the competency required for solving complex issues.

Nevertheless, the goal for this group is to handle 70%-80% of the user problems before finding it necessary to escalate the issue to a higher level. In other industries (such as banking, credit cards, mobile telephony, etc.) 1st level support is carried by a call center that operates extensive hours (or 24/7) acting as "initial sink" for user requests and, if required, creating an incident to notify other business teams/units to satisfy user request (provide new pin, blocking stolen credit cards/mobile phones/SIMMs). In some industries, 1st line support actually requires very good knowledge of the products, terms and conditions offered by the business rather than technical information itself (Retail/Wholesale). Most ISPs only offer tier 1 support.

Tier/Level 2(T2/L2)

This is a more in-depth technical support level than Tier I and therefore costs more as the techs are more experienced and knowledgeable on a particular product or service. It is synonymous with level 2 support, support line 2, administrative level support, and various other headings denoting advanced technical troubleshooting and analysis methods.

Technicians in this realm of knowledge are responsible for assisting Tier I personnel in solving basic technical problems and for investigating elevated issues by confirming the validity of the problem and seeking for known solutions related to these more complex issues. However, prior to the trouble shooting process, it is important that the technician review the work order to see what has already been accomplished by the Tier I technician and how long the technician has been working with the particular customer. This is a key element in meeting both the customer and business needs as it allows the technician to prioritize the troubleshooting process and properly manage his or her time. If a problem is new and/or personnel from this group cannot determine a solution, they are responsible for raising this issue to the Tier III technical support group.

In addition, many companies may specify that certain troubleshooting solutions be performed by this group to help ensure the intricacies of a challenging issue are solved by providing experienced and knowledgeable technicians. This may include, but is not limited to onsite installations or replacements of various hardware components, software repair, diagnostic testing, and the utilization of remote control tools used to take over the user's machine for the sole purpose of troubleshooting and finding a solution to the problem.

Tier/Level 3(T3/L3)

This is the highest level of support in a three-tiered technical support model responsible for handling the most difficult or advanced problems. It is synonymous with level 3 support, back-end support, support line 3, high-end support, and various other headings denoting expert level troubleshooting and analysis methods. These individuals are experts in their fields and are responsible for not only assisting both Tier I and Tier II personnel, but with the research and development of solutions to new or unknown issues.

Note that Tier III technicians have the same responsibility as Tier II technicians in reviewing the work order and assessing the time already spent with the customer so that the work is prioritized and time management is sufficiently utilized. If it is at all possible, the technician will work to solve the problem with the customer as it may become apparent that the Tier I and/or Tier II technicians simply failed to discover the proper solution.

Upon encountering new problems; however, Tier III personnel must first determine whether or not to solve the problem and may require the customer's contact information so that the technician can have adequate time to troubleshoot the issue and find a solution. In some instances, an issue may be so problematic to the point where the product cannot be salvaged and must be replaced. Such extreme problems are also sent to the original developers for in-depth analysis. If it is determined that a problem can be solved, this group is responsible for designing and developing one or more courses of action, evaluating each of these courses in a test case environment, and implementing the best solution to the problem.

Once the solution is verified, it is delivered to the customer and made available for future troubleshooting and analysis.

Tier/Level 4(T4/L4)

While not universally used, a fourth level often represents an escalation point beyond the organization.

This is generally a hardware or software vendor. Within a corporate incident management system it is important to continue to track incidents even when they are being actioned by a vendor and the Service Level Agreement (SLA) may have specific provision for this.

Remote PC repair or Remote Computer Repair

Remote PC repair or Remote Computer Repair is a method for troubleshooting software related problems via remote desktop connections. Technicians use software that allows the technician to access the user's desktop via the Internet. With the user's permission, the technician can take control of the user's mouse and keyboard, transfer various diagnostic and repair applications to the user's desktop, run scans, install antivirus programs, etc. If the remote service permits it, the technician can even reboot the PC and reconnect remotely to continue his work without the user needing to assist.

Common repairs available with online computer support providers are computer virus and spyware removal, computer optimization, Windows Registry repair, device driver issues, Web related issues, and Windows security updates. Generally, only software can be "repaired" remotely. A computer with a broken hardware component such as a motherboard or hard disk can in some cases be diagnosed and worked around, but must be repaired in person.

TRAINING FOR LIBRARY PROFESSIONALS IN THE NEW INFORMATION ERA

Prior to the advent of the new information era, the objective for the training of librarians was tailored towards developing their knowledge and skills for optimum performance as custodians and providers of information resources.

This direction in training programme no doubt facilitated the effectiveness of traditional (largely manual) library operations like acquisition, cataloguing, classification, serials control and user education services. Hashim (no date) associated the following traditional skills with librarians: information handling skills, training and facilitating skills, evaluation skills and concern for the customer.

These skills according to him covers cataloguing, classification, indexing, enquiry work and user education functions of the librarian. Creth (1996) had argued that the values of service quality, universal access and co- operation which are the foundation of the library profession should be maintained even into the next century. Lancaster (1997), equally argued that in order to justify its existence in the electronic environment, the profession must continue to perform one of the most important functions it now performs in the print-on-paper world: "to organize the universe of resources in such a way that those most likely to be of value to the user community are made most accessible to this community, physically and intellectually".

The above argument notwithstanding, it has been argued severally that the new information environment requires the fine-tuning or in some instances radical changes and additions in the librarianship skills. The challenges of the new information era, have attracted the attention of such authors as Ochogwu (1990, 2009), Turner (1991), Adams, (1999), Ochalla (2003), Diso and Njoku (2007) and Manir (2009). They were unanimous in their opinion that library education and training should be tailored towards developing ICT skills in the new professionals in addition to exposing them to the practical aspects of professional skills.

However Edoka (2001) posits that education and training of librarians in the ICT era should reflect international standards which should include, universal bibliographic control, universal availability of publication, trans- border transfer of information and globalization of information products. We are, however, of the view that while the above suggestions will necessitate a drastic re-ordering of the curriculum contents of the library schools, the "traditional" library skills mentioned above should be reassessed and their values to information services in the ICT era applied. For example, the skills of cataloguing, classification and indexing can be used to improve end user experience in information retrieval. It could equally be used to improve the usefulness of the search engines, database construction and management and electronic archiving. Using these skills in creating meaningful metadata files in the words of Lancaster (1997) can help users find needles in the internet haystack.

Commenting on the features of education and training programmes for library professionals in the present dispensation, Diso and Njoku (2007) argued that the integration of ICT in the Library and Information Science (LIS) schools in Nigeria is still in its infant stage noting that the majority of LIS schools have no competencies in the teaching of the courses. Also Manir (2009) after a review of some literature in LIS education in Nigeria argued that courses offered in LIS schools placed high emphasis in print orientation, print media with very little on post industrial information and communication technologies. He equally noted that most LIS schools teach these ICT courses theoretically because they have inadequate laboratories for computer and poor internet access.

The above arguments not withstanding, librarians are now regarded not just as professionals who physically handle information resources but as information managers that should be able to provide answers to every question related to information location, utilization and access irrespective of where such information is located. To this end we are of the view that librarians should be trained to function effectively as information managers who should be conversant with the global trends in information handling and dissemination. The aim of the training should be to inculcate the following skills into the students:

- Electronic information sourcing, cataloguing and indexing with emphasis in automatic indexing and abstracting;
- Website designing and maintenance with emphasis in the mechanics of search engines and internet surfing;
- Library automation systems including hardware and software selection and design.
- Text digitization, desktop publishing, electronic archiving and multimedia management;
- Current awareness services (CAS) and selective dissemination of information with emphasis in diagnosis and customization of information production and;
- Library advocacy with emphasis on information literary skills and user education for adapting in electronic environment.

It is our belief that if emphasis is placed on these areas in the LIS schools the profession should be able to produce professionals who would be able to place African knowledge where it would be visible to the rest of the world.

Ongoing Education for Professionals

The transforming effects of technology on libraries have challenged the library profession a great deal. Because libraries are at the epicenter of the information generation, storage and access the professionals have found themselves in great need for fundamental re-tooling due to the impact of information and communication technologies (ICT) on the profession.

They have been saddled with the challenge of learning the skills of these new ICT tools for effective practice in the profession. For formal student trainees who are learning the rudiments of the profession, it is easy to adjust the curriculum content of their programme to include the fundamental principles of these tools. For the practitioners it has been an uphill task trying to retool them for effective practice in the new information era.

The fundamental challenge facing the profession in this dispensation is to determine the extent of retooling in the profession. Some believe there has to be far reaching changes in the profession before we can function properly. This schools of thought believe that we should think and act like core ICT professionals (Computer Scientist and Electronic Engineers). Others believe that we have to concentrate on improving our professional techniques to incorporate skills that will enable us function effectively as information professionals. At the centre of these debate is the cataloguing, classification and indexing section of the profession which is saddled with the task of creating access to all forms of information resources be they manual or electronic.

Heinstron (2005) argued that our present information rich society demands increasingly more of our capacity to handle information, both in terms of quantity and quality. It is not enough to know how to choose relevant information from the flow around us, it is equally essential to be able to analyze and evaluate it critically.

The availability of web-based information resources and the shift by electronic information providers and vendors to web based services have made librarians with web technology skills an imperative in professional practice. Therefore Martell (2003) argued that the strength of the libraries in the twenty first century will not relate to the symbolism of the institutions but to the expertise of the librarians. To this end a number of arguments have been raised by researchers as to the changing roles and training needs of practitioners especially in the cataloguing, classification and indexing of information materials.

Edoka (2001) identified a seeming lack of exposure and breath of knowledge required for managerial library and information work in the training programmes. Nwachukwu (2005), Citing Reiham observed that the new information era has resulted to changes in the nature and mode of library work leading to reconfiguration in the ethics of information transformation and the resultant new role expectations for the library professionals.

Glasser (2007) skillfully enumerated a number of concerns affecting the technical services division of the library. She noted that since the late 1980's, the amount of knowledge and information available in electronic formats has grown considerably. Electronic books, electronic journals, internet sites and digitization projects are all relatively new forms of recorded knowledge in need of cataloguing.

Cataloguing departments have had to grapple with difficult issues of how best to bring electronic resources under bibliographic control.

A number of questions have been begging for answers, such as, what is the best way to catalogue electronic resources – the MARC format or another metadata scheme? What electronic resources should be catalogued, only those purchased or subscribed to or also freely available internet sites and other sites which the library may have access?

What is the best way to deal with the nonstatic, ever changing, ever moving nature of electronic resources? (Glasser: 2007). We may wish to note here that the essence of the profession is to contribute meaningfully to the world of bibliographic control no matter the source or the format. To this end what should be uppermost in any cataloguer's or indexer's mind is how to make the world of information resources available in the globe to be accessible to users. So the problem of the indexer or cataloguer is not actually organizing the information resources available in his local library but making same part of the world information resources.

Omekwu (2007) therefore argued that the most critical role of cataloguers, especially those of developing countries, is to develop or adopt cataloguing practices that will effectively mainstream their information resources into the global information network environment. Having this in their mind, he noted, their cataloguing systems would then become tools for access and controlled description of physical and virtual resources. Amidst these concerns a number of functional skills have been identified for cataloguers.

Glasser (2007) citing Ellero pointed out that 45% of advertisement for cataloguers in America required electronic resource cataloguing. Other skills identified for cataloguers and indexers include:

- the use of an increasing number of on-line tools;
- the management of materials in new formats;
- developing metadata schemes, metadata creation, extraction and manipulation
- heading Internet cataloguing projects;
- writing training manuals for higher skilled task such as the cataloguing of the newer formats;
- learning to read code: XML, SQL and CQL;
- Understanding more about how computers work, what they can do, and what they can't do.

Apart from the last item on the list, most training programmes organized for practicing librarians in developing countries do not lay emphasis on the others.

This has resulted on the cataloguers in developing countries not being able to keep abreast of developments in ICT with the resultant poor showing of African resources in the World Wide Web. The implication of these is that professional associations in Africa should design appropriate in-service training for staff in the areas highlighted above. Appropriate policy framework should be put in place at regional levels in Africa to ensure a fundamental retooling of professionals in core technical needs that will help them function as professionals in this ICT era. This should not be left to individual institutions in our universities.

ONLINE LIBRARY CATALOGUE

To regain the online catalogue's lofty status and win back its fair-weather fans, let's redesign an online library catalogue that embraces: (1) post-Boolean probabilistic searching, to ensure the precision of searches in online library catalogs bearing the full texts of digitized books, journal articles, encyclopedias, conference papers, etc., (2) subject cataloguing, to take advantage of the user's ability to recognize what they want or do not want during the course of the search, and (3) qualification cataloguing, to enable users to customize retrievals that are in keeping with their level of understanding and expertise in a domain.

Embrace Post-Boolean Probabilistic Searching

Long overdue is the replacement of our outdated Boolean-based catalogs with post-Boolean, probabilistic retrieval methods that characterize Google and other web search engines (University of California Libraries, 2005, 17). Why does post-Boolean probabilistic searching do so well? Susan Feldman (1998, 40-41) sums it up best:

> *"These systems are doing what you as [expert] searchers have learned to do yourselves. They look for terms that can distinguish one document from another, they ask for the terms to appear close together in the document, they stem words, and they count words that appear in the title more heavily than those appearing in the rest of the text... Some systems also try to match query concepts... They enlarge a search beyond the boundaries that the query originally defined." In the post mass digitization era, every word and phrase from millions of digital texts of all literary genres will be at the fingertips of online library catalogue users. Giving users a Boolean-based system to search digitized texts is comparable to giving Captain Kirk a Mercury-era space capsule to travel the galaxy.*

Embrace Subject Cataloguing

When people can search every word that has ever been written, one is hard pressed to find evidence in support of subject cataloguing. Yet such evidence has been right under nose for several years, thanks to a report Marcia Bates prepared for the Library of Congress. The evidence pertains to the 30-to-1 ratios that characterize access to stores of information (Dolby and Resnikoff, 1971). With respect to books, titles and subject headings are 1/30 the length of a table of contents, tables of contents are 1/30 the length of a back-of-the-book index, and the back-of-the-book index is 1/30 the length of a text.

Similar 30 to 1 ratios are reported for the journal article, card catalogue, and college class. "The persistence of these ratios suggests that they represent the end result of a shaking down process, in which, through experience, people became most comfortable when access to information is staged in 30-to-1 ratios" (Bates, 2003, 27). Recognizing the implications of the 30-to-1 rule, Atherton (1978) demonstrated the usefulness of an online catalogue that filled the two 30-to-1 gaps between subject headings and full-length texts with tables of contents and back-of-the-book indexes. In the post mass digitization era, subject headings, class numbers, classification captions, and entries from tables of contents entries and back-of-the-book indexes should figure prominently in the post-Boolean probabilistic catalogue's:

1. Ranking Algorithms: Such algorithms should be profiled to give much higher weights to subject headings, classification captions, and entries from tables of contents and book indexes than to words buried deep in the text.
2. Brief-document Displays: Everyone is familiar with Google's brief- document displays that list keywords, phrases, and sentence fragments from retrieved web pages. Users scan these displays to determine what the page is about and whether to link it. Even better would be document titles, subject headings and classification captions to expedite scanning for relevant items in long lists of retrievals.
3. Relevance Feedback ("find more like") Mechanisms: Relevance feedback algorithms should weight titles and subject headings much higher than words buried deep inside texts. North Carolina State University's new Endeca online catalogue gives us previews of relevance feedback for virtual classification browsing points and for faceted LC subject headings (Antelman, Lynema, and Pace, 2006). Mann (2005; 2006a) extols the benefits of maintaining LC subject headings in their current form; Anderson and Hofmann (2006) advocate faceting LC headings.

Expand with Qualification Metadata

Metadata that is essential for users in the post mass digitization age must facilitate their document-selection decisions. Here is a list of document attributes that would enable users to qualify retrievals with greater precision and customize them according to their level of understanding and knowledge of a domain:

- In a discipline: in biology, in computer science, in the history of art, in mathematics, in meteorology, in physics, in theology, etc.
- With knowledge of this subject at a particular academic level: with an elementary education, with a high school education, with a college education, etc.
- To what extent the author is an authority on the topic at hand.
- For a particular class of people: for teens, for seniors, for shut-ins, etc.
- Is a particular genre or of a particular literary nature: encyclopedias, law, newspapers, poetry, history, bibliography, research, diaries, statistics, state-of-the-art review, dissertation, first-person account, fiction, etc.
- When the particular subject took place: 16th century, Age of Enlightenment, Victorian Era, 1939-1945, etc.
- What can be done with the document: buy, read, solve, calculate, download, play games, chat, sell, gamble, search, listen, watch, etc.
- How others benefited from using the document, i.e., reviews and ratings.
- What kind of experience the user gets from the document: scary stories, sad pictures, funny jokes, break-your-heart lyrics, etc.

ONLINE CATALOGUES: WHAT THEY ARE

Online catalogues are a norm today. they are not static. they have developed rapidly and will continue to evolve further. By utilising the various capabilities of computers and telecommuni-cations, online catalogues are adding new features that make them totally different from traditional catalogues. Online catalogues are now gateways to larger information systems or, as Hopkins says, they are the 'one-stop information store'.

The online environment is an environment encompassing a wide range of information tools, both bibliographic and non-bibliographic. Library catalogues are now a small but very important component of the evolving online environment and are accessible through different tools in the networked environment, the public access computer system (PACS).

The global network is the Internet including various PACS components such as Gopher, WAIS (Wide Area Information Servers), Netscape and Mosaic and other access modes such as Archie and FTP (File Transfer Protocol) tools. The Webpages created by libraries and other information providers are becoming very pervasive and are often used both by librarians and endusers as linking sources for library information.

The same workstation serves as a means of navigating the whole world of the Internet. In the online environment not only are the information tools different from the traditional tools but also the whole concept of access to bibliographic information has changed. Time and location are irrelevant in searching the online environment.

Developments and Directions of Online Catalogues

As a result of a significant growth in scientific and technological information after the second world war and a resulting expansion in library collections, manual systems could no longer respond effectively to the ever-growing information needs of society.

In terms of fast and effective retrieval of bibliographic information, the card catalogue had many disadvantages. Its large size, complexity and high costs of maintenance made it more and more difficult for libraries to maintain as an up to date searching tool. It became obvious that a more flexible tool was needed to cope with the new conditions of libraries.

It was thus necessary to think of alternative ways of constructing library catalogues that could be cost-effective, manageable and easy to use. Following on the application of computers in other fields, librarians became assured that the computer's theoretical capability to control library operations constituted adequate grounds for embracing a mechanised approach. As Weihs and Howarth point out, "It was necessary to investigate the computer as a relatively cost-effective tool to provide library catalogs." Computer applications, however, first occurred in library activities other than the provision of public access to the catalogue. Computers were used in libraries mainly for house-keeping types of activities such as circulation control, acquisitions and serial control. This did not directly affect patrons' access to the library catalogue. Library automation began in the early 1960s with the rationale that "If a job could be done by computer, then the number of staff required to work at a defined level of expertise could be reduced".

Although some evidence of automation of library operations other than cataloguing is reported from the 1950s and 1960s, it is the MARC (Machine- Readable Cataloguing) project that has been considered as one of the most important factors in the development of automated catalogues.

With the beginning of the MARC Distribution Service in 1969, large libraries began to utilise MARC magnetic tapes mainly for automated cataloguing in the standard form provided by the Library of Congress. The usefulness of MARC services in cataloguing, along with the increasing availability of computer technology in the late 1960s, led to more developments in automated catalogues.

In response to the needs of small and medium-sized libraries without access to a mainframe computer, centralised cataloguing services gave way to the establishment of bibliographic utilities in the early 1970s.

The Online Computer Library Center, established in 1971, has been considered to be a significant factor in the development of automated catalogues. With the standard cataloguing services of such bibliographic utilities, libraries were able to utilise the power of computer technology in a cost-effective way.

The proliferation of MARC-based cataloguing led to the realisation of the importance of uniform, standardised bibliographic description as the nucleus of bibliographic services at national and international levels. The growth of bibliographic utilities in the early 1980s as well as developments in telecomm-unication technology accelerated the move towards centralised MARC-based cataloguing and the need for standardised descriptive cataloguing.

A significant factor further affecting the development of online catalogues was that some libraries began to use MARC bibliographic information for their circulation systems in an online mode. Using short bibliographic records rather than full MARC records for circulation operations, a number of libraries tried to help their patrons in checking whether an item was on loan, on order, or at binding.

This was a form of public enquiry module, which later developed into the online public access catalogue (OPAC). However, as Seal pointed out "The public enquiry module will often replicate the structure of a card or COM [Computer Output Microform] catalogue."

Another major factor leading to the rapid development of online public access catalogues was the contribution, by some library system vendors, of designing and developing public access modules as an important part of their turnkey systems. These vendors tried to incorporate a more sophisticated structure for the public enquiry module with more searching facilities. It should be noted that the early public enquiry systems were not integrated with other library modules, such as acquisitions and serials control.

Due to both the relative success and acceptability of online public enquiry modules, and pressures from patrons and librarians, libraries began to consider developing online public access catalogues (OPACs) with more bibliographic information, i.e., full MARC records and more searching capabilities, such as keyword access and Boolean searching.

The possibility of utilising MARC records as the foundation of bibliographic databases led to the development of the concept of the Integrated Online Library Systems (IOLS) in which "The information that was input at the acquisitions stage would form a basis for the catalogue record which, in turn, would support all library functions.

Thus, a number of integrated systems, such as GEAC, ULISYS, ATLAS, DOBIS, NOTIS and VTLS, were established incorporating this modular design.

The overall factors relating to the growing interest in online catalogues have been numerous. It is generally agreed that the most important factors that led to the rapid proliferation and development of online catalogues in the early 1980s were those related to their search, retrieval and display capabilities. Moreover, the opportunity of feedback from librarians and library patrons has provided a continuing momentum for upgrading the structure, contents and capabilities of online catalogues.

Tracing the historical development of online public access catalogues, Hildreth and Matthews identify three generations of OPACs. This categorisation is based on the features and capabilities of online catalogues in the processes of input, storage and output of bibliographic information.

Matthews claims that most of the existing online catalogues are still in the first or second generations and only a few systems have moved beyond first-generation. Added to the three generations identified by Hildreth and Matthews, recent advances in OPACs using graphical user interfaces (GUIs) have introduced a fourth generation to online catalogues.

First-generation Online Catalogues

Derived from circulation or cataloguing systems, first-generation online catalogues were in fact computerised card catalogues with almost the same traditional features. In contrast to the patrons' expectations from their use of computerised database systems, these new library catalogues provided limited author, title and controlled vocabulary subject heading access points. For this reason, first-generation online catalogues have been criticised as having no advantages over the card catalogue.

Searching in first-generation online catalogues was essentially based upon pre-coordinated information retrieval principles and was possible only through inputting the exact form of words or phrases. In contrast to searching in card catalogues, the patron had great difficulties as he/she had to input something into the system so that it could respond to his/ her query.

As this was possible only through inputting the exact form of words or phrases, which was difficult to remember, searching was not as successful as the searcher expected. Keyword access was not available and refining a search by further limiting it to elements such as date of publication, language or country of publication was not possible. The interfaces, which were usually menu-driven, replicated traditional catalogues in their form of access by providing mainly phrase access to separate subject headings, title, and author indexes. Output and display of search results generally had a single format.

Second-generation Online Catalogues

With further developments in information technology, it was possible to provide a more sophisticated system for input, storage and output of bibliographic information. Second-generation online catalogues are a departure from traditional card catalogues and incorporate many new features for the provision of effective access.

In contrast to the limited input, storage and output capabilities of first-generation online catalogues, second-generation online catalogues are characterised as being powerful tools for the searching of bibliographic information. Keyword search, Boolean keyword search, cross index search and increasing or reducing of search results are among the features of second-generation online catalogues. Hildreth writes:

Today's second-generation online catalogs represent a marriage of the library catalogue and conventional online information retrieval (IR) systems familiar to librarians who search online abstracting and indexing databases via DIALOG, BRS, ORBIT, MEDLINE, etc.

Improved card catalogue-like searching and browsing capabilities have been joined with the conventional IR keyword and Boolean searching approaches. Many online catalogs support the ability to restrict searches to specified record fields, to perform character masking and/or right-hand truncation, and to limit the results by date, language, place of publication, etc. Also, bibliographic records may be viewed and printed in a number of different display formats. However, it should be noted that there are a number of major differences between online catalogues and these IR systems that make second-generation online catalogues easier searching tools. With a combination of different search methods, the user is offered possibilities that were not available in first generation online catalogues.

Due to improvements in the design of database management softwares, the structure and content of bibliographic records in second-generation online catalogues may be enhanced by incorporating full records augmented by information such as tables of contents, summaries, content notes, abstracts and links to full electronic texts. Considerable increase in the length of fields was another improvement in second-generation systems.

Interfaces are usually in two modes, menu-driven and command-driven. this makes the interaction between the user and the catalogue more flexible. In terms of user assistance, these catalogues provide more options including, for example, help screens, error messages and suggestive prompts. Ease of use and user-friendliness are two major features of today's second- generation online catalogues.

Third-generation Online Catalogues

Only a few systems have moved beyond second-generation online catalogues into third-generation online catalogues with enhanced or more sophisticated features. Due to the growing sophistication and availability of technology, new capabilities are being added to online catalogues making them more adaptive to the needs of library patrons.

Free text search, enriched database search and simultaneous journal citation searching are among the retrieval capabilities in third generation online catalogues. Furthermore, the mode of interaction has been developed to the point of conversational, adaptive dialogue and the bibliographic format can be tailored according to user preference. Operational assistance such as automatic, context-based correction is also available.

Fourth-generation Online Catalogues

Beginning from the late 1980s, a most recent development in online public access catalogues has been achieved in providing easy access to bibliographic information by using graphical user interfaces (GUIs) such as Windows. These systems, which can be considered as fourth-generation catalogues, have moved away from the traditional menu-type interfaces and are more associated with client server and graphical user interface.

They use WIMP (windows, icons, mouse and pointers) interfaces to speed and simplify searching. With the Windows-style user interface available through PCs (personal computers, i.e., intelligent, and not dumb terminals), there is much more functionality. In these systems the user has the flexibility to click on various buttons, each of which carries a special function.

Nevertheless, these systems do not eliminate but augment the keystroke access. There is also the possibility of using function keys for different purposes when keyboards are involved.

In general, access is via mouse or keyboard or a combination of both. Searching capabilities in the Windows version of OPACs are greater than those found in other generations of online catalogues. Pointer capabilities allow the searcher to select exactly the term he/she is looking for, while pull-down menus provide additional options to make searching even more useful. By using scroll bars and pull-down menus, browsing in different indexes is very simple.

With the capability of post-Boolean searching, the search software also attempts to interpret users' search requests in order to present matches of greater or lesser interest to the user. This is called relevance ranking of the search terms. Similar to second and third generation online catalogues, these systems search for terms through using an implicit Boolean 'AND'.

Other Boolean operators such as 'OR' and 'NOT' can also be used to narrow down search results or such search strings can be constructed using the mouse alone. In addition, access has been enhanced by text retrieval qualifiers such as 'language', 'date' and 'form' of the text.

With this feature, it is possible to include new data elements that help in the better identification of the sought item. Integral or add-on text retrieval modules to provide range searching, related term searching, wild card features, adjacency and proximity are supplied by some systems.

One of the recent additional advanced features of fourth-generation OPACs is the 'hypertext' function. Through this function, any word that the user selects or highlights can be used to search all the fields and subfields in all the records in the database for any occurrence of that word. This dynamic feature helps the searcher to navigate the database to find more relevant sources of information.

ACADEMIC LIBRARIES USE OF INTERNET GENERATION

A tendency is up-and-coming in Internet access by K-12 teachers, students, and college freshmen that forecasts coming challenges for college and university librarians, computer administrators, and faculty. Because these students increasingly utilize the Internet to do research on their own initiative, as they enter higher education their library use is changing in ways that require new strategies to integrate traditional resources with Internet research. Many solutions to present and future challenges will be implemented by computer administrators in consultation with professions traditionally associated with the academic library.

Before the Internet's arrival, students were routinely sent off to the library by teachers and professors with little afterthought. In preparation for their research, students were given an orientation tour of the library during the first week of the semester, one that included a short class on how to use the online catalogue. Afterwards, they were largely on their own for the rest of their collegiate careers. If they encountered a problem, they could consult with a reference librarian or their professor. In those days, what was there to worry about? The farthest a wayward student might go in his or her search for information was the inter-library loan office, or a static computer database. As an information resource the academic library was a finite one that contained authoritative items for academic study.

Today, students on the collegiate and secondary school levels are conducting a significant portion of their Internet research on their own initiative. Anyone who taught in the pre-Internet classroom knows that this development, in itself, marks a sea-change in student behaviour. In those days most students faced the prospect of going to the library with trepidation. Not only are students now eager to undertake Internet research, by virtue of search engines and hypertext links they often perform a good portion of it without assistance. As recently reported in The Chronicle of Higher Education, Librarian John Lubans, Jr., of Duke University conducted two surveys of incoming college freshmen and 7th-10th-grade students. One finding was that the latter group was more "savvy" in its Internet use than the incoming group of college freshmen. Moreover, the members of the younger group were growing "more self-reliant" in their ability to find resources on the Internet, with the percentage of its sources that they used in tandem with traditional ones significantly greater. As a result the 7th–10th graders were less likely to ask the assistance of reference librarians. Another study conducted at Duke since the academic year 1991/92 has traced a steady decline in reference desk questions. The primary cause behind this continuing drop in 1997/98 was students' Internet use, based on its "genuine and timely ease of finding and using worthwhile sources."

The attractiveness of easy access to information via a quick search without specialized knowledge of reference materials, indexes, or the materials that constitute the inner pathways of the academic library should not be surprising. While a book in the stacks is easily located via an online catalogue search, many collections have to be accessed through special indexes (on microfilm, for example) that one must learn how to locate and access. A good example of how the Internet and personal computer have made the research library more accessible is a journal index. Before this technology was available one had to master the multi- volume reference guide to a particular discipline in order to find the appropriate journal article. Now a simple keyword search on CD-ROMs or Internet sites is often sufficient. We forget that before recent technological advances the academic library was an intimidating place for most undergraduates. Then, reference librarians and professors could count on frustrated students asking questions about what to look for, or how to find it. Today that is no longer the case, and several factors predict increasing student independence.

The vast resources being invested by both state and federal governments to provide Internet training to primary and secondary level students ensure that incoming classes of freshmen will be increasingly computer literate. According to the Benton Foundation, local school districts are making a $4 billion annual investment to provide Internet access, and in fiscal 1998 the Federal Communications Commission added $1.5 billion to achieve that goal. Based on Department of Education statistics the sum of this investment appears to be having a dramatic effect. The number of U.S. public schools that enjoyed Internet access rose from 35 percent in 1994 to 78 percent in 1997. And 87 percent of schools surveyed in 1996 that were not yet wired planned to be Internet-capable by the year 2000. By the millennium, well over 90 percent of public schools will have Internet access, though with only one or two connections per school. But progress is being made in this area as well. Schools with at least five Internet connections rose from 25 percent in 1996 to 43 percent in 1997.

One of the penalty of these outlays is that the Internet and its resources are becoming part of the everyday process of primary and secondary education. For example, a study conducted by Quality Education Data in February 1998 found that teachers' and students' leading use of the Internet on the K-12 level was for research. The discovery made by Lubans' study that 7th–10th graders had a higher level of confidence in their Internet research skills than incoming freshmen is partly explained by increasing Internet use and training on the K-12 level. Based on Lubans' belief that incoming freshman classes would be increasingly proficient in this regard, he thought this constituted a trend that should be "an early warning for college and university librarians who will be providing research help for these students in a few years." In other words, neither reference librarians nor faculty can assume students will seek out their help as in years past. If conducting a significant portion of research without such help becomes the norm, the role of the reference librarian and the academic library must evolve. In this environment the appropriate response is to integrate training in research techniques into students' online experience.

Respond to the Challenges

How can such a program be undertaken? The coming Internet generation will require the input of librarians, faculty, and fellow students in an ongoing project that seems best realized through enhanced university online catalogues and Internet server software.

Students in the Duke study suggested the addition of hypertext links in appropriate places in the library's online catalogue to cross-reference information between the library and the Internet. Of course, the opposite operation would allow students who use a college or university Internet server (either directly or from an off-campus location) to have advisory windows alert them to appropriate sources within the library itself when they perform an online search.

Even if this type of service listed only a handful of references, it would still remind students that other pertinent sources of information exist. And through such advisories in both directions, between Internet and the academic library, computer administrators can craft a partnership between those mediums. Because every academic library's collection is unique, a one-of-a-kind programming solution would be necessary for each university.

Another suggestion made by the Duke students to assist them in online research was, "all books in full text format should be available on the Web." However, such a digitization initiative is lagging far behind Internet training and access for K-12 students. To ideaualize the existing shortfall, consider the fact that the largest online collection—Michael Hart's Gutenberg Project—contains 10,000 digitized books, while approximately the same number of students at the University of Chicago enjoy over 13 million individual items in their library system.

Furthermore, the largest ongoing digitization project sponsored by the government has been undertaken by the National Archives and Records Administration to provide 200,000 archival holdings on its Web site. But Congress has appropriated only $4.5 million for the NARA project, a figure that pales in comparison to the approximately $5.5 billion annual investment in Internet access on the K-12 level.

Even if this imbalance was rectified in the near future, as it certainly should be, it will take considerable time to digitize enough print materials to provide exclusive support for even a segment of college and university level studies. Meanwhile, as the partnership between academic libraries and the Internet evolves, an ever more Internet-capable stream of students will be using the academic library in the coming decade. Both practical and pedagogical problems will face its administrators as a result.

An example of the practical problems of this transitional period is illustrated by the recent controversy surrounding the opening of San Francisco's new Main Library. According to the coverage of the new library's opening by the San Francisco Chronicle, confusion reigned from almost the very outset. Because the library featured over 300 computer terminals and multiple new meeting rooms, staff was shifted from traditional duties like cataloging and re-shelving books to assist with patron access to its new facilities.

Other patrons soon complained that they could not find books in the library's stacks; a backlog of unshelved books was the culprit. As the library tried to perform old and new functions, deficits increased to the point that the system had to cut staff and curtail all new book purchases. In hindsight, this disorganization and the budgetary crisis that it produced derived from trying to have the same staff and operating budget support two very different information mediums. Despite the library's attempt to integrate them both under one roof, it soon became clear that one librarian could not catalogue a book and assist a patron at a computer terminal at the same time. Although book and byte both convey information, they require very different staff administrations in their use and maintenance.

The pedagogical challenge for library management, computer administrators, and faculty is to encourage students to critically evaluate the authority of the sources they use, whatever the information medium. Yet another finding of the Lubans' study of 7th–10th grade students was that their Internet research was reasonably well informed in regard to its integrity as a source of information.

That group judged the authority of Web sites to be related to "page ownership," "links," and "e-mail link." While this approach demonstrates an impressive amount of discrimination, it should serve as a starting point for the formulation of a systematic method of judging Internet source reliability—not only because of pedagogical concerns, but because of a requirement of the recently enactedDigital Millennium Copyright Act.

It mandates that colleges and universities inform students on the proper use of Internet sources so that they do not violate the rights of copyright holders. Because this legislation will be defined by future court decisions as the Internet evolves, a new program of student orientation for the use of the academic library is requisite. It can no longer be consigned to the beginning of a semester for a week or two, but must be conducted throughout the year. Furthermore, its content must be under constant review to remain current.

With the proliferation of sources on the Web, there is an increasing concern that too much of its content is not authoritative as measured by the standards of the academic library. Yet, a review of federal government Web sites demonstrates the massive amount of legitimate data that is finding its way onto the Internet. Criticisms of the Web in this respect also overlook the fact that the academic library was not built overnight.

It took considerable time to formulate the necessary cataloging techniques (Thomas Jefferson being the most famous contributor), and centuries to accumulate the collections of our most outstanding academic libraries. As Elizabeth Eisenstein has explained, when "ideas are detached from the media used to transmit them, they are also cut off from the historical circumstances that shape them, and it becomes difficult to perceive the changing context within which they must be viewed." Although we tend to see the academic library as a ready-made information resource, processes that catalogue and legitimize its sources. This is the task that lies before us.

Require to Work Together

No single university profession will be able to accomplish this imposing undertaking exclusively. The expertise of librarians is cataloging and locating information; that of the academic faculty is in authoring and analysing sources on an authoritative basis; students' increasing Internet use has made them a powerful resource in gathering site data. The means to join all of these divergent groups is the creativity of computer professionals in devising new network features that can link academic libraries with the Internet and with one another to facilitate source retrieval within statutory guidelines. Cumulatively, all of these groups must lend assistance to one another in devising new strategies to locate, analyze, and collect sources of information, because there is no longer one building that identifies them. Previously, one did not have to think too hard about how to categorize or analyze a source's authority. Academicians and librarians had already performed these tasks by analysing and cataloging appropriate material. Today that model of information gathering has been transcended, and as we begin to realize the extent of its demise a new paradigm will find its beginning in collaboration across disciplines, professions, and age groups.

MANAGING A COLLECTION OF ELECTRONIC INFORMATION RESOURCES

Librarians are attempting to choose electronic resources to optimize access and value for their patrons. Electronic resources are now often available in several different formats. In some cases, the same material can be acquired from multiple vendors; each vendor will have different methods of access and different pricing options. This new class of material also impacts budgets. Vendors make technology choices that influence the availability and delivery of their material to library patrons. In some cases a vendor's choices are incompatible with a library's service approach.

Libraries often need to be creative in order to purchase and offer certain information resources. Some vendors are beginning to develop resources that are marketed directly to the end-user. The roles of libraries as intermediates in the information delivery process may be changed substantially.

The delivery technology chosen effects who can use the material and for what purpose. Since delivery is dependent on the type of equipment owned by patrons, a particular decision by the library may limit access by some patrons. For example the technology may allow a person to access information from his on-campus computer, but not from their computer at home. The choices are complex and interact with each other. Staff in the acquisitions, systems and reference areas are all effected by the collection of electronic information resources. More people have to be involved in the decision making and delivery processes. Extra skills are needed by all involved, both patrons and library staff.

The availability and use of electronic information resources change the interactions between patrons and librarians. Patrons no longer have to come to a library or wait for it to be open in order to use an electronic resource. A patron can now potentially access electronic information twenty- four hours a day from any computer, home or office. At present librarians are frequently called upon to trouble shoot the technology, rather than help a user find suitable content. New materials and strategies are being developed to provide help and service for this new model.

As the technologies evolve, the issues evolve as well. It is necessary for libraries to stay abreast of new publishing developments and be flexible in service options and strategies to help our patrons take maximum advantage of electronic information.

Dartmouth College

Dartmouth College is primarily an undergraduate liberal arts college with 3 graduate schools in medicine, engineering and business. It has approximately 4000 undergraduates, 1200 graduate students, 400 FTE faculty (not including the Medical Faculty) and 150 FTE library staff. The Dartmouth Library collection consists of approximately 2 million printed volumes, 2.5 million microforms, 20,000 journals and access to about 1000 electronic resources. The Dartmouth College Information System has over 250 local networked databases with about 150,000 connections per month.

The library catalogue is linked to the circulation system and bibliographic files are linked to the catalogue using serial numbers (ISSN).

The Dartmouth College Library consists of ten branches; technical services are centralized and public services are very decentralized. Dartmouth Computing has a Library-like service philosophy-users are not charged for services. Dartmouth has a ubiquitous network, there are ports in all offices and rooms and student ownership of computers is required.

The Dartmouth College Information System (DCIS) was a joint project between the library, computing and Apple Computer which started in 1989. It is a campus wide information system, which first started with the library catalogue and over time added additional electronic resources. DCIS also includes many department developed applications such as a Rental Housing Listing, a student employment database and the Hood Museum Catalogue. There is a graphical interface which includes the DCIS Navigator application (providing system directory and software delivery) and Online Library, a common search interface. The functions of these applications have also been implemented on the world wide web.

Computing Services operates the server computers centrally (including the Library's machines) and maintains the college network. Information Systems reports jointly to the Library and Computing Services. Information Systems does local software development to support DCIS, works on new electronic information projects and installs and maintains vendor systems for the operation of the library and the delivery of electronic information.

Selection of Online Resources

At Dartmouth, a number of people influence decisions regarding the selection of information resources, whether they are paper-based or electronic. Individual bibliographers suggest resources in their collection areas. The Director of Collection Services identifies large budget items and works on consortial purchases.

Academic Computing has made some electronic acquisitions to support particular projects. Faculty recommend resources in which they have an interest. The Collection Management and Development Committee works on items of general interest to bibliographers and has created a subgroup to concentrate on electronic information issues. Information Systems examines the technical requirements and suggests alternative integration approaches and delivery methods.

Dartmouth's acquisition of electronic resources has progressed through a variety of information types over the last 7 years. The earliest purchases were for bibliographic data as supplements to the online catalogue. These were followed by electronic reference works for quick information questions. Electronic full-texts of well known literature and philosophy works were added to support class room study. Currently the focus has shifted to web-based journals and article databases.

Funding for purchasing electronic information has evolved over time as well. Early acquisitions were made with special project funding. Consortial purchases were quite successful in acquiring several large bibliographic datasets with moderate budget commitments. Some Electronic Journals are now financed from bibliographer's budgets. Large purchase decisions, along with financing options, are made on an individual basis.

Contract terms have evolved as well. License agreements have gotten more complex and restrictive.

HANDLING OF ELECTRONIC RESOURCES

The Electronic Information Group, a subgroup of the Library Collections Management Development Committee recommended that all electronic resources be listed in the library catalogue. Each electronic resource is catalogued as a distinct entry. This was intended to help patrons find the relevant material in one location, regardless of the format. This approach avoids proliferation of resource lists which will result in maintenance problems. Each individual library can choose to advertise individual resources in a variety of ways for their patrons.

Dartmouth has preferred the option of campus-wide network delivery. We have frequently purchased data for local loading into databases on network servers for distribution. This allows for the best performance and maximum simultaneous usage. In some cases, we use CD-ROM for delivery within a local library LAN, or from an individual machine within a library. Dartmouth has developed a name directory system and that system is always preferred for access control. Information Systems has developed a protocol to allow sharing licensed databases among local consortia members.

Changes in Staffing

At Dartmouth, the Information Systems department was created by merging library systems and the DCIS development group. Information Systems reports jointly to Computing and the Library. The Acquisitions department has made processing changes to handle electronic sources, storing additional information about these materials and the necessary contacts in their electronic files. A project concentrating on electronic journals developed better communication between Information Systems, bibliographers and acquisitions. New cataloging procedures have been developed for cataloging staff to deal with electronic resources. Information systems has developed new tools to check active links in the catalogue and on local library web pages. The error reports are regularly processed by the catalogue maintenance department.

Are Faculty and Students finding these Resources?

Dartmouth is using the library catalogue as the primary locator for all library resources, including electronic ones. Hyperlinks have been inserted into cataloging records so users can easily jump from a found record directly to the source. In addition, the DCIS directory, which is an interactive part of the online interface, lists all locally mounted resources and includes pointers to some of the major remote sources. Web pages have been used to highlight and advertise the newest resources. Classes are being offered and articles are written for campus publications to educate patrons about the offerings and the technology needed to access them.

There are a number of issues that continually confuse users. Some resources need a particular hardware configuration or additional software for access. Networked CD-ROM towers are not necessarily accessible from all campus locations. Users are confused about the differences between full-text and bibliographic data, where they should start their search and which database to use. Additional electronic mail accounts have been created and links have been set up from the electronic resources directly to these electronic mail accounts. Help documentation and FAQs are being developed and mounted on web pages. Database specific documentation has been developed for each of our locally mounted databases.

Brown University

Brown is a University with an undergraduate college as well as a graduate and medical school. Brown University is probably best known for its distinctive undergraduate curriculum that offers students the opportunity to become architects of their own educational experiences. Brown has 7535 undergraduates and graduate students, 526 FTE Faculty (not including the Medical Faculty) and 180 FTE library staff. As of 1995-1996, the Brown University Libraries contained 2,810,163 volumes, 1,561,108 microform units, and over 5,746 linear feet of manuscripts and archives. The total number of items in the collection exceeds 6 million, and 13,101 serials are currently received. Upwards of 96% of the collection (1.45 million records) is fully catalogued in Josiah, the Library's integrated online catalogue. The Library, in conjunction with Computing and Information Services (CIS), successfully implemented Brown's first online catalogue in February 1988. One of the most important features of the catalogue then and now has been its ease of integration into the Brown computer network. Any terminal or workstation connected to the network or to the Internet can access the catalogue, thus permitting searching from offices, classrooms, dormitories, or personal residences. In 1994, the Library replaced the first online catalogue with a state-of-the-art integrated system from Innovative Interfaces, Inc.

The Library uses a combination of platforms to make resources accessible to the community. Public workstations in the reference areas have databases accessible through an Electronic Reference Desk (ERD) menu. These same resources are linked to the Library Web and may also be catalogued in the Library's OPAC. The Library maintains two local CD-ROM servers.

In 1992 the first server, called the "Electronic Library," became accessible to appropriately equipped PC's in faculty offices and public clusters. This server is currently being replaced to provide both PC and Mac accessibility. In 1995 a new technical platform, the Electronic Reference Library, allowed access to Brown users by way of Windows, DOS and Macintoshes both on and off campus. This server was upgraded in 1997 and now provides a Web client as well. The University has a complex, distributed computing environment including mainframe and minicomputers, approximately 5000 institutionally owned Intel-based and Macintosh personal computers, 500 UNIX workstations, and many specialized computers and servers. Nearly all of this equipment is connected to a campus network consisting of a fiber backbone and building connection, with structured in-building wiring that provides 8000+ connections in 160 buildings.

Selection of Online Resources

The Electronic Resources and Services Committee at the Brown Library reviews all requests for electronic products and resources. The majority of the recommendations are received from collection development librarians. The Committee decisions are made based on information from an electronic resource request form submitted by individual collection development librarians. The form requires the librarian and the committee to review the technical requirements for the product. The librarian must also suggest a preferred service tier, ranging from delivery over the campus network to access on a single workstation. The form includes an implementation analysis so that staff who are involved with the product are required to consider how the database will have an impact on the individual department. Once the request has been evaluated, the Committee may recommend approval and the best method(s) for making the resource accessible.

The major objective of the Library is to provide network access to resources when feasible. Factors to be considered include scope, cost, and number of users benefiting from the resource. Consortial agreements, such as NERL (North East Research Libraries) and BLC (Boston Library Consortium), are influencing decisions. The Library does not currently have a formula for determining the budget for acquiring electronic products. At this time, however, approximately 8% of the total library acquisitions budget is being spent on electronic databases, electronic journals, and CD-ROMs. Usage of databases is monitored annually to justify retention. Currently, the continued provision of multiple formats of resources electronic, print, and/or microform is being studied.

Handling of Electronic Resources

Once a product is approved for purchase, an implementation checklist is used to track the process from ordering to linking on the Library homepage. This checklist is critical to making the resource accessible in the current Brown environment. The traditional organization of the Library makes the provision of access to electronic resources challenging. The Library would prefer to make all resources available via the Web PAC but the multiple platforms (ERL, ELibrary, Web, and stand-alone CD's) make that an impossibility. The Library Web and ERD are the primary access points to electronic databases as this time.

Changes in Staffing

Beginning in 1994, reference areas in the libraries were redesigned so that librarians and other staff could work effectively in assisting users with both print and electronic resources. The public areas are equipped with sophisticated workstations possessing graphics capability, which can access a wide variety of databases and information formats on the Internet as well as those resident at Brown.

Reference and Information Centers also provide the physical environment in which all these scholarly resources conveniently come together, along with the professional assistance necessary to guide users through an increasingly complex world of information. Reference and Information Centers are now operating in the Rockefeller and Sciences Libraries, Orwig Music and John Hay Libraries.

Early in 1997, staff in the Brown University libraries expressed a strong desire to increase their overall technical competency in order to better serve the library of the 21st century. In response to this request, the Library instituted a program designed to introduce Library Staff at all levels to commonly used computer applications. It is hoped that a more computer-literate staff can better assist library patrons.

In addition, a task force organized to study the issue of the cataloging of electronic resources has recommended change in several areas. The lack of a physical object necessitates the need for better communication to be established across departmental lines to ensure appropriate and timely processing of electronic materials. Collection development and collection maintenance, currently the responsibility of collection development librarians, should include a mechanism for the notification of the technical services staff regarding decisions to acquire, cancel, or withdraw items.

Are Faculty and Students Finding these Resources?

As indicated above, Brown has two primary access points for electronic resources; the Electronic Reference Desk (ERD) and the Electronic Resources section of the Library Web. In the spring of 1997, Brown faculty and students expressed confusion about how to find electronic resources on the Library Web after using the Windows-based ERD in the library. As a result of this problem, and compounded by the recent acquisition of more than 20 new electronic databases, that made an alphabetical listing impractical, both interfaces were extensively redesigned. The ERD now presents the user with subject-based program groups that more closely reflect the subject-based presentation on the Library Web.

In addition, collection development librarians created an "about" page for each electronic database. These pages contain information "about" the database, including a description, extent of coverage, and related print and electronic resources.

Attempts to introduce Brown faculty and students to Electronic resources have been met with varying degrees of success. Until recently, Brown libraries have been dependent on the Computing and Information Services department for classroom space. Scheduling instructional sessions at times convenient to our user population has been difficult. This will change in November of 1997 with the dedication of the Hecker Center for Library Technology, a state-of-the-art training room in the Rockefeller Library, which will allow for more flexibility in designing a bibliographic instruction program for users.

Summary of Current Issues

Publishers are experimenting with the electronic medium and changing the way they distribute electronic resources on a frequent basis. This ever-changing environment leaves us with a number of open questions that need to be addressed. Prices for the materials are rising.

New pricing models need to be created. Libraries are looking hard at consortial licensing arrangements in order to be able to afford electronic information and provide these services. Vendors are now attempting to sell directly to the consumer. The library's intermediate role is unclear.

A number of years ago, the library world was excited about the benefits of the Z39.50 standard. A patron would be able to search a multitude of different databases, but her search interface would be the same. This web interface. Users are having trouble understanding how the different systems work. This diversification has made it more difficult to use a variety of sources.

Access control is a complex problem. The most common vendor solutions are userid and password or IP address restrictions. Userid and password is complex to administer for both the publisher and the library. IP address control prevents reasonable use by patrons traveling or working from home and using independent internet service providers. Better solutions exist but require more cooperation between the vendor and the library.

Vendors have tended more toward mounting their own data and having subscribers connect to their system. This can cause performance problems, elimination of usage statistics and loss of library control over the quality of service.

These new information resources make it convenient for the user to search large amounts of information from one site, but make describing and identifying the content being searched very difficult or impossible. Some other organizational tools need to develop to make these collections more useful.

A number of the factors that go into selecting and delivering electronic resources for an undergraduate college have been briefly outlined. The challenges to libraries are large and so are the potential benefits.

❐

6

Digital Library: Elements, Concepts and Scope

The idea of easy, finger-tip access to information-what we conceptualize as digital libraries today-began with Vannenar Bush's Memex machine (Bush, 1945) and has continued to evolve with each advance in information technology. With the arrival of computers, the concept centred on large bibliographic databases, the now familiar online retrieval and public access systems that are part of any contemporary library. When computers were connected into large networks forming the Internet, the concept evolved again, and research turned to creating libraries of digital information that could be accessed by anyone from anywhere in the world.

Phrases like "virtual library," "electronic library," "library without walls" and, most recently, "digital library," all have been used interchangeably to describe this broad concept. But what does this phrase mean? What is digital library? And what are the issues and challenges in creating them? Moreover, what are the issues involved in creating a coordinated scheme of digital libraries? It has been suggested that digital libraries will only be viable within such a scheme.

Of course, the concept of digital library has multiple senses that one might invoke in various contexts. For example, the concept may refer simply to the notion of collection without reference to organization, intellectual accessibility or service attributes. This extended sense seems to be in play, for example, when we hear the World Wide Web described as a digital library. The concept might also refer to the organization underlying the collection, or even more specifically to the computer-based system in which the collection resides.

The latter sense seems to be most operative in the NSF digital library initiative programme. Digital libraries might also be distinguished from digital archives to emphasize the nature of the works collected or, as in *Preserving Digital Information:* Report of the Task Force on the *Archiving of Digital Information,* to stress the preservation function.

One could, of course, revise, refine, and otherwise improve this comprehensive definition. However, it is meant here mainly to suggest that there is a set of attributes that gives coherence to the concept of digital libraries.

These attributes include functions of collection, organization, preservation, access and economy. A programme for the development of "federated" digital libraries needs to be defined and measured in terms of the development of these attributes.

However, the proposed definition also emphasizes that "digital libraries" need to be defined and measured in relation to the communities they serve. Thus, the DLF programme aims to situate the development of digital libraries in a larger context of service.

MAIN ELEMENTS

Digitizing

Digitizing or digitization is representing an object, image, document or a signal (usually an analog signal) by a discrete set of its points or samples.

The result is called "digital representation" or, more specifically, a "digital image", for the object, and "digital form", for the signal. McQuail identifies the process of digitalization having immense significance to the computing ideals as it "allows information of all kinds in all formats to be carried with the same efficiency and also intermingled". (2000: 28)

Analog signals are continuously variable, both in the number of possible values of the signal at a given time, as well as in the number of points in the signal in a given period of time. However, digital signals are discrete in both of those respects, and so a digitization can only ever be an approximation of the signal it represents. A digital signal may be represented by a sequence of integers. Digitization is performed by reading an analog signal A, and, at regular time intervals (sampling frequency), representing the value of A at that point by an integer.

Each such reading is called a sample. A series of integers can be transformed back into an analog signal that approximates the original analog signal. Such a transformation is called DA conversion. There are two factors determining how close such an approximation to an analog signal A a digitization D can be, namely the sampling rate and the number of bits used to represent the integers.

The term digitization is often used when diverse forms of information, including text, sound, image and voice, are encoded in a single 0-1 binary code. Digital information exists in only one of two forms-0 or 1-which are called bits (a contraction of 'binary digits'), and the sequences of 0s and 1s that constitute information are called bytes. The term is often used for the scanning of analog sources, such as printed photos or taped videos into computers for editing, but it also can refer to audio (where sampling rate is often measured in kilohertz) and textures map transformation. In this last case, as in normal photos, sampling rate refers to the resolution of the image (often measured in pixel per inch). Digitizing is the primary way of storing images in a form suitable for transmission and computer processing.

Digitizing is making a digital representation of geographical features within a raster image or vector using a geographic information system, i.e, the creation of electronic maps, either from various geographical imagery or by digitizing the traditional paper maps. Since the advent of digital video the term continues to be frequently used, as of 2005, to refer to the process of importing footage into a computer via a Fire Wire cable. But this is not technically accurate, as the footage is already digital, so it is not really being digitized, but rather encoded into whatever format the non- linear video editing software uses.

"Digitization" is also used to describe the process of populating databases with files or data. While this usage is technically inaccurate, it originates for the previously-proper use of the term to describe the part of the process which involved converting the analog sources (printed pictures, printed brochures, etc.) into the digital representation before uploading to the target database(s). Digitizing is also used in the field of apparel where an image is recreated by artists with the help of embroidery digitizing software tools and saved as embroidery machine code. This machine code is fed into an embroidery machine and embroidered onto apparels. The most supported format is DST file. Digitizing also refers to the process of acquiring precise dimensions from a real world object, such as a car, using a CMM (Computer- Aided Manufacturing Measurement) device. Common digitization methods include optical 3d (laser) scanners as well.

Analog to Digital

Analog signals are continuous electrical signals. Digital signals are non-continuous. Nearly all recorded music has been digitized. About 12 percent of the 500,000+ movies listed on the Internet Movie Database are digitized on DVD.

Processes

The broad use of internet and the increasing popularity of Lean philosophy has also increased the use and meaning of "digitalizing". It is now often used in order to describe the work of improving organizational processes. This will often involve some kind of a Lean process in order to simplify process activities. In many organization this will be followed up with an effort of improving the efficiency in the new "lean and mean" process by digitalizing data and activities. There are no doubt that internet technology have improved many valuechains and also shifted the focus on organizational cooperation into the "battlefield" of value chain cooperation and competition.

Analog Texts to Digital

About 5 percent of texts have been digitized as of 2006. Older print books are being scanned and optical character recognition technologies applied by academic and public libraries, foundations, and private companies like Google. Unpublished text documents on paper which have some enduring historical or research value are being digitized by libraries and archives, though frequently at a much slower rate than for books. In many cases, archives have replaced microfilming with digitization as a means of preserving and providing access to unique documents.

Implications of Digitalisation

This shift to digitalisation in the contemporary media world has created implications for traditional mass media products, however these "limitations are still very unclear" (McQuial, 2000: 28). The more technology advances, the more converged the realm of mass media will become with less need for traditional communication technologies. For example, the Internet has transformed many communication norms, creating more efficiency for not only individuals, businesses also. However, McQuail suggests traditional media have also benefited greatly from new media, allowing more effective and efficient resources available (2000: 28).

Collaborative Digitization Projects

There are many collaborative digitization projects throughout the United States. Two of the earliest projects were the Collaborative Digitization Project in Colorado and NC ECHO-North Carolina Exploring Cultural Heritage Online, based at the State Library of North Carolina.

These projects establish and publish best practices for digitization and work with regional partners to digitize cultural heritage materials.

Additional criteria for best practice have more recently been established in the UK, Australia and the European Union. Wisconsin Heritage Online is a collaborative digitization project modeled after the

Colorado Collaborative Digitization Project. Wisconsin uses a wiki to build and distribute collaborative documentation. Georgia's collaborative digitization programme, the Digital Library of Georgia, presents a seamless virtual library on the state's history and life, including more than a hundred digital collections from 60 institutions and 100 agencies of government. The Digital Library of Georgia is a GALILEO initiative based at the University of Georgia Libraries.

In South-Asia Nanakshahi trust is digitizing manuscripts of Gurmukhi Script.

Library Preservation

Digital preservation at its most basic definition is a series of activities aimed towards ensuring access to digital materials over time. Digitization is a means of creating digital surrogates of analog materials such as books, newspapers, microfilm, and videotapes. Digitization can provide a means of preserving the content of the materials by creating an accessible facsimile of the object in order to put less strain on already fragile originals.

The prevalent Brittle Books issue facing libraries across the world is looking towards a digital solution in long term preservation.

For centuries, books were printed on wood-pulp paper, which turns acidic over the period of its decay. As the paper ages, it deteriorates to a point of being completely unusable. In theory, if these widely circulated titles are not treated with de-acidification processes, the materials upon those acid pages will be lost forever. As technology evolves, it is increasingly becoming a preferred method of preserving these materials-mainly because it can provide easier access points and significantly reduced amounts of physical storage space.

Google, Inc. has taken steps towards attempting to digitize every title with "Google Book Search". While some academic libraries are in contract with the service, issues of copyright law violations threaten to derail the project. However, it does provide-at the very least-an online consortium for libraries to exchange information and for researchers to search for titles as well as review the materials.

Fiction

Works of science-fiction often include the term digitize as the act of transforming people into digital signals and sending them into a computer.

When that happens, the people disappear from the real world and appear in a computer world (as featured in the cult film Tron, the animated series Code: Lyoko, or the late 1980s live-action series Captain Power and the Soldiers of the Future). In the video game Beyond Good and Evil the protagonists holographic friend digitizes the players inventory items.

TYPES OF DIGITAL LIBRARIES

The term digital library is diffuse enough to be applied to a wide range of collections and organizations, but, to be considered a digital library, an online collection of information must be managed by and made accessible to a community of users.

Thus, some web sites can be considered digital libraries, but far from all. Many of the best known digital libraries are older than the web including Project Perseus, Project Gutenberg, and ibiblio.

Nevertheless, as a result of the development of the internet and its search potential, digital libraries such as the European Library and the Library of Congress are now developing in a Web-based environment. Public, school and college libraries are also able to develop digital download websites, featuring eBooks, audiobooks, music and video.

A distinction is often made between content that was created in a digital format, known as born-digital, and information that has been converted from a physical medium, e.g., paper, by digitizing. The term hybrid library is sometimes used for libraries that have both physical collections and digital collections. For example, American Memory is a digital library within the Library of Congress. Some important digital libraries also serve as long term archives, for example, the ePrint arXiv, and the Internet Archive.

Digital Archives

Archives differ from libraries in several ways. Traditionally, archives were defined as:

1. Containing primary sources of information (typically letters and papers directly produced by an individual or organization) rather than the secondary sources found in a library (books, etc.);
2. Having their contents organized in groups rather than individual items;
3. Having unique contents.

The technology used to create digital libraries has been even more revolutionary for archives since it breaks down the second and third of these general rules. The Oxford Text Archive is generally considered to be the oldest digital archive of academic physical primary source materials.

Academic Repositories

Many academic libraries are actively involved in building institutional repositories of the institution's books, papers, theses, and other works which can be digitized or were 'born digital'.

Many of these repositories are made available to the general public with few restrictions, in accordance with the goals of open access, in contrast to the publication of research in commercial journals, where the publishers often limit access rights.

Institutional, truly free, and corporate repositories are sometimes referred to as digital libraries.

THE CONCEPT OF THE DIGITAL LIBRARY

The Internet has contributed to the creation of a new information environment— the digital library. At the base of the digital library is the capability to retrieve, manage, store, and publish information in numerous formats. Lucier (1995) describes an effort to build a digital library for the health sciences (DLHS) at the University of California, San Francisco. He suggests that the current structure of print-based libraries that integrate electronic resources is not sufficient to support a true digital library. He views the DLHS objectives as driven primarily by the expectations of its users, and suggests that it has three primary roles:

1. information storage, retrieval, and preservation;
2. information access and delivery;
3. the online publishing of biomedical knowledge (knowledge management).

Although these roles are consistent with current information transfer principles, Lucier emphasizes that the DLHS is not the :

> *...exclusive performer of these roles. In many functions, the DLHS plays a minor role, while other collaborators, such as publishers and individual scientists, make more significant contributions. However, the DLHS adds value in partnership with others through every step of this cycle.*

To accomplish this evolution to a digital library, Lucier outlines an approach that advocates reduction in physical storage of information, an increase in housing of personnel who manage information, and a collection development policy that focuses on filling users' critical information needs rather than on building a comprehensive collection.

Impact on Professional Roles

As Internet access has spread within the library community, professionals have begun to incorporate use of the Internet into their areas of responsibility. These changes have begun to be reflected in job titles, ranging from direct service positions to upper-level administrative jobs. Titles such as "Networked Information Resources Librarian," Internet Services Coordinator," or "Electronic Resources Librarian" simply did not exist five years ago.

Allen (1995) observes that libraries as organizations can adapt to technological change by creating new types of positions that eventually help to integrate the new technology into the mainstream of library operations. Unlike the earlier position of Online Search Coordinator established in the 1970s, Internet and networked resources positions cross over departmental boundaries, and they are equally likely to be found in the Reference or in the Library Systems departments, depending on the amount of technical skill required to perform the job.

An examination of 23 postings for librarian positions in a single issue of the Chronicle of Higher Education (September 15,1995) revealed nine position descriptions in which responsibilities that include use of Internet or networked resources is a noted component of the position. Job titles include the following:

- Systems Librarian (I)
- Electronic Systems Librarian (I)
- Law Librarian for Internet Services (I)
- Network Services Librarian (I)
- Public Services/Reference Librarian (with emphasis on Internet resources (2)
- Database Coordinator (I)
- Network Coordinator (I)
- Electronic Information Services Librarian (I).

Four of the nine positions are located in the Reference or User Services departments of their respective libraries and two report to the Director of Library Systems; the other two position descriptions do not indicate a home department. The following statements were found among the qualifications required for the nine positions:

- "Advanced work in computing and information science."
- "Experience with online integrated library systems, campus networks, the Internet, and electronic information resources."
- "Strong public service orientation, experience with searching electronic resources (online, CD-ROM, Internet), and interest in library instruction essential."
- "Expert knowledge of HTML and extensive experience with Web administration and operations."

Bosseau (1995) notes that the changes brought about be the availability of networked information have affected higher level administrative positions in academic settings, resulting in the creation of combined titles for managerial positions such as "University Librarian/Associate Vice President for Information Resources," with library directors being placed in charge of "an expanded set of library and other media responsibilities." Bosseau asserts that this, among other changes, reflects recognition of the library's active role in managing technology and infrastructure services that support the delivery of effective information content to users in academic settings. He characterizes the change in the library's role in the academic setting as one that has moved from the cliche phrase "the heart of the university" to a more active and critical role as the "cardiovascular system of the university."

The presence of the Internet in the professional library arena has further blurred the traditional distinctions between technical and public service responsibilities. The major distinction may now be between primarily technical development and support skills and those that are used to help provide some method of organization and access to electronic resources. As computer and networking technologies become increasingly sophisticated, and the technical knowledge threshold is lowered, staff with traditionally lower technical skills are able to connect to and navigate the Net without assistance.

Concurrently, librarians who now enter the profession seeking reference and public service positions possess more computing and networking skills than those who entered the profession as few as five years ago. This combination of simplified technologies and the increased likelihood that professionals with enhanced computing skills will enter the library market has resulted in increased professional facility with the Internet and networking resources.

Along with a shift of roles within the library profession is the overlap in training and support services between library and computing enter personnel. In a recent survey of library and computing center professionals, Shiller (1994) reported more involvement by computing services staff in providing Internet access and training. However, the survey results also indicated that librarians have considerable involvement in Internet training and support. Some survey respondents reported that team training programs were being offered through collaboration between the library and the computer center. She states that a number of respondents viewed the roles as complementary, distinguishing between "physical access," which was attributed to the computing center, and "intellectual access," which was attributed to the library.

Communication

The Net in libraries has also created the potential for change in the professional communication of librarians and other staff. This change is the result of increased opportunities for communication with individuals or collegial groups-through any number of common channels, ranging from e-mail to listserv and other interactive or asynchronous discussion groups.

While the *potential* for change exists, the expansion of professional communication depends on the administrative commitment of the library to support convenient staff access to the Net and the individual's commitment to learn to use the necessary communication protocols and software (Ives, 1995). Ives includes support staff use of the Internet as an important component of how networking (electronic of non-electronic) can empower staff, and improve library service.

He suggests that use of the Internet, particularly as a communication and a current awareness tool, will enable libraries to accomplish more without increasing staff and other resources. He identifies several types of Internet use that should be of value to library staff in carrying out daily responsibilities:

* *E-mail:* communication-in-house, group, organization, or committee communication; obtaining evaluative information about products; sharing information about policies and procedures; "electronic mail is the most pervasive means of tapping into a large number of knowledgeable people across the expanse of the planet" (Ives,1995).
* *Listervs:* electronic discussion groups, usually focusing on a specific topic; there are many devoted to specific library-related topics (e.g., CDROMLAN, LIBREF-L: reference, BI-L: bibliographic instruction); listservs facilitate ongoing, daily discussion about numerous issues, but they are most useful for finding a resolution to a problem when the in-house expertise is not enough.
* *Remote access:* for free of fee, a large selection of library and information resources is accessible through the Internet, including remote online catalogues, software archives, full-text papers, and other documents, bibliographies, and numerous numeric and bibliographic databases.
* *Use-Net newsgroups:* Discussion and news groups on all topics, including libraries, that require specific software for access—usually installed by the computer center for an organization. Very useful for current awareness, they do not clutter up individual e-mail boxes as list-servs tend to.

Some library administrators harbour concerns that staff will misuse the Internet for nonwork activities, thus lowering productivity. Ives argues, however, that library administrators limit the growth potential of their organizations by not enabling staff to use the Internet to discover potentially useful work-related information.

Perhaps the question is not whether to provide Internet access but, rather, what types of access are appropriate to enhance a staff member's knowledge of his or her area of speciality. This issue will likely resolve itself as library staff and administrators alike discover and exchange Internet resources that further enhance their work.

Strictly limiting an employee's focus to what is already known to exist prevents the serendipitous discovery of equally or perhaps more useful information. Listservs or e-conferences comprise a substantial portion of the mainstream methods of asynchronous communication among groups on the Internet. Based on a survey of fifty-seven library-related scholarly e-conferences, Kovacs et al. (1995) concluded that library and information science professionals used e-conferences to gather research and professional information for their personal use as well as for information to enhance service to library patrons. They suggest that participants view the information they obtain from e-conferences similarly to the more established sources upon which they rely to find and verify information-journals, conferences, mail, and telephone contacts. Most of the respondents were librarians or paraprofessionals in academic libraries.

Changing Perspectives on Service Provision

McClure et al. (1994) claim that libraries need to rethink the provision of information services for a networked environment. They suggest that libraries will need to change traditional assumptions about their clientele and their information seeking behaviour. They envision that networked library services will become more demand-based than they currently are, citing the point that users will gravitate to the Internet services that best meet their needs, regardless of physical location. McCombs (1994) suggests that the provision of flexible electronic access to information that often has no physical format requires that librarians, especially those in technical services areas, will need to rethink traditional attitudes toward the access and processing of information.

Holt (1993) believes that electronic networks in general can have an important role in democratizing access to library resources. His library, the St. Louis Public Library, has already established "equity sites" in such inner city locations as YMCAs, homes for the elderly, and high schools.

As Holt puts it, these:

...Provide access to library materials for those who have trouble getting to their public library and/or those without computers in their homes.

Nevertheless, for various reasons, public libraries have lagged behind academic libraries in the exploitation of the Internet resources. Speaking from a British perspective, the Library Association (1995) has recommended that, given access to the Internet, public libraries should:

* use their skills to identify information, whether in text, image, or sound, and route it as appropriate to people in need of it;
* Provide network access points, free or charged, as appropriate, & provide opportunities for education and training in the use of the network;
* use open information systems and broadband communications to intergrate use of the network with mainstream library services;
* publish appropriate information e.g. catalogues, community information, and archives over the networks;
* apply their skills to the management of the vast amounts of information on the networks;
* as appropriate and in partnership with the academic sector, provide information from the network to students and distance learners.
* Ways in which the Internet is being used by British public libraries are discussed by Batt (1996a).

Perhaps the best way to understand the impact of the Internet on libraries is not by speculation or through denial, but through examination.

McCLure and Lopata (1996) propose a set of evaluative methods for assessing the impact of networking on the academic environment.

They suggest using standard social science research methods, such as focus groups, critical incident technique, surveys, observation and site visits, as well as collecting and analysing standard system-generated network performance and feedback statistics. Their manual contains an overview of methods and applications, as well as sample data collection forms and information about software that can be used to measure network services and their level of use. A section of the manual is devoted to online catalogue measures. They pose a series of questions for each area of network use in the academic environment. The overall network and library use questions center on the network's impact on a user's ability to find information, both inside the library and within the broader campus community:

1. Has the network affected your use of electronic information resources (Faculty, student, and librarian perception)? If yes, how?
2. Has the network affected your ability to access information in the library (Faculty, student, and librarian perception)? If yes how?
3. Has the library provided public access to the network (Faculty, student, and librarian perception)?

4. Has the network affected your ability to find the information you need in the library (Faculty, student, and librarian perception)? If yes, how?
5. Has the network affected the types of services provided by the library (Faculty, student, and librarian perception)? If yes, how?
6. Has the library been involved in developing and providing access to campus information resources on the network? (Faculty, student, and librarian perception)? If yes, how?

Their work is further evidence of the Internet's impact in bringing service units like the library and the computer center closer together with instructional units in an academic environment.

Reid (1996) has described a "process model" for the increasing integration of the Internet into library services :

> *The process model is divided into five phases spaning from the acquisition of Internet experience, redesign of library processes for the networked environment to a possible revisi.on of the organization's information management processes.*

Instruction and Training

With respect to Internet instruction and orientation, librarians appear to be finding a unique and useful niche. While Internet access providers normally furnish instructions or training in how to connect, and what general types of information are available, librarians have quickly begun to fill the void of content-based-training—e.g., how to find information on a particular topic. The traditional role of bibliographic instruction has broadened to encompass Internet use as another means for gaining access to information that is available through a librarian's assistance. The recent action by the Association of College and Research Libraries (ACRL), to change the Bibliographic Instruction Section's name to simply "Instruction Section," reflects this broadened approach to instruction and training in the library profession, regardless of whether the tools are print or electronically-based.

Since the early 1990s, several Internet self-help and instructional guides have appeared. A search in the University of Illinois online catalogue, in September, 1995, revealed approximately twenty books published on Internet use since late 1992, with most appearing in 1994 or later. Authors include both computer professionals and librarians. Among the "self-help" handbooks and manuals, works by Krol (1994) and Kehoe (1993) assist all types of Internet users in better understanding how to get connected to the Net and how to locate various resources. Benson (1995) provides a handbook that is tailored to the information searching activities of librarians. Jaffe (1994) provides one of the most complete training manuals that can be used for presenting Internet workshops.

Kalin and Wright (1994) describe an Internet instruction program that exemplifies how librarians have begun to collaborate with computing professionals to offer instruction and training that helps users learn both the technical and content ends of Internet use. Other approaches, such as that of Pask and Snow (1995), advocate the integration of Internet training into overall instruction for research information retrieval, particularly in the academic setting. They point out that librarians can apply their important knowledge of subject classification to the searching of the Internet.

Learning what the Internet is, and why it ought to be used, involves the teaching of database structure, information retrieval, and critical evaluation concepts, as well as the practical aspects of getting connected. Librarians have embraced the challenging task of designing instruction that combines the teaching of skills as well as evaluative techniques. Since the early 1980s, librarians involved in instruction have found themselves training on an increasingly conceptual level about the skills needed to correctly characterize an information need and to locate relevant information, whether in print or electronic form. Perhaps one of the greatest challenges in teaching use of the Internet lies in training learners to employ "work around" techniques when they encounter common communications or other network problems.

Numerous authors have commented that the two critical components of Internet training are the use of systematic search techniques and concepts, and critical evaluative skills. These skills, many suggest, are the ones that will enable Internet users to sift efficiently through the information they retrieve from disparate sources of varying degrees of validity. Connell and Franklin (1994) point out that the Internet has had a significant impact on how work and study is accomplished in academic and commercial settings. They suggest that varied approaches to instruction and training, that incorporate critical thinking and collaboration, will enable users to best locate and exploit Internet resources.

Networking, Data Sharing, and Standards

For libraries, one of the most attractive features of the Internet is its capability to support connections among remote systems. Within recent years, the library community has become increasingly involved with computer and other information professionals to create and implement standards for networking and for data sharing. Since the early 1980s, libraries have been working to implement the basic component layers of the OSI (Open Systems Interconnection) communications protocols. OSI comprises a complex see of communication protocols designed to enable different systems to communicate across a network. More recently, the ANSI Z39.50 protocol suite was developed and implemented by groups of libraries and by vendors of commercial library systems. These protocols provide guidelines and structure so that, for example, two libraries could design software that enables a user from Library to formulate a search using the familiar commands of its own online catalogue, execute the search across the network on Library 2's online catalogue, retrieve the result set, and display it through Library's online catalogue. A number of libraries have implemented Z39.50 in collaboration with reciprocal partners or in consortia as a means to enable users to search across different online catalogue systems without having to learn the commands for the unfamiliar system. Carson and Freivalds (1993) describe one of the first such Z39.50 implementations. Numerous vendors have incorporated Z39.50 into their current OPAC systems and Z39.50 development continues, with both national and international involvement and an organized group which meets regularly to shape the content of changes and enhancements to the suite. Michael and Hinebusch (1995) provide an excellent analysis of the development of the Z39.50 protocol and its implementation in libraries.

OOKS IN DIGITAL LIBRARY

Publishers and printers are constantly working on how to make better, cheaper hard bound books since the time of Gutenberg. The only noticeable improvement achieved was the introduction of convenient, low cost paperbacks. It was about 60 years ago. These days, there are much more cost effective, convenient, simpler, and more importantly, environment friendly options are available. Just think about creating paper books. You have to kill trees for the paper (reducing the global ecosystem's capacity to generate oxygen and getting rid of poisonous carbon dioxide from the air we breath). Warehousing and transporting paper supplies back and forth uses a great deal of resources which also pollute the environment.

On the other hand, an electronic book [eBook] has none of these harmful side effects. An eBook can be stored and transmitted at virtually zero cost. When you consider the economic and environmental prospective, eBooks are an obvious choice of any cost conscious person. We would like to think, in the near future, all published books and works will use an eBook format instead of paper.

A close observer of publication dates will note that one of these books has been sitting on my 'to be reviewed' shelf for rather longer than it ought to have been. However, perhaps that has turned out to be for the best, since it offers the chance to examine three books that deal with the concept of the digital library.

Rather ironic, to have so many 'old-fashioned' artefacts like books that deal with such a modern idea. Two of the books (Ar ms and Borgman) are in the same MIT Press series on Digital Libraries and Electronic Publishing (the series editor is Arms), while the third, and earlier publication is in the Morgan Kaufman Series in Multimedia Information and Systems, edited by another well-known figure in the digital libraries field, Ed Fox of Virginia Tech. As might be expected when three books deal with essentially the same subject area, there is some overlap — this is most readily seen in Arms and Lesk: for example, both deal with text conversion standards, information retrieval, usability issues, multimedia, archival concerns, economics, and intellectual property.

However, they cover these topics in different ways, and each includes topics that they other omits: for example, Lesk deals to a greater extent with digital library initiatives around the world, while Arms says more about meta-data and about organisational issues. Lesk's work has more and better illustrations, a better index (although neither is a perfect model), and a bibliography. Shamefully, Arms provides neither footnotes nor a bibliography, leaving his readers scrambling to find, 'A 1998 article in the New York Times...' or other, similarly disguised citations, as well as the appropriate sources for the numerous standards he mentions — how the publishers can have allowed this is beyond me. Although these two books cover much of the same ground, they are complementary and both will be of value anyone seeking an understanding of what the digital library idea means today.

For the student, Lesk's book is probably the most useful and it could be used as a standard text on the subject. Arms's work is also of value to students, but perhaps of more value to the library manager seeking to map out the future of the library in whatever community he or she serves. Borgman's book differs from the other two in adopting what she calls 'a social informatics perspective' in her examination of this phenomenon. In my opinion 'social informatics' is a particularly obscure term, since it does not convey what is meant by its adoption. 'Informatics' is from the French, informatique, meaning simply (according to Larousse) 'data processing' — adding 'social' clarifies this not at all, since it seems to convey the idea of some kind of collective data-processing.

To say 'adopting a social perspective' would have served just as well. And, indeed, that is what emerges in what is an excellent text — excellent in more ways than one: where Arms provides us with no bibliography, Borgman gives us one of forty pages, along with a much better index. Part of this significant body of literature is Borgman's own work in the fields of human-computer interaction, digital libraries, and on-line searching — along with her consultancy work in Eastern Europe under the auspices of the Soros Foundation Open Society Institute.

The result is a rich, well-informed text, which deals with digital libraries as social phenomena, as well as with some of the technological aspects dealt with by Arms and Lesk. For example, Borgman also touches on the economics of electronic publishing, on retrieval systems and on text-encoding standards, but her analysis of these topics feeds into the intended, more socially informed perspective. What makes Borgman's work different, and in my opinion, more interesting than that of either Arms or Lesk, is not only the social perspective but also the concept of the 'global information infrastructure', found in the sub-title. She presents a serious analysis of the concept of 'infrastructure', based upon Star and Ruhelder's eight dimensions of embeddedness, transparency, scope, learnt nature, practice conventions, standardisation, installed base and visibility on breakdown, and shows how these dimensions are applicable to an information infrastructure. Borgman believes, rightly, we think, that the adoption of technological innovation is a matter neither of revolutionary or evolutionary change but of what she terms 'co-evolution', that is change in social and organisational practices along with the adoption by people of such innovations as work for them. This process results not only in changes in work practices, for example, but also in the innovations themselves as they are adapted to work practices. On the basis of this analysis, a 'global information infrastructure' or GII is:

> *...a technical framework of computing and communications technologies, information content, services and people, all of which interact in complex and often unpredictable ways.'*

Where the problematical concept of a 'digital library' is discussed: is a digital library an institution like a university library, which happens to enable access to its resources digitally, or is it distributed, digitised content to which digital access is enabled. The first, says, Borgman, is favoured by librarians, the second by researchers into the digital library. My own feeling is that the distinction is disappearing and cannot persist: the institutional base of the digital library cannot persist because users have access from their office desks, their student halls and their homes to digital resources well beyond the bounds of any institution to which they may belong and not necessarily requiring access to be negotiated by any library. This leaves, of course, the question, 'What, then, happens to the institutions we call libraries?' (a question I have tried to answer, at least in part, elsewhere (Wilson, 1998)) and Borgman debates this issue, 'Whither, or wither, libraries', but, to a degree, leaves the answer to both questions hanging. Libraries are social and cultural phenomena as well as institutions for access to information and, rightly, Borgman believes that their roles and functions need to be re-thought. How they might be rethought is less than clear, however, and she concludes that:

'In developing new approaches to managing distributed information resources, it should be possible to draw on the best theories, principles and practices of libraries, archives and museums. The fundamental goal is to balance cooperation and competition in implementing social strategies that continue to support cultural values for a digital age.'

From which we take it that she believes that the principles of librarianship will survive in the digital age, since they are the principles of information organisation and access, but that the institution of library will need to map out new functions in order to complement new forms of information access and services and, having done so, will find itself competing for users and, hence, resources in the global information infrastructure.

Naturally, some things are happening in the intervening chapters, Borgman considers the nature of access to information in digital libraries, including topics such as meta-data, which are covered by Arms and Lesk; electronic publishing in general, and scholarly publishing in particular; why digital libraries, with the present state of the technology, are so hard to use and what might make them easier to use.

Most of this is concerned with setting out a research agenda under various headings. Enough topics are mentioned to keep several research teams busy for some years to come: some of them are the old questions in a new light — such as how to improve upon IR systems to make them both easier to use and more effective (a lost cause in my opinion, given the dead end of the present research paradigm), and other issues, such as the transferability of information from pre-digital library systems to digital libraries, which are brought about by the existence of this new phenomenon.

The issue of 'Acting locally, thinking globally', that is, how to ensure that 'global' information resources are accessible globally — in other words how to achieve interoperability, when resources may be prepared in different languages and in different character sets, and so forth. What standards will be required, based upon those that are now available, to ensure the existence of the true global library?

The other chapter takes this further by asking how the technology available is to be scaled up, how access is to be provided, and how to transfer the technology and services to '...parts of the world with different traditions and practices than those of the Group of Seven major industrialised nations that laid the technical and political framework for a global information infrastructure.'

This last point is perhaps the most significant challenge: those of us who use the Internet every day and live in conditions that enable and foster its use, may forget that we are privileged and that, as a recent correspondent (Grosser, 2000) to the pages of Communications of the ACM reminds us, 'Half of the total [of the world's population] have never seen a computer or even made a telephone call.' and that more than two-thirds are illiterate — there is a great deal to be done before any truly 'global digital library' can have any relevance for the greater proportion of humanity, and most of what needs to be done has nothing to do with computer technologies.

DIGITAL ERA LIBRARIANSHIP

The Traditional Days

In the initial days, books were few and far between; copied by scribes, almost always backed by the royal patronage. Users were the royalty and the topmost rung of the social layers; whereas a few very scholarly people, favoured by the affluent class might have allowed sniffing perfumes of the knowledge fragrance. With printing, there came a fresh bridge of hope in the knowledge field with books printed in multiplied numbers and more and more people came into contact of books. Gradually the Public Library Movement in different countries brought in the concept of 'People's University' and the commoners were included in the priviledges of enjoyment of knowledge embodied in books.

The Role in Traditional Librarianship

With the flourishing of the libraries as a centre of knowledge, it became evident that a librarian and his team were needed for preserving the books and later the periodicals. The establishment had become vast and the basic service of preserving books along with occasional readership had multiplied into acquisition, processing, storage, dissemination, preservation and conservation. Gradually all of those blossomed into intricate branches with many library scientists offering theoretical and practical treatises on different aspects of librarianship. All of that literature was of the same opinion on one count: all were preaching custodianship.

The Paradigm Shift

The new age librarianship brought out several changes, the most important being the shift from possession cum custodianship to access. There were several dramatic changes in the realm of LIS. The formats were diversified from print to digital via other non-print mediums. Some such changes are listed below:

- From possession to access
- From rigidity to flexibility
- From ascetic environment to informal environment
- From specified/strict norms to Information Commons

- From custodianship to facilitator
- From guardian to friend
- From reader to user
- From time-bound access to any-time-access
- From space-bound access to anywhere-access
- From librarian (or library-centred) to user-centred
- From strict disciplined library to relaxed pursuit of knowledge
- From one format to diversified formats
- From direction (from library staff) to participation (in the decisions)

From Copybook Leadership to Heuristics

Leadership is a quality to lead a team of workers. This is one of the most important qualities in the managerial capabilities. As is always said the strength of a chain is in the point of its weakest link, the librarian as a team-leader has always the role of motivator in such a way that all his team members become capable to work (at least) adequately as per the requirements of the job in hand. In the traditional era, all the roles of staff employed at different sections were well defined. The main consideration was monitoring the routine work and to supervise the exigencies. In the digital era—many changes occurred to change this status quo. In fact, it is a time for constant change. In this transition period for being a dynamic leader, the librarian needs to consider several aspects:

- Leading from the front
- Practice before preaching
- Arranging invited lectures by eminent Library & Information professionals
- Better among equals
- Friendly- not bossy- attitude
- The depth of subject knowledge in the area of the job-at hand
- Awareness of the personal as well as social limitations of the staff (as well as himself)
- Assigning right person to right work
- Understanding the special aptitudes of staff
- Keeping in mind likings and disliking of staff while allocating jobs
- Remembering the invisible presence of the users while designing services and passing this attitude to co-staff
- Instituting proper orientation training for the new recruits
- Organising regular refresher courses for the staff
- Regular ICT Workshops for staff

- Giving extra priviledges to staff as a reward and recognition of good work
- Allocating suitable infrastructure for every service points
- Providing ergonomic as well as aesthetic furniture for the staff

From Custodian to Facilitator

Librarianship has traversed a long journey and we have to weed out some of our older concepts while adopting quite a few new ones to suit our changing needs. The role of library leaders are now to nurture a breed of techno savvy, skilled manpower equipped to serve a new brand of techno-savvy users. Users of digital era know a lot of things beforehand. So the library team has to go a step forward and to be aware of the quality resources available in the digital (as well as print) scenario.

Challenges of Digital Era

Due to its radically different nature from the traditional era, digital era provides multifarious benefits but it also offers manifold challenges. So the leadership in today's environment needs many skills and competencies in today's multi-user, multitasking online learning environment.They should have adequate technical knowledge of Operating System Software, Word Processing Software, Power Point Presentation Software, Spreadsheet, Graphics, Database Management Systems, Webpage Development and Content Management Software, CD ROM Database Searching, Networking Concepts, Digital Library Management Software, etc. Free and Open Source Software are to be used as much as possible. They should have a thorough understanding of knowledge resources (both in traditional and digital form), very adoptive towards change, pro-active, strategy-planner, flexible.

Towards Knowledge Economy

Physical as well as virtual space has now been utilised for library/ information activities. In this changed and challenged environment, copybook leadership is no help. So, a library leader in the digital era has to be innovative, enthusiastic, and pro-active. With clarity of vision and the judicious use of the web 2.0 tools as well as heuristic knowledge, his mission is to create a user-centred library. The journey towards 'Knowledge Economy' will only be fulfilled if all stakeholders in the knowledge chain take active and interactive participation in the whole process.

Across Digital Libraries

The peer-to-peer (P2P) approach allows handling huge amounts of data of digital libraries in a distributed and self-organising way. These characteristics offer enormous potential benefit for search capabilities powerful in terms of scalability, efficiency, and resilience to failures and dynamics. Additionally, such a search engine can potentially benefit from the intellectual input of a large user community.

However, recent research on structured P2P architectures is typically limited to exact-match queries on keys. This is insufficient for text queries that consist of a variable number of keywords, and it is absolutely inappropriate for full-fledged Web search where keyword queries should return a ranked result list of the most relevant approximate matches. This stage builds upon the MINERVA system architecture presented in and brings current challenges to ultimatively making distributed search across digital libraries feasible. MINERVA provides ranked search on data and an efficient query mechanism that adheres to reasonable space and bandwidth limits. Unlike the approach criticised in, we do not spread inverted lists across the directory, but use only pointers to promising digital libraries as compact metadata and utilise these pointers to efficiently answer multiple-keyword queries. We leverage the extensive local indexes to incorporate features that are impossible in the approach studied in, such as phrase matching or proximity searches. Our bandwidth requirements are well within the postulation that a query should send no more data than the size of the documents ultimatively retrieved.

Related Work

Recent research on structured P2P systems, such as Chord, CAN, Pastry, or P-Grid is typically based on various forms of distributed hash tables (DHTs) and supports mappings from keys to locations in a decentralised manner such that routing scales well with the number of peers in the system. We briefly discuss some prior and ongoing projects towards P2P Web search. Galanx is a P2P search engine implemented using the Apache HTTP server and Berkeley DB.

The Web site servers are the peers of this architecture; pages are stored only where they originate from. PlanetP is a publish subscribe service for P2P communities, supporting content ranking search. PlanetP distinguishes local indexes and a global index to describe all peers and their shared information. The global index is replicated using a gossiping algorithm. The system appears to be limited to a few thousand peers. Odissea assumes a two-layered search engine architecture with a global index structure distributed over the nodes in the system. A single node holds the complete, Web-scale, index for a given text term. Query execution uses a distributed version of Fagin's threshold algorithm. The system appears to cause high network traffic when posting document metadata into the network, and the presented query execution method seems limited to queries with at most two keywords. The paper actually advocates using a limited number of nodes, in the spirit of a server farm. The system outlined in uses a fully distributed inverted text index, in which every participant is responsible for a specific subset of terms and manages the respective index structures. Particular emphasis is put on minimising the bandwidth used during multi-keyword searches. considers content-based retrieval in hybrid P2P networks.

The peer selection for forwarding queries is based on the Kullback-Leibler divergence between peer-specific statistical models of term distributions. In addition to this recent work on P2P search, prior research on distributed IR and metasearch engines is also potentially relevant; see for overviews. However, their work has assumed a relatively small number of digital libraries or databases and a fairly static configuration.

System Design

The system design has already been given in, we only present a brief overview here and refer the interested reader to this prior work. We view every library as autonomous. A conceptually global but physically distributed directory, which is layered on top of a Chord-style dynamic hash table (DHT), holds only very compact, aggregated information about the peers' local indexes and only to the extent that the individual peers are willing to disclose. Every peer is responsible for a randomised subset of the global directory. The global directory consists of aggregated information (Posts) that contains contact information about the digital library who posted this summary together with statistics to calculate IR-style relevance measures that try to estimate the relevance of a particular digital library to a query. These measures are used to support the peer selection process, i.e., determining the most promising libraries for a particular query. If, at query time, the local query result is considered unsatisfactory by the user, a library retrieves a list of potentially useful libraries. Using collection selection methods from distributed IR and metasearch, a number of promising libraries for the complete query is computed from these PeerLists. In we have studied promising and efficient techniques for this purpose. Subsequently, the query is forwarded to these libraries and executed based on their local indexes.

The results from the various libraries are combined at the querying peer into a single result list; this step is referred to as result merging. The goal of finding high-quality search results with respect to precision and recall cannot be easily reconciled with the design goal of unlimited scalability, as the best information retrieval techniques for query execution rely on large amounts of document metadata. Posting only compact, aggregated information about local indexes and using appropriate peer selection methods to limit the number of peers involved in a query keeps the global directory manageable and reduces network traffic. We expect this approach to scale very well as more and more peers jointly maintain the moderately growing global directory.

Challenges

Our work is driven by the question of how a collaborative search across digital libraries can benefit from the unique nature of the P2P paradigm.

We want to address the shortcomings of centralised search engines and further benefit from the intellectual input of a large user community.

Democratic Community Search

To overcome the danger of the infiltration of a centralised index by (commercial) interest groups we leverage the indexes from potentially thousands of digital libraries, making it harder to bias the final query results.

Implicit User Feedback

Additionally, we want to incorporate the fact that every library has its own local index, e.g., by executing all queries first locally at the initiating library and using implicit-feedback techniques for automated query expansion.

User Recommendations

We want to incorporate local user bookmarks into our query execution. Bookmarks represent strong recommendations for specific documents. Also, user bookmarks can be considered as compact samples of peer indexes that describe their fields of interest. Queries could be exclusively forwarded to thematically related libraries with similarly interested users, to improve the chances of finding subjectively relevant pages.

Replication

In order to achieve service levels comparable to today's search engines and in order to actually benefit from the infrastructural advantage of a distributed system, we are going to introduce a certain degree of replication to the directory. Currently, as dictated by the DHT-style maintenance approach, a peer gracefully leaving the system forwards its share of the global directory to another peer. Analogously, a library entering the system asks for its appropriate share of the directory. While one approach to ensure a valid, complete, and up-todate directory is to simply rely on the libraries to regularly re-send their Posts to the directory, it is also necessary to replicate parts of the directory to avoid data loss as libraries ungracefully leave the system. Also, replication can serve as a load-balancing measure, relieving the burden from peers that host popular parts of the directory, and increases data availability. Adaptive, self-tuning strategies for choosing appropriate degrees of replication and placing replicas are an open issue in our ongoing work.

Caching and Proactive Dissemination

To further enhance query efficiency, statistical summaries and also the results of queries from across the network may be cached in a way that allows other peers not only to instantly benefit from the existing query results but also to benefit from click streamst that were recorded on the occasion of similar queries. Statistical summaries may also be disseminated proactively among thematically related peers. Finding good strategies to this end is a widely open issue.

Overlap-aware Query Routing

Peer selection has been a research issue for years. Most of the existing literature estimates the expected result quality of a collection, typically using pre-computed statistics, and ranks the collections accordingly. We believe that this is insufficient if the collections overlap, e.g., in the scenario of digital libraries that share an arbitrarily large fraction of documents. We argue for the extension of existing quality measures using estimators of mutual overlap among collections. Preliminary experiments show that such a combination can outperform popular approaches based on quality estimation only, such as CORI. Taking overlap into account during collection selection in this scenario can drastically decrease the number of libraries that have to be contacted in order to reach a satisfactory level of recall, which is a great step towards the feasibility of distributed search across digital libraries.

Benefit/Cost Optimisation

Ultimatively, we want to introduce a sophisticated benefit/cost ratio when selecting remote libraries for query forwarding. For the benefit estimation, it is intuitive to consider such measures. Defining a meaningful cost measure, however, is an even more challenging issue. While there are techniques for observing and inferring network bandwidth or other infrastructural information, expected response times are changing over time. One approach is to create a distributed Quality-of-Service directory that, for all peers, holds moving averages of recent response times.

LARGE-SCALE DIGITAL PRESERVATION INITIATIVES

It is pertinent to note here that many research libraries and archives have begun or are about to begin Large-Scale digital preservation initiatives (LSDI's). The main players in LSDIs are cultural institutions, commercial companies such as Google and Microsoft, and non-profit groups including the Open Content Alliance (OCA), the Million Book Project (MBP), and Hathi Trust. The primary motivation of these groups is to expand access to scholarly resources.

LSDIs: Library Perspective

Approximately 30 cultural entities, including the 12-member Committee on Institutional Cooperation (CIC), have signed digitization agreements with either Google or Microsoft. Several of these cultural entities are participating in the Open Content Alliance (OCA) and the Million Book Project (MBP). Some libraries are involved in only one initiative and others have diversified their digitization strategies through participation in multiple initiatives.

The three main reasons for library participation in LSDIs are: Access, Preservation and Research and Development. It is hoped that digital preservation will ensure that library materials remain accessible for future generations. Libraries have a perpetual responsibility for their materials and a commitment to archive their digital materials. Libraries plan to use digitized copies as backups for works in case they go out of print, deteriorate, or are lost and damaged.

As is obvious from the previous discussion, the first use of the term digital library in print may have been in a 1988 report to the Corporation for National Research Initiatives The term digital libraries was first popularized by the NSF/DARPA/NASA Digital Libraries Initiative in 1994. The older names electronic library or virtual library are also occasionally used, though electronic library nowadays more often refers to portals, often provided by government agencies.

METADATA FOR DIGITAL LIBRARIES: A RESEARCH AGENDA

"Metadata" is the Internet-age term for structured data about data. Typical examples are library catalogue records, bibliographic headers in Web pages, "terms of use" statements, and ratings. Different user communities—from librarians and computer scientists to government agencies, cultural heritage organizations, publishers, businesses, and the legal community—scope and purpose metadata differently. International communities in areas such as biodiversity, the space sciences, and museums seek to refine the semantics of specialized metadata for the rapidly evolving needs of their fields. Likewise, publishers and other content providers are seeking agreements on standards to enable new forms of electronic commerce.

The creation and management of metadata is a sizeable and rapidly expanding industry. In the scholarly communities, libraries and abstracting and indexing services invest heavily in the creation of metadata to manage the published literature. Scholars are increasingly publishing their work in electronic journals or in less formal Web forums, and scientific datasets are proliferating. Metadata will be needed for these materials. As libraries and museums digitize cultural heritage information, they must create metadata to organize and manage it; indeed, the cost of creating this metadata is often comparable to the cost of digitization itself. In the consumer world, metadata in the form of ratings and reviews has long been important. Now it is becoming clear that good metadata is needed to allow consumers to find products for sale on the Web as well. As we look towards worldwide commerce in intellectual property over the Internet, metadata to support rights management will be an essential part of this new marketplace.

In all such contexts, metadata helps people find what they need, verify its authenticity, process it in an appropriate format, and perhaps to order or pay for it online. Some types of metadata will be used by humans; others will be processed automatically by new types of software tools and systems. No single type of metadata can suit every such application, every type of resource, and every community of users. How the diverse forms of metadata will co-exist and interoperate is a complex issue for research.

The EU-NSF Working Group on Metadata focused on the architectures, tools, and models needed for managing metadata in a distributed, networked environment and on aspects very broadly related to the problem of resource discovery. We did not cover specialized uses of metadata within information services, such as using thesauri to reformulate queries. Also outside our scope was metadata for knowledge representation in the broader sense of natural-language ontologies, classification schemes, domain-specific terminologies, and controlled vocabularies of element values.

Architectural Issues for Metadata

A number of high-level issues concern the management of metadata and the relation of metadata to the overall design of networked information systems.

Models for Metadata-Resource Association

There are several models for associating resources and metadata. For simple text documents on the Web, descriptive information is most commonly embedded in documents using the META tag of the Hypertext Markup Language (HTML). No additional infrastructure is needed for this other than the Web itself. The metadata can be created by authors and others who build networked resources, and it can be harvested automatically by indexing robots. Alternatively, metadata can be tightly coupled with a resource and transported together with that resource's contents in Web transactions using the Hypertext Transport Protocol (HTTP). This allows metadata and resources to be maintained separately, but at the cost of a somewhat more complex infrastructure. A third model finds metadata located physically apart from a resource in a separate database, managed in some cases by the owners of the information described, in other cases by third parties. Research is needed to understand the implications of these models for performance, cost, scalability, interoperability, implementation, maintenance, and systems design.

Trusted third-party resource description has long been provided by libraries, archives, and indexing services in a well-established metadata industry that predates the Internet, with well-established standards such as the MAchine-Readable Cataloguing format (MARC). Since the rise of the Web, new entrepreneurial metadata services have emerged, including ratings bureaus, which may operate in conjunction with filtering systems in browsers, and full-text search engines.

Search engines typically derive their metadata algorithmically, rather than intellectually, from a statistical and semantic analysis of full-text documents on the Web. This metadata is used only to resolve queries and is not made available directly to users.

As work advances on metadata in areas as diverse as resource discovery, electronic commerce, and rights management, it is becoming clear that interoperability will depend on a clearer understanding of data models for information objects. Efforts are underway to explore the relationships among the data models underlying the so-called Digital Object Identifier (DOI), the Dublin Core Element Set for resource description, and INDECS (INteroperability of Data in E-Commerce Systems), a metadata initiative for supporting global commerce in intellectual property. One common reference point for these various communities is the Functional Requirements for Bibliographic Records of the International Federation of Library Associations and Institutions (IFLA), which describes a range of possible "states" for information resources from the abstract work through the physical item. Defining a logical framework that subsumes or reconciles a variety of data models is a major research challenge with implications for the exchange and reuse of different types of metadata for a broad range of applications.

Metadata Creation and Management

Producing metadata has long been the task of professionals such as librarians and indexers. Today, metadata is also being produced by non-specialists (e.g., ordinary users), publishers, for-profit commercial agents, and even software systems. Creating metadata is often labour-intensive, though automated procedures and new types of tools for creating and managing metadata are evolving and will continue to become more sophisticated. Some word processors, editors, and format filters generate embedded metadata tags when a document is first created. Other tools automatically extract metadata values from the documents themselves.

Metadata may be generated or updated at various times in the life cycle of a resource, so workflows must be designed accordingly. Declarative rules or prescriptions can be used to explicitly describe how, when, and by whom a metadata element will be produced or updated.

Research on metadata creation and management will enable systems to use document analysis to automate metadata capture, automatically extract subject classifications, trigger the update of metadata when a resource is modified, support the capture of temporal metadata, certify metadata at the time of publication, and remove metadata when a resource is obsolete. Such tools must become integrated into a variety of environments from Web site management utilities to databases, data warehouses, and legacy resources. If used on a wide scale, they could significantly improve the quality and cost-effectiveness of metadata in the networked environment.

Metadata for Repositories and Services

Proprietary digital resources will increasingly be stored in data repositories and may not be accessible to external Web harvesters. Publishers may want to use metadata to advertise their materials, which would then be available for a fee. Metadata will play a crucial role as a surrogate which makes the contents of such restricted resources and services visible to searchers. Some services, such as weather forecasts, may make their contents accessible only through dynamic interfaces that cannot be harvested. Metadata will not just serve as advertising for content; some kinds of metadata, such as reviews, will have markets in their own right.

Designing effective mechanisms for such repositories will enable large- scale commercial publishing on the Web. One repository model, the Kahn- Wilenski Digital Object Repository, supports formal specification of the services, policies, and transaction methods associated with a collection of resources. Research on repository architectures and their metadata will need to balance market forces and organizational needs to ensure that the technological options enable rather than constrain the expression of policy.

Simplicity, Complexity, and Interoperability

Current approaches to metadata, such as the Warwick Framework, assume that complex metadata needs are best met by a multiplicity of separate but functionally focused metadata schemes, relatively orthogonal and independently maintained by communities of expertise and practice, which can be mixed and matched as needed, rather than by just one comprehensive but monolithic set of elements. The metadata associated with a given object would be separated into a series of "packages" that would be marked as using these various metadata schemes. The foundations for such modularity are already in place. Further research is needed now to scope and elaborate new schemes and to specify the interrelations among packages.

There are also research issues involved in the management of multiple packages for an object under the Warwick Framework within various distributed computing environments, including questions of consistency, overlap, relationships among packages, and the linkage of packages to nested or complex objects.

Core Metadata Sets

Metadata schemes that meet fundamental functional needs of users in a wide range of fields and applications are called "core element sets." The most important work in this area to date has been in resource description, where the Dublin Core forms a central reference point of fifteen broad categories onto which more complex or specialized descriptive schemas can map. Such core element sets are needed now for functions complementary to description, such as structure and navigation, administration of digital objects, authentication, certification and provenance, terms and conditions, trust and quality, privacy, and longevity.

Particular communities will develop discrete (but possibly overlapping) packages of metadata for various purposes. For example, structural metadata for display and navigation is needed for specifying the range of file formats a library can deliver, the size of particular documents, or the parts of documents that are accessible individually, such as tables of contents and chapters. Administrative metadata can cover the creation of an object (such as date of capture or digitization technology used), identify an instantiation (version or edition), or specify the technology needed to view or use an object (e.g., storage or delivery file format, compression scheme, or location). Metadata on trust might include certifications or ratings of the quality of services or content offered by information providers. It is probably impossible, at this stage of development, to establish a comprehensive enumeration of core element sets; however, the need for a number of such sets is clear, and managing their evolution and scoping will be a challenge.

Metadata Pidgins and Complexification

In all forms of human communication there is a tension between the virtue of simplicity and the need for complexity. Historically, attempts to create simplified common languages such as Esperanto have often splintered between those who wanted to keep it simple to promote mass usage versus those who called for larger vocabularies and grammatical nuance. Pidgins— simple languages improvised by speakers of different languages who need to work together or conduct trade—also start with small vocabularies and simple grammars. When adopted by entire communities, however, pidgins typically evolve into more complex and expressive "creoles."

Such dynamics have been evident in efforts to define global standards in metadata. The effort to simplify and hybridize the resource description conventions of various communities has led to the pidgin-like (unqualified) Dublin Core Element Set. Such core schemas are extensible via additional elements or local refinements, but complexified adaptations can compromise or at least reduce interoperability. As users seek greater nuance of semantics and syntax, the natural follow-on to this pidginization is a re- complexification, or creolization, resulting in metadata that may be more precise and expressive, yet less compatible with the global standard.

This tension between simplicity (hence interoperability) and greater semantic richness is a natural feature of evolving metadata conventions. A search for balance has been evident in the evolution of the Dublin Core, particularly in the differences between qualified and unqualified approaches. Each new core metadata set will pose the same problem of balance as it is extended and specialized beyond its original core use.

Metadata for Complex Digital Resources

There are well-established conceptual models and practices for describing the contents and structure of traditional resources. For example, the consensus understanding of component parts of texts (titles, chapters, paragraphs) is so strong that it is often implied by layout and typography.

This understanding can be formalized, along with higher-level structures, through constructs such as the Document Type Definitions (DTDs) of the Standard Generalized Markup Language (SGML) or word processor style templates. Other practices surrounding the use of text (e.g. citation and quotation) are also relatively well established, as are means of associating metadata with texts (e.g., independent MARC records, HTML META tags, and DTDs of the Text Encoding Initiative). A relatively limited number of encodings are in popular use for text documents—ASCII, word processor formats, PDF, HTML, SGML, and perhaps soon XML—and viewing software often allows users to convert among these formats.

For non-textual data the variety of encodings in use is much wider, and the problem of conversion is accordingly more complex. Many of these conversions will need to be controlled and automated by new types of metadata. Time-based media such as audio and video will need "mechanical" metadata for controlling processes such as synchronization (e.g., sampling rates and frame sizes), which will need to be linked to higher-level descriptive metadata through abstractions that are still very much at the research stage. For describing the intellectual contents and structure of resources that are more complex and less well understood than normal text documents—such as collections of documents, time-based media, and dynamically generated objects—there are few conventions in general use.

A "Multimedia Content Description Interface" (MPEG-7) is currently under development within the Moving Pictures Experts Group (MPEG), a committee of the International Organisation for Standardisation that focuses on the encoding and processing of motion pictures, audio, and related multimedia formats. MPEG-7 is intended to include not just basic description, but metadata on terms and conditions, ratings, encoding formats, and "scenarios" of how multimedia components are combined in presentations.

More broadly, we have a relatively good understanding of traditional publication genres such as printed newspapers, magazines, journals, books, music CDs, and movie videos. Each of these genres is associated with a relatively clear, often long-standing analytical, intellectual, economic, and legal framework. However, we do not yet have such an understanding or consensus about evolving genres of digital publication. We may need to define new genres as the sum of multiple dimensions relevant for their management and handling, such as their encoding format, publication type, access controls, description, and terms and conditions of use. For all genres, including text, we need metadata conventions that support versioning.

Collections may be purely administrative entities, or they may be characterized by attributes such as medium, subject, or provenance. Collections may exist within other collections, such as a reference collection within a library. Distinctions between "whole" and "component" collections could facilitate navigation by helping users discover specific databases. Collection description could also provide at least some access where no item-level descriptions exist, such as in certain image databases and manuscript archives.

Metadata Diversity and Resource Discovery

While we have much experience with homogeneous descriptive metadata (i.e., the library catalogue), very little is known about how to effectively repurpose and integrate the much broader range of metadata now being associated with digital objects into the discovery process. Moreover, the availability of various types of metadata will be highly variable in practice, and it is unclear how best to use types of metadata that may be only sparsely or spottily available. We face the challenge of breaking a vicious circle: without enough metadata of a given type, people will not build harvesters, but if that type of metadata is not widely used, there will be no motivation to create it in the first place. Solutions to this problem will advance metadata deployment, discovery systems, and networked services in general.

Infrastructure

Interoperability among applications benefits from common conventions on semantics and syntax. Semantic interoperability may be achieved either by agreeing on shared meanings or by using mediating software to create coherence across applications. Syntactic interoperability requires standard formats and protocols for expressing metadata structures.

Metadata and Information Architecture Standards

A number of standards that are emerging for the Internet and the Web will provide much of the basic architecture and context for digital libraries. For example, a working group of the World Wide Web Consortium (W3C) is developing the Resource Description Framework (RDF), a set of standards for supporting the exchange of metadata on the Web. This group has recently published the public specification of a general model for metadata. Its underlying encoding syntax is the eXtensible Markup Language (XML), which is expected to become a primary format for document encoding on the Web. RDF has been designed to support the encoding of metadata semantics in discrete functional packages that can be used by applications in the modular, plug-and-play manner called for by the Warwick Framework. The use of Dublin Core metadata in RDF will provide early deployment experience that should expose some of the strengths and weaknesses of this evolving infrastructure.

RDF uses metadata schemas to specify the structure and semantics of formal metadata standards in a way that is usable both by humans and by machines. Schemas will be extensible, either by referencing other schemas or by adding local refinements or specialized elements. Sharing a common set of elements across multiple metadata schemas will promote semantic interoperability by allowing the creation of new schemas that inherit and preserve (while perhaps specializing) the semantics of a parent schema. Languages, techniques, and systems for expressing such schemas will remain an important area for research. The refinement of a generalized metadata architecture based on RDF will require several iterations as it is deployed for digital libraries and in commercial applications.

Generalized formal models of metadata, such as RDF, provide a common language for defining the structure of the many types of metadata used in digital libraries. Within such overarching frameworks, more specific models may be needed to define specialized domains or facets of resources, such as intellectual property restrictions or geospatial coordinates. These formal models may exist in a hierarchy of description, with general models such as RDF pointing to more specific models. For example, the Federal Geographic Data Committee Content Standard might describe specialized aspects of geospatial data, while a more general model is used to associate that data with related non-geospatial resources. The combination of general and specific models is more practical and flexible than monolithic approaches and supports the integration of heterogeneous resources into coherent collections.

The metadata activity of W3C also includes work on standards for privacy and rating services. PICS (Platform for Internet Content Selection) and P3P (Platform for Privacy Preferences) are intended to provide a foundation for this work. Metadata for both will be expressible in RDF. These standards, however, have not yet been widely deployed. Research is needed both on technical and social aspects of their use and on their interaction with other metadata sets.

Other evolving standards involving substantial use of metadata will require continued refinement through deployment experience. In many cases, metadata-using standards have developed somewhat independently of the efforts of the metadata research community, and considerable work relate to work such as RDF and the Warwick Framework. Examples include the Common Object Request Broker Architecture (CORBA) under development by the Object Management Group, which enables applications to manipulate distributed computing objects; the various proposals for electronic rights management and digital identifier systems (such as the DOI); and the Z39.50 protocol for information retrieval, which includes methods of providing metadata to characterize databases and servers.

The standard ISO/IEC 11179 (Specification and Standardization of Data Elements) will need to address the varied requirements of metadata for digital libraries and electronic commerce. ISO's Basic Semantic Register will be relevant to the future standardization of metadata vocabularies and to the development of ontologies across schemas.

Crosswalks and Registries

A variety of constructs allow users to search and retrieve across different metadata schemas by translating the elements of one system or subject organization into the terms of a second. Mappings, whether based on tables or on formal definitions, represent relationships that are unambiguous; they support transparent searching across domains.

Crosswalks are more complex frameworks that establish the relationship between schemas that have significantly different syntaxes or semantics. They can be based on thesauri or on more elaborate semantic frameworks, such as ontologies, which describe the metadata elements for each domain and map their internal relations. Crosswalk tools could use ontologies to help users understand semantic complexities across systems, but further work is needed on formalisms for expressing such linkages.

The metadata schemas available on the Web will form a global collection of namespaces that will effectively function as a distributed registry. These registries will need to be managed, coordinated, and ultimately connected.

Registries will define the elements of metadata schemas in a machine-readable syntax (e.g., RDF) and offer authoritative listings of legal values, local extensions, mappings to other schemas, and guidelines for good usage. They will serve both humans, with readable text, and programmes, with structured content that can automatically be parsed. Their role will be both to promote and to inform, thereby encouraging the use of standard formats.

Like good dictionaries, registries will need to describe actual usage while prescribing good practice. They will help providers of content in languages other than English both in keeping their translations of global standards up-to-date and in constructing specialized local schemas that are as compatible as possible with global standards. They will also assist in aligning element definitions among diverse existing and proposed schemas, thus reducing duplication of effort. At a more complex level, registries could offer knowledge bases that support the automatic translation of metadata into other languages and schemas, automatic validation, and the automatic updating of remote metadata to new versions.

The interaction between metadata registries and particular user communities will never be simply a technical problem. Like natural languages, metadata languages will evolve with use. Interoperability over time can be ensured only if registries are supported by a public forum with formal processes that allow user communities both to negotiate meanings collectively and to adapt these rules to local needs. Since the shared semantics of communities differ in complex ways, the definition and maintenance of crosswalks and registries imply support for complex social processes. Building such systems must draw on our understanding of how ontologies, whether of specialized vocabularies or of natural languages, can formally be related or linked among themselves. Constructions used in federations of thesauri, such as "interlinguas," could be adapted for linking ontologies of metadata.

Metadata element sets will be managed by agencies that are responsible for their development and maintenance. An ecology of registries will emerge that reflects a diversity of organizational motives, market forces, and user requirements. A distributed model for registries will reflect this diversity by supporting cooperation at multiple levels—global, regional, domain (by subject or resource type), and sector. The development of such infrastructures will provide an important focal point for international collaboration.

Policy and Management

The Web has substantially reduced barriers to information flow and access around the world and we now see increased interaction across sectors and disciplines on an international basis. Content and metadata are both moving rather casually between communities and across national boundaries. This radical change in accessibility has major implications for creating and managing both content and metadata.

Trans-Border Information Policy

Legislators and policy-makers are paying increased attention to the Internet environment and to harmonizing both intellectual property law and a wide range of information policies (e.g., privacy, content rating, commerce, and censorship) on a global basis. However, national differences in policies and legislation on such issues will inevitably become more prominent.

The semantics of metadata, the operational characteristics of applications that use metadata, and the interaction of diverse forms of metadata will receive substantial scrutiny.

Libraries, archives, museums, government agencies, and publishers—as well as their constituents—will need to take account of international implications as they establish metadata standards and infrastructures in support of their goals and interests.

Various classes of assertions embodied in metadata may well have legal status, at least in some usage contexts and legal regimes. We need to understand the implications of this within a complex diversity of national and international law and practice, especially when metadata crosses borders and jurisdictions.

In some situations, it may be necessary to translate metadata values between languages to another or to map metadata packages from one legal regime to another. The assertions embodied in metadata and the sources of metadata will raise issues of liability and accountability; in order to cross borders, for example, some metadata may have to be digitally signed.

Metadata Research and the International Standards Process

Much of the value of metadata comes from its character as a shared community understanding. This means that progress in metadata rapidly moves into the arena of standardization. Work on metadata standards— and particularly the sort of cross-community standards discussed in much of this paper—is particularly challenging because it demands collaboration from historically autonomous and specialized communities of practice and their standards development organizations. This is creating significant difficulties as the various standards organizations struggle to define their roles and establish processes for coordination and collaboration with other groups.

It is becoming clear to many communities of practice that as their activities and information resources move into a highly distributed network- based environment they will need to evolve community metadata standards. Research is needed to develop faster, more effective and efficient ways for these communities to develop, achieve consensus upon, and document community practices, processes, and data models. Streamlining such efforts could have a high impact on a range of fields, from scientific disciplines to the cultural heritage community.

The development of standards for digital libraries and networked information is a very important process for establishing consensus about intellectual models and for translating research into practice. Standards development, particularly at the international level, is a slow and costly process that has in the recent past been dominated by commercial interests and government representatives with the resources to participate. It is essential that resources be made available to permit the metadata and digital library research communities to participate fully in these ongoing efforts.

Integrity, Accuracy, and Authenticity of Metadata

As metadata becomes more important both for discovering information and for expressing assertions about networked content, it will become increasingly necessary to verify its accuracy, integrity, and trustworthiness. One can already see situations in which content providers attempt to mislead Web indexing services with irrelevant index terms in order to make their content more visible to searchers. In the present environment, Web indexers can inspect the actual source content of Web pages to check for such subterfuge, and the major commercial services have developed proprietary algorithms that attempt to filter out indexing misinformation. As metadata use expands to capture more abstract assertions about objects (e.g., ratings or subject analysis), the design of such validation algorithms and heuristics becomes an extremely challenging and largely unexplored problem for research.

An alternative to verifying metadata is to consider the source of each metadata assertion associated with an object. This suggests research in at least two areas. The first is the design of systems to verify the source of metadata assertions, presumably in conjunction with digital signatures and a public key infrastructure, in a highly distributed international environment. The second is how to factor user-provided (and third-party-provided) constraints about the relative trustworthiness of metadata providers into processes such as resource discovery.

Evaluation and Metrics

The deployment of metadata through standard mechanisms such as RDF provides an opportunity to explore the evolving use of metadata within various communities. The sampling and analysis of metadata will provide a valuable window onto the Web as a medium for distributing the cultural, scientific, and technical products of a society and onto the practices used to describe them. Knowledge gained from tracking the diffusion of metadata use can be applied to the further development of metadata schemes and to the creation of dictionaries that track the transition from pidgin to creole. Usage patterns can serve as a guide for developers of schemas and feed back into the design of core metadata sets and functional packages.

A fundamental question about the use of metadata, particularly in areas such as resource discovery, is cost-effectiveness. Is intellectually derived descriptive metadata sufficiently better than algorithmically computed metadata to justify the cost of its creation? Benchmarks and experimental evaluation frameworks similar to the Text Retrieval Conference (TREC) for full-text databases will be needed. Tracking deployment will also help identify which data elements users consider to be important in processes such as resource discovery and show how these elements are being used. Such data will guide the further evolution of core metadata sets.

Conclusion

This paper identifies numerous topics for research on issues that will be central to fostering the growth of networked information resources, digital libraries, electronic commerce, and network-based publishing. In the near term, a commitment to work on registry infrastructures could provide an important focal point and source of cohesion for research and development in many of these areas, as well as being an important research project in its own right. The Dublin Core seems poised to provide a metadata system for resource discovery that is consistent across a wide range of applications and domains, usable by both experts and non-experts, interoperable with existing library catalogs and legacy databases, and coherent across many languages (over twenty to date). RDF is a deployment vehicle not only for Dublin Core but also for a wide range of new core and discipline-specific metadata sets that will be developed.

Effective research progress on metadata will need to involve intense collaboration between metadata specialists and communities trying to solve functional problems, such as rights management, resource discovery, archiving and preservation, or the organization and management of data specific to various disciplines. The definition and maintenance of metadata standards over time is a complex social process requiring negotiation, consensus-building, and iteration. Learning to manage such processes effectively and to coordinate the ever-growing activities of many disparate communities of interest is clearly a long-term research undertaking involving complex economic, technical, and social questions.

The world has never had information systems of this scale, nor has it ever tried to provide consistent organization and access to sets of resources and services as large and diverse as those appearing on the Internet today. We must seek not just to serve specific disciplines or communities of practice, nor must we focus just on facilitating the use of information across communities. Rather, we must seek to provide the emerging global information infrastructure with coherent methods of organization and access that transcend the historical boundaries of nations, languages, and cultures. Addressing these challenges will require a two-pronged research approach: engagement in near-term, applied questions involving specific metadata sets and architectural issues raised by developments such as RDF, and a continued investment in theoretical and foundational work that can abstract out broad principles and model the effects of scaling.

❐

7

Strategic Planning

A Definition of Strategic Planning

Strategic planning is a tool for organising the present on the basis of the projections of the desired future. That is, a strategic plan is a road map to lead an organisation from where it is now to where it would like to be in five or ten years. It is necessary to have a strategic plan for your chapter or division. In order to develop a comprehensive plan for your chapter or division which would include both long- range and strategic elements, we suggest the methods and mechanisms outlined in this manual.

The plan must be:

- Simple
- Written
- Clear
- Based on the real current situation
- Have enough time allowed to give it a time to settle. It should not be rushed. Rushing the plan will cause problems.

Benefits and Pitfalls in Strategic Planning

Since, the beginning of Special Libraries Association in 1909, it has experienced phenomenal growth in membership and influence. In the past ten years, growth has been particularly significant. Changes in the fields of special librarianship and information science have been dramatic and fundamental to the very way of doing business. The advent of on line systems and the computer age rapidly changed the way librarians/ information managers operate. The Association recognises that it can no longer merely react to issues as they emerge. If it is to continue as a leader in improving the profession, it must begin to anticipate future change rather than merely react to change. The Association as well as each chapter and division needs to consider this long-term future. Drawing on the resources it has, both human and financial, it needs to continue to grow. These resources are limited, and careful thought must be given to the allocation of these resources.

To meet obligations to the profession, the public, and the membership, it is essential that the Association and its units use these resources in the most efficient manner by determining priority areas on which to concentrate. This means the identification of goals, pursuing those goals, and achieving them. Strategic planning will help build continuity in the Association's programmes, particularly in the areas of continuing education and publications. The Association has the gift of a great deal of diversity among the membership. The Association draws its strength from this diversity but at the same time, that diversity lessens the Association's impact in key areas because of a lack of cohesive focus by the organisation.

Therefore, it is necessary for each chapter and division to have a plan that is compatible with the overall strategic plan of SLA thus concentrating its efforts and greatly increasing its impact. There are several pitfalls associated with strategic planning. First, the plan may not turn out as well as expected because of changes in the environment in which the plan is supposed to operate. Also, strategic planning is worthless in getting an organisation out of a major crisis.

A crisis is a current problem not solved by a strategic plan. And, if the planning process itself is weak, the resulting plan may be weak and not satisfactory to the organisation. George Steiner in his Strategic Planning lists 50 major common pitfalls in starting, doing, and using strategic planning.

Strategic Planning Model

In choosing the strategic planning model, two main things need to be considered. The first is whether you want the Association unit to plan as a not-for-profit, or as a profit organisation. Association planning is not the same as the planning for universities or businesses or government agencies. Associations need to be consistently receptive to the needs of the membership- at-large. The main purpose is to serve the members more than to make a profit or to increase the size of the organisation. The strategic plan needs to include a Mission Statement, Objectives, Goals, and an Action (or Implementation) Plan.

Mission Statement

This is the agreed-upon statement by the organisation and explains the reason for its existence. It is necessarily broad to encompass the diversity within the Association. The statement is not precise in its measurements nor does it need to be, but it does need to be periodically reviewed by the Association to see whether it still encompasses all of the relevant activities of the Association.

Objectives

The objectives are the areas of emphasis within the Association. Rather than specific statements with a specific goal, objectives state that the Association plans to continue to do quality work in the following areas. These objectives or areas of emphasis need to be attained by discussion and review of the organisation's current activities as well as activities in which it would like to participate.

Goals

These need to be both long-term and short-term goals; six months, one- year, threeyears, and ten-year goals need to be set so that the strategy for reaching these goals can be outlined in the plan. Most organisations recommend setting the long-term goals first and then setting short-term goals: those goals which can be reached as steps to attaining the long-term goal.

Action Plan

The Action Plan should be designed after the main goals and objectives have been set in order to attain the mission in a straightforward and measurable way. With an Action Plan, the goals themselves can be obtained. Without the Action Plan, and the measures it entails, it would be impossible to implement the plan and measure its success. Being able to measure success would certainly be important both for maintaining our tax status as a not-for-profit organisation as well as to explain the use of it to the membership-at-large.

Strategic Planning Processes and Mechanisms

The publications 'A Guide to Nominal Group and Delphi Processes' by Andre L. Blebecq, et al, and "Guide for Leaders Using Nominal Group Technique" by James G. Cope and Carl Moore, describe the combination of nominal group and Delphi processes. Using these techniques, an organisation that is geographically separate can communicate and develop the working document in fairly rapid fashion.

Gathering of Background Information

Background information is used by your Strategic Planning Committee for its review. By shifting through that information, the Committee would be able to develop a sound basis to continue their work. After existing information has been gathered, another information gathering activity should take place.

Develop a survey questionnaire to poll all members for their viewpoints on the directions your chapter or division should take. After the information has been synthesised from the questionnaires as well as from information already gathered, move to the second step.

A Planning Workshop

The title of the article is 'Strategic Planning: Lead Your Association With a Plan for Tomorrow'.

Based on this article, your chapter or division needs to gather information on five basic questions:

- Where are we now? (The Situation);
- How did we get there? (Our Momentum);
- Where are we going? (The Direction);
- Where should we be going? (Desired Direction);
- How will we get there? (The Strategic Plan).

Bailey recommends that after gathering the background information, the planning workshop should take place. The first session would assess the current situation and how you arrived at that present situation. The second activity of this first workshop is to try to figure out where you are going and where you want to be. This is a very hard-hitting and difficult time for any association or business given the economic conditions and the change within our profession itself.

Designing A Planning Workbook

The planning Workbook will bring together all of the information gathered during the Planning Workshop, sift through the ideas put forward, and organise them into a meaningful body for review by the Planning Workshop attendees and other interested parties in the organisation.

Second Planning Workshop

After the Planning Workshop information has been gathered into a workbook, another workshop should be planned. At this workshop (which should not be held too long after the first one), several things need to be accomplished. In the first half-day a Mission Statement should be adopted for the Association. The Mission Statement will include what the Association intends to stand for; what it hopes to contribute to the world-at-large. It should set goals for the Association and then, having set the goals, fulfill the Mission Statement by translating each goal into a specific objective. This means that the Mission Statement will be carried forth into a strategic plan.

The Committee Structure

The Strategic Planning Committee should be composed of people who understand the organisation of Special Libraries Association, but also who have a constant feel for the Association and your chapter and division in general, and where it is moving. The Strategic Planning Committee should be made a permanent standing committee within the chapters and divisions with a rotating membership. This will encourage constant review and updating by the membership.

Thoughts Regarding Short and Long Range Planning

In order to achieve a sound basis for the development of programmes and activities, systematic planning efforts must be undertaken. The following is a stream of ideas about planning which have been able to find their way to paper. They are presented merely for a point of departure and not meant for any other purpose--a 'Plan for Planning' so to speak.

Planning

Planning includes the ability to identify opportunities, analyse problems, establish priorities and needs, and allocate available resources. This also includes the establishment of priorities and needs, and allocate available resources.

This also includes the establishment of policies and procedures, objectives and standards of performance, forecasts and budgets, programmes and schedules:

- Planning is necessary:
  - — Provides direction
  - — Gives perspective
- Planning facilitates:
  - — Involvement of concerned people and groups.
  - — Communication
  - — Coordination
- Steps in Planning:
  - — Organising
    - a. Establish a structure
    - b. Group involvement
  - — Setting objectives
    - a. Nature of objectives
    - b. Basis for objectives
  - — Establishing priorities—based on needs, opportunities, interrelationships between elements.
  - — Designing activities
  - — Dividing action into feasible steps

a. Short range
b. Long range
— Implementing action
— Disseminating information
— Evaluating—a continual process
— Revising—at least annually

Programme

- Conceptual—why the programme should be undertaken:
  - — Problem statement
  - — Objectives
  - — Hypothesis
  - — Review of existing information
- Methodological—what has to be done and how it will be done:
  - — Design Programme
  - — Sampling
  - — Analysis

a. Quantitative
b. Qualitative
— Instrumentation selection or development.

Contents of Planning Document

- Statement of philosophy:
  - — General philosophy of the organisation
  - — Philosophy of special libraries
- Needs assessment
- Goal of the Association
- Objectives of the Association
  - — Something we want
  - — Output—end product
  - — Means—end product
- Establish programme alternatives
  - — Fiscal—costs of conducting the programme:

a. Time
b. Resources
   i. Human
   ii. Non-human
c. Money
— Programme—set of activities which are combined into some structure and are carried out to achieve some previously stated objective.
— Limits and constraints:

a. An analysis of what we have to work with and work against
b. Specify time, money, programme requirements, people, and facilities within which the Association must operate
c. The statement of ground rules under which the Association must operate

— Types of constraints:
    a. Social
    b. Technological
    c. Administrative
    d. Political
    e. Legal
    f. Economic
— Forces affecting programme development:
    a. Political
    b. Outside interest groups
    c. Administrative hierarchy
    d. Users
    e. Professional organisations
— Establish programme priorities
— Select best programme alternative
— Action plan
— Evaluation of programme

❑❑❑

INDEX

□□□